The Quest for Law

The Quest for Law

– Law Libraries and Legal Information Management of the Future

Peter Wahlgren

Jure AB

Stockholm 1999
Jure AB
ISBN 91-7223-047-9

Elanders Gotab 23296, Stockholm 1999

Acknowledgements

This study that is documented in this book was carried out between the years of 1993 and 1997. The financial means were provided by the *Swedish Council for Planning and Coordination of Research*, FRN. The financial support for travel of relevance to this study has been generously provided by the *Edvard Cassel Foundation,* and initially also by the *Law Faculty at Uppsala University*.

The *Law Faculty at Stockholm University* and the *Swedish Law and Informatics Research Institute* (IRI) have provided the necessary administrative and practical means for the work. To all these organisations I express my sincere gratitude.

A factor facilitating the completion of this study has been the stimulating environment at the Law Faculty at Stockholm University, and my daily contacts with numerous colleagues at IRI, many of whom also actively participated in the evaluation of legal IT products on the Swedish market – the latter being a sub-project within the framework of this study. In this context mention should especially be made of (in order of appearance) *Johan Palm, Daniel Westman, Pernilla Skantze, Cecilia Wikander, Erik Woodcock, Roger Persson Österman, Britt-Marie Svensson, Anna Gentzschein,* and *Ulf Färjare*.

Thanks are also due to *Ingrid Cantwell* at the *Stockholm University Library*, who made it possible for me to follow the development of the *European Legislative Virtual Library Project*, ELVIL, to *Kathleen Price* and *Marie Louise Bernal*, who inspired me by inviting me to one of the first meetings concerning the project *International Access to Legslative Information*, ILIN, at the *Library of Congress* in 1992, and to *Teresa Bjelkhagen* who has reviewed this book from the point of view of the English language with enduring patience.

Stockholm, March 1998

Peter Wahlgren

Table of Contents

Chapter 4 Legal Issues

List of Abbreviations

AALL	American Association of Law Libraries
ADB	Automatisk databehandling (Automatic Data Processing)
AI	Artificial intelligence
BBS	Bulletin Board System
BGIC	Business and Government Information Center, University of Nevada
BIBSAM	The Royal Library's Office for national planning and coordination, Sweden
CCL	Common Command Language
CCTA	Central Computer and Telecommunications Agency (UK)
CD-ROM	Compact Disk - Read Only Memory
CPU	Central Processing Unit
DDS	Decision support system
DIB	Data Inspection Board (Sweden)
DIFS	The official publicaiton of regulations of the DIB
Dir	Direktiv
DPA	The Data Protection Act (Sweden)
Ds	Departementspromemoria/or
DTD	Document Type Definition

EDI	Electronic Data Interchange
EC	European Community
EF	European Community
EG	Europeiska gemenskapen (European Community)
ELVIL	European Legislative Virtual Library
EU	European Union
FPA	The Swedish Freedom of The Press Act (TF)
FUD	Företagens uppgiftslämnardelegation
GILS	Governmental Information Locator Service
GLIN	Global Legal Information Network
HTML	HyperText Markup Language
ID	Identification
ILIN	International Legal Information Network
IMPRIMATUR	Intellectual Multimedia Property Rights Model And Terminology for Universal Reference
IPR	Intellectual Property Rights
IR	Information Retieval
IRI	Institutet för rättsinformatik (The Swedish Law and Informatics Research Institute)
IT	Information technology
JILT	The Journal of Information, Law and Technology "http://elj.warwick.ac.uk/jilt/"
JT	Juridisk tidskrift vid Stockholms universitet
Ju-dep	Justitiedepartementet (The Swedish Ministry of Justice)
LIBRIS	LIBRary Information System
MB	Mega Byte
Mhz	Mega Hertz
MIT	Massachusetts Institute of Technology
MÅHS	Målhanteringssystem (Computer system for Swedish courts)

NC	Network Computer
NJA	Nytt Juridiskt Arkiv
NÅR	Nordisk årsbok i rättsinformatik (Nordic Yearbook of Law and Informatics)
OECD	The Organisation for Economic Co-operation and Development
OSA	Official Secrecy Act, Sweden
PIN	Personal Identification Number
RAM	Random Access Memory
RRO	Reproduction Rights Organisation
SFS	Svensk författningssamling, Official publication of Statutes, Sweden
SFSR	Database containing a register over Swedish Statutes
SFST	Database cotaining the full text of Swedish Statues
SGML	Standard Generalised Markup Language
SOU	Statens offentliga utredningar
SUB	Stockholms Universitetsbibliotek
SvJt	Svensk Juristtidning
TF	Tryckfrihetsförordningen (FPA)
TOC	Table Of Contents
TRIPS	Trade Related Aspects of Intellectual Property Rights
URL	Upphovsrättslagen (The Swedish Copyright Act)
UN	The United Nations
WIPO	The World Intellectual Property Organisation
WTO	The World Trade Organisation
WWW	World Wide Web
XML	Extensible Markup Language

1 Introduction

1.1 The Quest for Law

The object of this study is various foreseeable trends of relevance for effective legal information management and the accompanying consequences for the legal profession as such. Special attention has been paid to the changing situation of law libraries, although the analysis is not restricted solely to this area, and should be of relevance to anyone interested in legal information management.

It has been the ambition that the work should contribute to the identification of the future requirements of the legal domain, with regard to legal information systems and other services traditionally related to law libraries. The intention is also to discuss strategies and appropriate features that may be developed in order to meet such requirements.

The study is motivated by the ongoing development in the field of information technology (IT) and its continuously increasing impact on the legal profession: a development characterised by features such as digitalisation, Cyberspace and the Internet, but also by the growing experience among the users and the producers of legal IT products and services.

Another important assumption of relevance for this study is the ongoing internationalisation of law, which affects the legal material in several ways. The fact that different legal systems are approaching each other does not only mean that the amount of legally relevant material constantly show a dramatic increase. It is also evident that the rate at which the legal material is published grows all the time. These circumstances are, in turn, of crucial importance for the organisation of the modern law library, entailing far reaching consequences for almost anyone working within the legal domain.

1.2 Objectives

The Quest for Law is a study whose ambition it is (i) to make an inventory of requirements that may be related to legal information, (ii) to identify and analyse factors of relevance for thc evaluation of legal IT products, and (iii) provide an overview of legal issues that may impede the effective utilisation of IT in legal work and legal information management. In addition, (iv) the work provides a discussion of "external" (i.e. not necessarily domain dependent) aspects that may affect the future development of the legal work process in an environment increasingly affected by IT.

In the following sections each of these objectives are described in some detail. However, the reader should keep in mind right from the start that these aims are interrelated. That is to say, effective legal information management presupposes not only a good understanding of adequate needs for legal information, but also an awareness of the relevant legal frameworks, and proper insight into what aspects that need to be examined when it comes to evaluating products and services based on legal IT. Likewise, in any project concerning development of legal information systems a large number of other external aspects must be taken into consideration.

1.2.1 Requirements of Legal Information

A considerable part of the study is devoted to the requirements connected with legal information, as these may be understood from an analysis of legal work processes and legal work situations of various kinds. In this analysis a large number of different types of needs have been investigated.

Legal information is viewed in this context from the point of view of methodology. That is to say, this is not a study trying to make an inventory of emerging legal problems and accompanying requests for regulations. Nor is this an attempt to try to predict legal issues of a substantial nature that can be expected to gain interest in the future. Instead, the focus is set on how legal information as such is employed and utilised in legal work processes, as they can be described at various levels. In other words, the ambition is to provide a general description of the requirements that may be related to legal information – disregarding the legal domain they appear in. In this undertaking various functions of legal information and their relationship to legal work situations have been investigated. The assumption being that an analysis of this kind may be useful for the development of future strategies of law libraries and other institutions and persons concerned with the administration of legal information.

Thus, a somewhat more precise goal has been that the study should enhance the understanding of the kind of legal products and services that may be useful to develop, and, furthermore, that the work should provide some indications of how legal information management resources ought to be allocated. In this undertaking three different levels at which various types of legal requirements can be defined have been addressed – the position of the government with respect to the administration of public legal information, the presuppositions of the organisations working with legal information, and the situation of the individual lawyer.

1.2.2 Evaluation of IT Products for Law

The second objective of the study has been to present a model that can be used in order to evaluate IT related products and services and, more precisely, to formulate some criteria for the evaluation of phenomena of this kind. This approach has been motivated by the fact that in the legal domain the knowledge of this development is rare and not very well documented. At the same time, there is little doubt that in many cases it is necessary to make choices regarding future IT investments in order to survive as a lawyer or a legal organisation. In this respect the potentialities with respect to rationalisation and quality enhancements are too important to be neglected. Consequently, the ability to evaluate various products and services is crucial.

With few exceptions, early studies on IT-based products for the legal domain have focused on technical aspects.[1] In Sweden, for instance, during the 1970s and 1980s several user surveys focusing on the first national legal information retrieval system, *Rättsbanken,* were completed. These attempts were tentative and the questionnaires used in these studies basically reflected concrete technical issues, mingled with vague ideas about user friendliness. Simultaneously, an awareness of the need for legal standards was present. Any general considerations about such standards remained, however, inarticulate, and the relevant aspects to be investigated were by no means obvious.[2] Technical aspects are, of course, still important, but as the development of IT continues, it becomes more and more obvious that systematic evaluation must include a number of additional aspects. To accomplish this, several approaches are possible, and in this study a few of them have been outlined. An attempt has also been made to relate a number of such aspects to each other, in order to create a practical model for evaluation. The model of evaluation is related to ongoing activities and to various suggestions for future solutions, as they have been presented. In addition, a number of products and services developed for the legal sector are discussed.

1.2.3 Legal Issues

A third part of the study is devoted to an inventory of regulatory issues related to the digitalisation of legal information and to the development of new products and new services in the legal sector. The necessity to include regulatory aspects in the study is simply a reflection of the fact that all realistic IT related enterprises in this field must be adjusted to a legal framework. The latter is reflected, for instance, in the facts that any producer of information products must take copyright issues into consideration, that a developer of case managing systems for public authorities, or law firms, must adjust the solutions to issues related to secrecy, that a governmental decision concerning, for example, the

---

[1] Bing, Jon, *Legal Decisions and Computerized Systems*, 1990 at 224.

[2] *See*, as an example and for further references, Wahlgren, Peter, *Rättsdata: En användarundersökning*, 1983.

utilisation of telecommunications in the legislative process must be issued in accordance with the principle of freedom of information, and so forth.

Moreover, it is obvious that future IT-based development in the legal sector will generate problems that need to be considered from the traditional legal angle. Consequences related to IT developing activities may be of many different kinds and the relevant issues that may have to be looked into may range from, for instance, privacy issues to contracting, and liability problems related to economic losses occasioned by malfunctions in the system.

The reason to include an inventory of regulatory issues in a study focusing on legal information management is furthermore motivated by the fact that a large number of the issues related to regulations are of such a kind that they must be given attention already in the initial stages of projects concerning changes. The alternative – trying to adapt a more or less complete and perhaps also implemented solution to a legal framework – is in most cases simply impossible or, at least, often connected with high costs and practical problems.[3]

1.2.4 Aspects Affecting Change

The future development of IT and its impact on legal information management and legal work are depending not only on the possibilities of technological adjustments to a more or less rigid regulative framework. Nor is it sufficient to rely on development activities based on analyses of legal requirements or effective evaluations of IT matters. The number of projects that have failed due to the fact that various aspects of a non-technical and non-legal nature have been overlooked are too many to be disregarded, and in professional legal information management a number of other factors must also be given serious attention.

The factors that may be relevant to look into in this context may initially appear as being of different kinds. Some of them are directly linked with the characteristics of the legal domain, whereas others are of a more general kind in the sense that they play an important role also in other system

[3] Magnusson Sjöberg, Cecilia, *Rättsautomation: Särskilt om statsförvaltningens datorisering*, 1992 *passim.*

development projects performed outside the legal sector. Examples range from project organisation and implementation strategies to user education. Each of these "external" factors may be nevertheless of crucial importance for the planning of practical activities in order to make the analysis of legal information management more complete. Some of these factors are therefore discussed in more detail.

1.3 Scope

1.3.1 Studies of the Future

The subtitle of this book is *Law Libraries and Legal Information Management of the Future*. From the methodological point of view such a formulation imposes certain general limitations on the study: viz. that it is impossible to study the future, aiming to reach any degree of exactness. The future as such does not exist in the physical world and as it approaches it constantly changes its shape. Hence, studies of the future will always reflect a certain amount of speculation.

The fact that it is difficult – or even impossible – to reach any indisputable results should not be, however, used as an argument against studies of this kind. Analyses of the future are in many cases essential: to follow the changes and to adjust to them is always necessary. It is also clear that certain kinds of future studies are less problematic than others. A number of things can be easily predicted with a high degree of plausibility. It is furthermore possible to pinpoint various factors that may affect the prospects of reaching positive results.

It is well-known, for instance, that the degree of difficulty in extrapolation increases with the increase in time span one tries to cover. Likewise, all speculations about the future depend on the knowledge available to the investigator about the addressed topics. An important aspect of future studies is, of course, also the nature of things under analysis – more complex objects of study are, as a rule, more difficult to speculate about. Yet another factor that influences the possibilities of future forecasts is the pace of change exhibited by a given phenomenon.

Complexity and pace of change are thus factors that greatly affect studies about the future of technical achievements, which are multifaceted and can take many forms. These factors naturally also has bearing on this study and a consequence of this is that one needs to be very cautious when trying to analyse the future of the combined field of law and IT.

A considerable difficulty connected with an undertaking of this kind is thereby to predict the course of the IT development, which is, of course, quite impossible. The visions vary a lot here[4] and the expectations are sometimes set very high. A citation from *Nicholas Negroponte*, influential director at the prestigious Media lab at MIT, may illustrate this point: "Possibly. The idea that twenty years from now you will be talking to a group of eight inch-high holographic assistants walking across your desk is not farfetched. What is certain is that voice will be your primary channel of communication between you and your interface agents."[5]

To some extent difficulties concerning the ability to understand the future may be eliminated by keeping the analysis outlined at a general level. Such an approach, may be perceived, in turn, as a limitation however, as it may obviously lead to misinterpretations and misunderstandings of the true potentialities of various kinds of subject matters, especially when technical features are involved, due to the fact that some important aspects may be overlooked.

In this context it should therefor be also made quite clear that this is not primarily a technical investigation. That is to say, that although technical aspects concerning IT are under scrutiny, they are investigated from the strictly functional perspective, and from the point of view of the user. Another consequence of this approach is that the study adopts a broad view as concerns the ways in which applications of potential interest for law libraries have been selected for in depth analyses. In practice this means that all types of systems and services are taken into consideration, disregarding the kind of technology that they are based on. In this respect this study

---

[4] *See, e.g.*, Denning, Peter J. & Metcalfe, Robert M., (eds.) *Beyond Calculation: The Next Fifty Years of Computation*, 1997, Gates, Bill, *The Road Ahead*, 1995, Janlert, Lars-Erik, *Hemma i cyberspace*, 1995, *and* Dertouzos, Michael L., *What Will be*, 1997.

[5] Negroponte, Nicholas, *Being digital: The road map for survival on the information superhighway*, 1995 at 148.

differs a little from various other undertakings which quite frequently start out from some given technological features trying to analyse and understand the ways in which that kind of technology will affect the environment, e.g. the law library.[6]

1.3.2 The Notion of Legal Information

In this context it must be further recalled that the intention of this work has not been to identify any specific kinds of publications, documents, or series containing the core legal information that may be expected to be requested in the future. Nor is this a work aiming to indicate future areas of law or some special kinds of legal issues which may emerge as prime objects of interest for the law library or the legal information manager.

The objective is different and, naturally, from the strictly practical point of view, this may be considered as a weakness in the sense that the work does not give any clear-cut answers to the question of the identity of products and services that may be useful and interesting. Nor does this work give any methodological advice on how existing publications series and other forms of legal information systems may be utilised. In these respects this is not a handbook.[7] The reason for this is quite simple, viz. that the changes in this respect are quite impossible to predict. A fact which may be illustrated by the political changes in Europe during the last decade – with far reaching consequences for a large number of affected national legislative systems.

---

[6] *See, e.g.*, Hodd, Rebecca A. & Karp, Rashelle S., *Library Automation Technology*, 1993.

[7] As illustrations of more practical works, in which also lists of core legal materials in the form of publication series, etc. are included, *see, e.g.*, Bernitz, Ulf, Heuman, Lars, Leijonhufvud, Madeleine, Seipel, Peter, Warnling-Nerep, Wiweka, Victorin, Anders & Vogel, Hans-Heinrich, *Finna rätt: Juristens källmaterial och arbetsmetoder*, 1996, Bertnes, Pål, A. & Kongshavn, Halvor, *Praktisk rettskildelære: Juridisk kildesøking i Norge, øvrige nordiske land og EF*, 1992, Clinch, Peter, *Using a Law Library: A Student's Guide to Legal Research Skills*, 1992, Cohen, Morris, L. & Olson, Kent, C., *Legal Research in a nutshell*, 1992, Holborn, Guy, *Butterworths Legal Research Guide*, 1993, MacEllven, Douglass, T., *Legal Research Handbook*, 1986, Moys, Elisabeth, M., *Manual of Law Librarianship: The Use and Organization of Legal Literature*, 1987, Thomas, Philip A., *How to use a Law Library: Introduction to Research Skills*, 1996, Wren, Christopher, G., *The Legal Research Manual: A Game Plan for Legal Research and Analysis*, 1986, *and* Youngs, Raymond, *Sourcebook on German Law*, 1994. (The list of works of this kind can easily be elaborated.)

1.3.3 The Aspect of Legal Culture

Another general limitation consists in the fact that the perspective adopted in this study is basically a Swedish one, and that the regulative aspects being discussed reflect primary the Swedish legislation. Although, this limitation should perhaps not be looked upon as a very serious one. Many of the topics addressed here constitute truly international phenomena, which indicate that there are good reasons to make national solutions explicit and to discuss them in a broader context. It is important to keep in mind here that the Swedish legislation is to a large extent a reflection of the Scandinavian perspective. Equally relevant is that the Swedish legal system is currently being integrated into the regulative framework of the EU. It can be therefor assumed that some of the national solutions that are discussed here can be of interest to others working with similar matters elsewhere.

The aspect of legal culture does not only affect, however, the wording of legal rules. Also the ways in which legal work is performed vary among different legal cultures. For one thing, it is obvious that the ways of measuring the relative importance of different legal sources are different in different jurisdictions, and that these differences have a decisive effect on the ways in which the legal work is actually conducted and organised.

To illustrate this, it is possible to look at the differences in the perception of the importance of rules as components in legal decision making. Whereas in the Scandinavian countries, as well as in continental jurisprudence, legal rules play a decisive role in the understanding of the legal decision making process, the conception of legal rules is often criticised within the common law system, which to a larger extent is suggested to be relying on cases and the notion of case based reasoning.

At first glance the existence of rather considerable differences between various legal cultures may be apprehended as a limitation in the sense that a study reflecting only one cultural aspect may appear to be of little interest to anyone active outside the jurisdictions sharing the same presuppositions. On closer inspection it becomes clear, however, that several earlier studies combining IT and jurisprudence indicate that these initial conclusions may have to be revised, and that IT development projects within the legal sector may bring about changes making that the perception of legal work may become less diversified.[8]

A more uniform attitude towards law and legal work would therefore be a natural consequence of the fact that any advanced employment of IT will make it necessary to describe a given component in a more or less process-like fashion, disregarding the ways in which the legal material is represented. This is simply to say that from the legal information manager's point of view, the question of whether the law is best understood as a system of rules or as a system of cases may not be the most urgent one to find an answer to. Instead, for anyone trying to develop efficient tools for the management of legal work, more intriguing and practical issues may concern the question of how to make the material available and how to restructure the legal knowledge in order to make it as easily comprehensible as possible.

Thus, although restricted national perspectives may be viewed initially as limitations, from the jurisprudential point of view it appears that studies of this kind may contribute to a more uniform understanding of law and legal work by means of articulating previously unidentified common conceptions. And, if this development continues, one may ask whether many of the previously emphasised epistemological and methodological differences between the various jurisdictions eventually will turn out to be of little practical meaning.

1.4 Method

The topic is investigated by means of an in-depth analysis of the requirements of law, as they can be perceived at various levels – in law libraries, and in different kinds of legal work places. The results of this analysis are then used in order to discuss future IT development alternatives. In other words, this means that the methods employed are basically of a theoretical and analytical kind. From this also follows that this work does not describe any attempts to build practical IT systems for legal

[8] *See*, for illustrations and further references, Wahlgren Peter, *Automation of Legal Reasoning*, 1992 at 157-60.

work. Nor have any experiments with prototypes of such systems been undertaken.

The selection of analytical methods as a starting point has been motivated in turn by the conviction that all studies of IT and internationalisation in the field of law ought to be of a general kind at this time. It may even be argued that the rapid technical development and the ever increasing number of new and diversified products make the general approach more or less necessary. That is simply to say that all investigations focusing on some special product or service run the risk of being too narrow, or of a too limited interest, except for a very short time.

The overwhelmingly rapid development of IT also indicate that a study of this kind cannot rely too much on traditional components and established conceptualisations, especially if the ambition is to discuss possible future scenarios. Rather, it may be argued, an investigation should start afresh from a new perspective, without the limitations of previous undertakings reflecting more or less outdated strategies and assumptions which are no longer adequate.

The consequences of these initial considerations are quite far reaching, and perhaps somewhat controversial, in the sense that this study does not assume that there exist any indisputable library perspective which can provide a firm framework for predictions about the future. Nor have any aspects of legal information been taken for granted. Observing that the library concept is formed and developed from the accumulation of paper documents and books, and taking the emerging influence of IT and digitalisation into consideration, it appears to be a good idea to find a starting point that is less restricted in these respects.[9]

The methodological approach adopted in this study is, however, not entirely theoretical. Several practically oriented undertakings have been initiated and one of the main efforts has been to elaborate a structured model for the evaluation of IT related products and services in the legal sector. The model has been developed in connection with a review of available IT products and services on the Swedish legal market. In this undertaking tentative versions of the general model for evaluation have also

[9] "The most radical issue [concerning the future] is whether or not libraries will be needed at all" Hagerlid, Jan, *Studenternas bibliotek,* 1996 at 23 (original in Swedish).

been elaborated and tested in a more systematic way.[10] It is assumed that this model may not only be of use in many situations, but if thoroughly elaborated and properly implemented, it may also have a considerable impact on the long-term perception of IT products and services.

In addition, a comparatively large amount of time has been devoted to the identification of foreseeable IT trends of relevance to the legal profession. As a consequence of this, a survey of reported activities that relate to this project in various ways has been completed. The survey is based in this respect on the investigation of available system development projects, reports on technical innovations, and the analysis of theoretical contributions.

1.5 Related Work

The choice of the approach to start this work from the analysis of legal requirements has not been randomly made. On the contrary, the discussion in this book is to a large extent an extension of various investigations of legal work and legal reasoning undertaken at *The Swedish Law and Informatics Research Institute* (IRI), where various theoretical analyses and empirical studies focusing on IT and legal work have been completed.[11] A number of discussions in this study are also related to experiences drawn

[10] The evaluations are continuously being documented in JT. *See* Palm, Johan & Wahlgren, Peter, *Utvärdering av juridiska databaser och IT-produkter: Rättsbankens rättsfallsdatabaser AD01 och HD01*, JT 1994-95 at 1098-1104, Westman, Daniel & Wahlgren, Peter, *Sveriges rikes lag CD-ROM: C-LAG X*, JT 1995-96 at 206-213, Skantze, Pernilla, *CELEX*, JT 1995-96 at 517-524, Wikander, Cecilia, *RIXLEX – riksdagens databaser*, JT 1995-96 at 902-08, Palm, Johan & Wahlgren, Peter, *Lexis-Nexis* JT 1995-96 at 1200-06, Skantze, Pernilla & Westman, Daniel, *Infolex*, JT 1995-96 at 1193-1200, Woodcock, Erik, *Pacta*, JT 1996-97 at 194-204, Österman, Roger, *Akelius skatt*, JT 1996-97 at 514-519, Skantze, Pernilla & Westman, Daniel, *CD-Lag X*, JT 1996-97 at 821-27, Svensson, Britt-Marie, *Rättsbankens författningsdatabaser SFST och SFSR*, JT 1996-97 at 1044-49, Wahlgren, Peter, *Notisum – Rättsnätet via Internet*, JT 1997-98 at 254-62, Gentzschein, Anna, *Rättsbankens litteraturdatabaser*, JT 1997-98 at 587-96, Wahlgren, Peter, *Sveriges rikes lag: Lagbokskommentaren*, JT 1997-98 at 870-76, and several forthcoming.

[11] The work of the IRI is continuously documented in the IRI-report series. Summaries of previous work of relevance to this study are given in Magnusson Sjöberg, Cecilia, *supra* note 3, and in Wahlgren, Peter, *supra* note 8.

from the ongoing activities at the IRI and the *Faculty of Law* at *Stockholm University*.[12]

Among other things, these earlier studies have shown that the critical factors for further positive development are not primarily of a technical nature. A large number of studies have also made it clear that it is no longer a crucial issue whether or not it is possible to utilise IT and telecommunications within the legal sector. Instead, it has become quite clear that a more important prerequisite for further positive development is to increase the understanding of how the existing technical potentialities should be utilised.[13]

The conclusion that practically interesting results cannot only be achieved through additional undertakings with system prototypes has thereby also strengthened the assumption that a theoretical and analytical investigation should be selected. The approach to start out from an in-depth analysis of the requirements of law, trying to elaborate a model of evaluation for legal IT products, is thereby further motivated.

In this context it is also appropriate to say a few words about the relationship of this study to other studies focusing on IT and law, and the ways in which such works are referred to. As related elsewhere,[14] the terminology concerning studies focusing on computers and law is not always homogenous. A variety of terms are used simultaneously, and as the technical development continues, the ways of describing studies of this kind changes also. Computers and Law, Law and Informatics, Artificial

---

[12] The most important project is the so called Lexlab project, through which computer based law teaching methods have been introduced quite extensively. *See, e.g.*, Seipel, Peter, *Informationssökning och rättsutbildning*, 1994 at 31-50. Mention can also be made of Corpus Legis – an ongoing legal document management project, Magnusson Sjöberg, Cecilia, *Corpus Legis*, 1996, and IT-Case, a current system development project concerning legal teaching tools, Diesen, Christian & Wahlgren, Peter, *Multimedia som juridiskt läromedel*, 1996. Recently also special courses in legal information management have been held. *See* Skantze, Pernilla, (ed.) *Essays in Legal Information Management*, 1996.

[13] *See, e.g.*, for reflections of this shift of focus, the bi-annual *International Review of Law, Computers and Technology* (previously the *International Yearbook of Law, Computers and Technology, Nordisk årsbok i rättsinformatik* (The Nordic Yearbook of Law and Informatics), the *CompLex* series of the Norwegian Research Center for Computers and Law, *and* Susskind, Richard, *The Future of Law: Facing the Challenges of Information Technology*, 1996.

[14] Wahlgren, *supra* note 8 at 126-34.

Intelligence and Law, and IT and Law are just a few examples of the variation of this area.[15]

This terminological indeterminacy implies that many of the topics that are relevant for this study have been investigated and analysed before under different labels, even though legal information management has not always been conceived of as a topic of its own. It should also be noticed that some of the core aspects of legal information management have been given considerable attention for a comparatively long period of time, e.g. litigation support[16] and information retrieval.[17]

From the general perspective it is possible, however, to gain some distance to the matters of terminology. The ongoing development indicates that it is rather pointless to try to elaborate any detailed classification schemata reflecting different kinds of studies, or try to relate this work to previous studies in any indisputable way. From the general perspective it appears more adequate to perceive this study to be merely the consequence of the fact that computers, IT, and telecommunications are becoming irreversibly integrated into the legal sector, and into almost any sector of society. In this respect, this undertaking – with its overall objective of analysing the integration of IT in the legal profession – can be looked upon as being nothing more than a modest enterprise in the field of general theory of law, or analytical jurisprudence, reflecting social changes of a more profound nature.

---

[15] *See*, for further examples and references, Saxby, Stephen J., *Public Policy and Legal Regulation of the Information Market in the Digital Network Environment*, 1996 at 3-5.

[16] *See, e.g.* Cwiklo, William E. (ed.), *Computers in Litigation Support*, 1979.

[17] *See, e.g.*, Bing, Jon, *Handbook of Legal Information Retrieval*, 1984.

2 Starting Points

2.1 *Law Libraries*

Systematic collection of knowledge in written texts and libraries is nothing new. One early, well-known example of this is the library of *Alexandria*, founded in about 300 BC which is estimated to have held some 500.000 volumes, all in the form of book scrolls.[1] As regards libraries in which law has been a crucial component the *Imperial Library* in *Constantinople*, founded by *Justanianus* in the 6:th century, encompassing some 600.000 volumes stands out as the most distinguished historical example.[2]

Besides numerous antique and medieval libraries founded by monarchs, many early collections of legal books appear to have been first brought together by individuals more or less formally appointed to legal services, e.g. judges and other officials.[3] Moreover, during the Middle Ages a large number of important libraries were compiled by the church and monasteries. Systematic collections of law books later on appear at a larger scale, parallel with the institutionalisation of the court system, the formation of

[1] The library, or parts of it, existed for some 700 years, but now only fragments of its content remain. *See*, on the general history of libraries, Wiegand, Wayne A. & Davies, Donald, G. Jr. (eds.), *Encyclopedia of Library History*, 1994 (especially on the ancient library of Alexandria at 19-21).

[2] Wiegand, *supra* note 1 at 332-36, *see also*, on the development of law libraries, Wedgeworth, Robert (ed.) *World Encyclopedia of Libraries and Information Services*, 1993, at 436-52.

[3] *Cf.* Göranson, Ulf, *Juristen i biblioteket*, 1996.

other official authorities, and the emergence of a more distinguishable legal sector.[4]

At present almost all important law libraries are part of, or are related to, some sort of an institution, e.g. a court or a university, their main function being to serve that institution.[5] From this in turn follows that law libraries can differ in kind, depending on the type of end users. In a recent Swedish survey four types of libraries where legal materials can be found are mentioned: large research libraries, specialised legal libraries, other special libraries with legal material, and public libraries.[6] Using a somewhat different basis for classification it is possible to make a separation between university libraries, government libraries, court libraries, law firm libraries,[7] and electronic libraries.[8] A similar classification recognises also practitioners' libraries, academic libraries, national libraries, and legislative libraries.[9]

For natural reasons private libraries are becoming less important – the growing magnitude of legal information makes it very cumbersome to develop and maintain high quality libraries even on a small-scale basis. Libraries are also difficult to maintain due to the facts that modern information management presuppose technical competence and an ability to administer a large number of different functions, as well as skill in licensing, contracting, etc., which makes that managing a library becomes a very difficult task if done without the support of a larger organisation. Another troublesome factor is in this context, of course, the increasing cost of legal information.

On the surface, libraries may seem to be one of the best examples of quiet, peaceful places where changes seldom occur and, when they do, they

---

[4] Modéer, Kjell Å, *Historiska rättskällor*, 1993, *passim*.

[5] In 1990 the two largest law libraries were the *Law Library of Congress*, and *The Harvard Law School Library*, each containing some 1.5 million volumes. Wiegand *supra* note 1, at 332-36.

[6] Bernitz *supra* chapter 1 note 7, at 198. An full list of libraries in Sweden is given in TLS, *Bibliotek i Sverige*, 1997, As for other countries various list can easily be found on the Internet, *see, e.g.*, "http://www.catalaw.com/", "http://www.yahoo.com/Government/Law/ Legal_ Research /Libraries/", *and* "http://www.law.indiana.edu/law/v-lib/lawindex.html".

[7] Wedgeworth *supra* note 2.

[8] The first and probably most well known illustration of the latter is the initiative at Chicago Kent Collage of Law. *See, e.g.*, "http://www.infoctr.edu/misc/eloise.htm".

[9] Blunt, Adrian, *Law Librarianship*, 1980.

do so at a slow pace. Looked upon in the long-term perspective, however, it is possible to perceive the history of libraries as a rather dramatic one, filled with more or less constantly ongoing revolutions. In this view the present situation with its digitalisation and various initiatives concerning electronic libraries represents merely the latest occurrences in a long chain of events.

The perhaps somewhat surprising suggestion indicating that law libraries can be looked upon as places of continuos change is probably best illustrated by the methodological development and the utilisation of new tools. This development can be decomposed in turn into a number of fundamental shifts in the ways of the handling of legal information. It can be noticed here that the physical medium of information shifted from clay plates, papyrus and pergament to paper; and from book scrolls to books in the form of volumes and publication series. Other fundamental changes include, of course, the shift from hand-written to printed material, and the fact that a large number of technical innovations have been made available, spanning from enhanced copying facilities to the integration of microfiche and other forms of storing and retrieval, etc. Likewise, better communication facilities, improved possibilities of information search, interlibrary loans, and similar matters, have radically changed the possibilities of retrieval and access to legal information. In addition, various kinds of new techniques have made it possible to manage information in the form of sound and vision. The list of improvements and changes of this kind can easily be extended.

Throughout the centuries also several "library methods" have evolved. Most important in this respect is the fact that more uniform ways of classifying and storing the material have been accepted, e.g. alphabetical catalogues listing authors and titles, classifications by subject matter, as well as development of numerous specialised catalogues. Extremely important has naturally also been the build-up of searchable card catalogues and other form of indexing systems, in recent decades replaced by computerised catalogues and reference databases. And although several competing systems have been introduced,[10] these phenomena have had a considerable

[10] In the American sphere, Shepard's Citations, providing the history and treatment of each reported case, as well as the legislative history of statutory law, legislative enactments, etc., provide an important starting point in many situations of law search. As concerns overall classification schemata for law library material mention can be made of the Library of Congress Classification, the Los Angeles County Law Library Classification, the Stanford Law Library

impact on the availability of library collections.[11] The introduction of uniform means of classification is also reflected in various ways in the development of the legal domain. Of relevance is furthermore the fact that general knowledge about the organisation of law libraries has been treated as a natural element of legal education for a long time now.

Yet another change, closely related to the internationalisation and the development of technology, is the magnitude of the accumulated material, as well as the fact that lately libraries have become important places of study on a large scale. In this context it may also be noticed that public libraries are a late, basically a ninetieth and twentieth century phenomenon,[12] and that many law libraries have changed from being private collections reflecting the needs of an individual or of a certain authority, to official institutions with the objective of providing broad services to the general public.

It is also clear that since substantive material changes all the time, law libraries must be able to revise and restructure the core material more or less continuously. In practice this means that political changes may have often made large volumes of legal material obsolete or inaccurate. For similar reasons, sometimes entirely new jurisdictions may have evolved. In Europe the most recent examples of this is the EU project, the democratisation of Eastern Europe, as well as changes related to the ongoing internationalisation process.

In the historical perspective it is furthermore noticeable that considerable changes stem from shifts in the use of legal language. It may thereby be recalled that for a long time Latin was the main medium of communication in law and that the shift to the use of the vernacular was a rather dramatic occurrence. In Europe this state of affairs has been succeeded by a situation where various versions of legal (EU) texts are available in different source

---

Classification, and the Classification schemata developed by Moys. *See*, for further examples, Wiegand *supra* note 1, Wedgeworth *supra* note 2, Mueller, Heinz Peter & Kehoe, Patric E., *Law Librarianship: A Handbook*, 1983, *and* Moys, Elisabeth, M., *Moys Classification and Thesaurus for Legal Materials*, 1992.

[11] An illustration of this is the LIBRIS Web Search, recently made available via the Internet without any costs. The database contains 3 million titles representing the holdings of more than 160 Swedish libraries, mainly research libraries. Swedish literature is almost completely covered from 1866 until today. *See* "http://www.libris.kb.se".

[12] *See* Blume, Peter, *Fra tale till data*, 1989 at 68, and 387-90.

languages. A state of the matter which sometimes makes it possible to make choices between several versions of core material.

To take into consideration is also that a traditional law library has several different functions. The most obvious one is its function as an information or documentation centre. In practice this means that the objective is to provide services to the customers by means of collecting, registration, storing, disseminating and making available all types of legal material.[13] From the practical point if view this has come to mean that it is necessary for the library staff to make overviews and conduct surveys in order to be able to follow and understand the development in various legal domains. Likewise, it is important to make use of various technical means in order to be able to access and retrieve various kinds of legal information.

Besides practical undertakings concerning physical objects, such as large volumes of books and documents, the functions of the library include also undertakings aiming at restructuring the available information in such a way as to reflect the requirements and objectives of the organisation which the library is set to serve. An important presupposition is thus also that any adequate collection of legal information must be based on good understanding of the needs of the users, or potential users of the library.

In recent years a number of additional functions have come to be related to libraries: compilation and distribution of course literature to students; provision of printing and copying facilities; serving as an interface towards other libraries, and thus forming a part of an information transfer network are just a few of these functions. From the fact that various functions may have to be developed for various users, as well as that they may have to be elaborated in various ways, it also follows that it may become necessary for libraries to become autonomous and able to make independent decisions

[13] An early discussion concerning the objectives of a documentation centre for legislative materials can be found in SOU 1973:23, *Bättre överblick över lagar och andra bestämmelser*, at 147-55. A general summary of common library objectives is also given by Hagerlid, *supra* chapter 1 note 9 at 31, who suggests that a library "[f]acilitates overviews and understanding by means of creating collections from the needs of a certain user group and by means of organising them in a meaningful way. Helps the users to filter less useful information through selection criteria of quality. Facilitates and enriches the possibilities of the users to access information through cataloguing, indexing and user-friendly search systems. Gives the users advice and teaches them how to search, Offers a ... uniform gateway to globally distributed information." (Original in Swedish).

concerning a large number of different activities oriented towards various kinds of user groups.

In addition to the more or less obvious objectives and functions connected with the practical handling of the material, in some cases there may exist more or less implicit objectives that may have to be considered. For a public library, for instance, one common underlying function would be to minimise the importance of economic obstacles, which makes accessing legal information in an efficient way more or less impossible for large groups of persons. In a similar way the function of a university library may be to provide crucial presuppositions for legal education taking place at the university by providing a place of study, which often also serve as a meeting place and a social institution. Likewise, for a company library, important implicit objectives may be to provide news reporting facilities as well as other services, including educational activities, for instance, on how to use information retrieval facilities in a more efficient manner. Moreover, a well maintained and updated specialised library may be crucial to the development of a research institution, and the possession of a well organised library may enhance the status of a law firm, and so forth.

To take into consideration is thereby also the fact that different law libraries must be differently organised in order to meet various specific needs and objectives of its users, depending on the location and the primary functions of the law library.[14] Noticeable is furthermore that this may be a cumbersome and difficult task, due to conflicting interests and limited funding, for example.

All this suggests that a law library can be defined and looked upon from many perspectives. It is also quite clear that all the changes described thus far are, of course, a reflection of the ways in which society, and therefore also the legal profession, develop. From this point of view it is also obvious that until very recently law library organisation used to be an undertaking in which the management of legal books and paper documents was the sole object of concern, – and that this is a presupposition which is quickly changing.

---

[14] Blunt *supra* note 9 at 105-06 "The identification of those needs usually presents little difficulty; the problem is that they tend to be many, varied and often mutually conflicting."

2.2 Digitalisation

The legal domain has been relatively conservative for a long time in the utilisation of IT and its possibilities. In the Swedish courts, for instance, it is still common to let legally educated clerks ("notarier" in Swedish) manually update the available legislative information. This is done by means of circulating the official law publication SFS (encompassing well over 1.000 alterations and amendments each year, and distributed several times a week) and instructing the personnel to make hand-written notes in the law books in the margin.[15] In several respects this hesitant attitude has not changed, and while this is being written (in the spring of 1997) many lawyers still lack adequate computer support.[16]

Examples of this kind are easy to find and, as concerns law libraries, they often reflect the lack of standard for the integration of international on line materials,[17] reliance on outdated and rigid classification systems,[18] limited resources for computerised research,[19] and administrative difficulties in the effective organisation of IT related user education.[20]

The slow integration of modern information management methods may in some cases be a consequence of administrative and economic difficulties.

[15] This somewhat surprising state of affairs was commented on already in 1988 by the Swedish Minister of Justice, Mrs Laila Freivalds, who then mentioned that school classes used to visit the courts in order to study the way in which work used to be organised "in the old times", In Wahlgren, Peter (ed.) *Det goda kunskapssamhället: Ett perspektiv på rättsinformatiken*, The Swedish Law and Informatics Research Institute, Stockholm, 1988 (IRI-report 1988:5) at 18.

[16] *See, e.g.*, on the situation for Swedish prosecutors, Bergström, Ann Marie, *IT-stöd blev åklagarnöd*, Jusektidningen nr 4, 1997, 4, *and* concerning Swedish court personnel, Nilsson, Åsa, *Vingklippt MÅHS gäckar domstolar*, Computer Sweden, nr 12, February 12, 1997 at 4-5. *See also*, for further references and a recent analysis of "the disappointingly low take up" by members of the legal profession, Paliwala Abdul, Cartwright, Andrew & Terrett, Andrew, *User Needs in Electronic Law Reporting: A Research Study of The Law Reports*, 1997 JILT (2). "http://elj.-warwick.ac.uk/jilt/leginfo/97_2pal/".

[17] *See, e.g.*, *Proposal for The European Legislative Virtual Library, ELVIL*, photocopy, Stockholm University, 1996.

[18] Seipel, Peter, *Law Libraries and Information Technology*, JT 1993-94, at 323 "stiff and from many viewpoints awkward".

[19] *See, e.g.*, on the situation of university libraries in general, Hagerlid *supra* chapter 1 note 9, at 13-14 *and passim*.

[20] *See, e.g.*, Seipel *supra* chapter 1 note 12, especially at 30-33, with further references to SOU 1991:72 *En kreativ studiemiljö: Högskolebiblioteken som pedagogisk resurs.*

Hampering factors may be found, however, also at the individual level. A conservative attitude, and sometimes even the fear of all too elaborated and advanced legal information systems are still the reality for many professionals in the legal sector. Important in this respect is obviously also the fact that very few IT products have attained such high quality as to constitute a true alternative to the traditional legal information systems. From the practising lawyer's point of view the majority of IT applications must still be looked upon as complementary tools, which is why it may seem that sometimes the conservative attitude may be an expression of sound scepticism.

Considerable changes are, however, predictable also in the legal sector. Several things make such development more or less obvious. Increasing possibilities for rationalisations and money savings, a continuously growing computer literacy, the integration of IT and legal education, and a more mature market for digital legal information are a few such factors.

Looking somewhat closer at this issue it becomes apparent that changes of many different kinds can be expected. New roles can be predicted, for instance, for law libraries as well as legal publishing companies. Of relevance here is that products and services of entirely new kinds will be introduced and integrated into legal work. Early signs of this are reflected in the fact that computerised information retrieval systems and CD-ROMs are being accepted at a larger scale. In the future perspective, however, it is also possible to predict a more widespread use of, among other things, decision support systems and other kinds of advanced computerised systems for legal information management. This development, in combination with the growing use of telecommunications and the Internet, will make that many of the functions that where traditionally connected with law libraries and legal publishers will be possible to overtake by small organisations, or even by individual lawyers.

Of relevance here is that the technique continuously becomes cheaper. From this also follows that IT becomes more widespread and that more people working with different tasks are becoming affected. This is a new situation. A decade ago access to computers and electronic communications presupposed considerable resources, and adequate facilities were only accessible to a few. Today, in practice everyone can get access to the technique, if not through own equipment, at least by means of using facilities provided by employers, schools, and public libraries. From this also follows that it in many situations no longer is possible to avoid the technique. The need to co-operate with others, to fit into organisations, and to handle professional tasks, makes it necessary to be proficient in IT matters, at least to some extent.

Already today it is possible for anyone with access to a computer and telecommunication facilities to reach, not only hundreds of library catalogues, but also a large number of legal databases, conference systems, and services through the Internet. In some cases it is also possible to access commercial vendors and forward requests or make orders, more or less instantaneously, e.g. concerning computer programs and jurisprudential literature.[21] Other Internet facilities range from interactive counselling;[22] access to official documents; possibilities to come into contact with public authorities, law firms (including on-line assistance with the filling in and submission of forms), people prepared to act as expert witnesses (listed by topic), legally trained computer consultants, etc.; calculating and administrative services; access to forms and legal document assembling programs,[23] so called chat systems;[24] legal newsgroups,[25] pedagogic overviews over administrative and legislative processes,[26] and electronic law journals,[27] etc. Likewise, it is possible to retrieve or download legal documents and texts reflecting various kinds of digital sophistication.[28] The material may then be further elaborated and incorporated into various individual working

---

[21] *See, e.g.*, "http://lawbook.com/".

[22] Swedish examples are "http://www.awapatent.se/dnet.html" *and* "http://www.jit.se/help/rhelp.html".

[23] *See, e.g.*, "http://www.ilrg.com/forms.html".

[24] *See, e.g.*, "http://www.legal.net/cgi-bin/nph-webchat.pl".

[25] *See, e.g.*, "http://www.kentlaw.edu/lawnet/lawnet.html".

[26] *See, e.g.*, "http://www.riksdagen.se/arbetar/frbeslut/index.htm".

[27] *See, e.g.*, "http://www.ilrg.com/journals.html".

[28] *See,* as starting points, *e.g.* "http://www.ilrg.com/" and "http://www.hj.se/hs/bibl/juridik.html".

processes. Noticeable is also that the number of services of this kind increases all the time.[29]

The fact that the technique becomes more widespread obviously will have far reaching consequences, of which only a few are possible to predict. Taken as a whole, however, it is not unrealistic to assume that a more widespread use of IT – in connection with the fact that in reality all legal information is becoming available in digital form – will make it necessary to look upon the law from a completely new perspective. In this respect it is possible to assume that legal information – which for centuries has been more or less consciously equalised with paper documents, printed volumes, and books – eventually will have to be separated from the printed media and handled in other forms.

Likewise the transition of information from physical to electronic form is likely to impose that the communication of legal information will change in a radical way and that many new forms of products and services will appear.

2.3 Internationalisation and the Growth of Law

Any study of law libraries and legal work must presently take the question of the internationalisation of the law into consideration. The fact that several legal systems are approaching each other implies, among other things, that the volume of legally relevant material is growing drastically. In addition, the rate at which legal material is published increases all the time.

Internationalisation makes it necessary to integrate legal sources of different origin. From the perspective of the law library this means not only that the allocation of resources, but also that the routines for the administration of the material must be adjusted in order to fit in with the

---

[29] Paliwala, *supra* note 16, in relation to primary legal sources mentions Cornell's Legal Information Institute at "http://www.law.cornell.edu/", the Australian Legal Information Institute "http:/ /austlii.law.uts.edu.au/", the United Kingdom decisions of the House of Lords published on ["http://www.open.gov.uk/index.htm" address changed], individual decisions of lower courts at ["http://www.open.gov.uk/" address changed], and *Sweet and Maxwell's* web based service for ordering case transcripts at "http://www.smlawpub.co.uk/smlawts/tcq/search/". The latter service, however, was withdrawn in December 1997. Swedish legislation is available at "http://rixlex.-riksdagen.se/", "https://www.infotorg.sema.se/cgi-bin/infotorg/", "http://www.notisum.se/", and "http://www.jit.se/aspscripts/default.asp".

new presuppositions. Great volumes of previously unknown and unclassified documents must be related to the traditionally available material in a legally acceptable way. Completely new issues are related to choices to be made between different source languages. In addition, evaluations and selections of various information retrieval channels emerge as practical problems.

Today, the most urgent task is to be able to administer and integrate the EU material. The EU material is greatly diversified and must be thoroughly analysed before any classification and storing can be carried out. For example, an accepted distinction within the EU is the division between primary and secondary law – a distinction previously not elaborated on in Swedish jurisprudence. Primary law consists of basic treaties as well as extensions and amendments of these, and unwritten, general legal principles, extracted from case law. Secondary law is composed of regulations, directives, decisions, recommendations and statements. In addition, decisions of the *European Court of Justice*, access to court cases and commentaries from the various member countries must be taken into consideration.

Internationalisation of law is not a solely European phenomenon. In a broader perspective it can be seen that contacts between different states as well as co-operation between various international organisations become more intensive. Political changes and advancements of IT and telecommunications are, of course, contributing factors in this development, which means that intensification of legal information exchange is becoming a global concern.

Various strategies have been observed as a response to this development. In some countries special centres for legal documentation and legal information have been established or proposed.[30] Parallel to this several international projects have been initiated. One example of such a project is the *International Legal Information Network* initiative (ILIN), later developed into *The Global Legal Information Network* (GLIN) initiated by the *U.S. Library of Congress*.[31] In Europe a project labelled ELVIL,

---

[30] *See, e.g.*, De juridiska fakulteternas europautredning, *Europagemenskap och rättsvetenskap*, 1992 at 20, *and* Seipel, Peter, *En Strategi för datarätten: IT:s juridik*, 1995 (IRI-PM 1995:13).

[31] *See* "http://lcweb2.loc.gov/glin/".

European Legislative Virtual Library,[32] has recently been launched and simultaneously a variety of international legal information collections and research projects are being presented.[33]

Internationalisation affects the professional lawyer's need for law libraries in many ways. The higher rate at which materials are published and the fact that they originate from many different sources implies that the standards of authenticity, completeness and methods of compilation change. It is furthermore remarkable that classifications and routines which have been in use for a long period of time, may suddenly become impractical and even obsolete. One must also remember that the relative importance of the old and the well known may be affected when it is restructured in order to fit into the new context. In Sweden, it has even been suggested that the legal profession faces the emergence of a new doctrine of legal sources.[34]

In this respect the situation will vary between various legal fields. In some cases it may be necessary to utilise previously unexplored search paths in order to retrieve previously unknown and unidentified collections of documents. In other fields of law the changes may be less noticeable, and there will be little or no need for altering the major information systems. In all cases, however, internationalisation, as well as the ever growing volume of legal information, will make it necessary to look upon market surveillance, selection, acquisition, evaluation, and updating of legal material from new angles.

Keeping in mind this development and the series of assumptions outlined above, it also becomes obvious that also the internationalisation makes it necessary to look upon legal information from new perspectives in order to try to better understand how various emerging IT phenomena should be evaluated and managed.

---

[32] *See* "http://www.sub.su.se/elvil.htm".

[33] *See, e.g.*, "http://www.lib.berkeley.edu/GSSI/eu.html#documents", "http://europa.eu.int/", *and* "http://www2.echo.lu/libraries/en/projects.html".

[34] *See, e.g.*, Pehrson, Lars, *EG-samarbetet och den svenska rättskälleläran*, JT 1991-92, at 626-37.

3 Evaluation of Legal Information Systems

3.1 Introduction

In this part of the study criteria for the evaluation of computerised support systems in the legal domain are discussed. The analysis leads up to the formation of a model for the evaluation of legal IT applications.

Models of evaluation may be, of course, of many different kinds: they may be more or less ambitious, more or less elaborate, and, they may be developed for different reasons.[1] In this context the overall purpose is to develop a tool which may help to answer some of the questions that various consumers of law will meet in the foreseeable future, due to the IT-development, the internationalisation, and the changes this development will bring about.

The intention, however, is not to present a complete and final solution concerning the evaluation of legal IT. On the contrary, the rapidly changing

[1] *See, e.g.*, Kracht, D, de Vey Mestdagh, C.N.J. & Svensson, J.S. (eds.) *Legal Knowledge Based Systems: An Overview of Criteria for Validation and Practical Use,* 1990. *Cf. also* JILT *IT Reviews* at "http://elj.warwick.ac.uk/jilt/sw/default.htm", *and,* especially on evaluation criteria for legal websites, BGIC "http://gordo.library.unr.edu/~bgic/fed/criteria.html", *and,* generally on IT adaptation of library functions, Brümmer, Anna & Åstrand, Lotta, *Biblioteken på Internet: en undersökning av elektroniska biblioteks hemsidors form, innehåll, struktur och användarstöd,* "http://www.ub.lu.se/UB2proj/LIS_collection/AnnaLotta/toc.html", Dickinson, Gail K., *Selection and Evaluation of Electronic Resources,* 1994, and Head, John W., MacCabe, Gerard B. (eds.) *Insiders Guide to Library Automation,* 1993.

technical presuppositions, the extension of the legal domain, and the multifaceted nature of law, among other things, make fulfilling such an ambition impossible. The objective is more limited, viz. to provide a sketch and to outline some aspects which may, hopefully, function as points of reference in future discussions concerning legal information management.

It is also important to notice that the objective is not to provide a complete inventory of legal IT applications. Effectuating an exhaustive investigation of legal IT products and services is hardly a practicable undertaking – the solutions that have been presented are simply too numerous. An inventory that aims to include as many products as possible is probably also a less profitable approach due to the fact that many of the systems in use are of a similar kind, and that not all of them can be expected to have more than a short life span.

Thus the analysis focuses on *various types* of suggested tools, including different forms of interactive services and related methodological proposals. For practical reasons, the investigation is also limited in the sense that the majority of the applications that have been investigated are national systems, primarily developed for the Swedish market. Although this restriction is not absolute, the ambition has also been to make comparisons with other solutions, which have been presented or suggested in various connections.

3.2 Models of Evaluation – Requirements

3.2.1 Generality

A model intended to support the evaluation of computerised IT applications in the legal domain must be of a general nature. This conclusion is obvious from the fact that any meaningful discussion of the pros and cons of various solutions must start out from system components, which are, to some extent, universal. Such a strategy is in turn motivated by the fact that the available, legally relevant products and services are of very different kinds. At the same time it is apparent that the legal profession is of a very diversified character and that the presented solutions may be intended to support a large number of different work situations.

A further important reason for giving the model of evaluation a general character is that individual users, as well as various groups of users of legal support systems, have different priorities, and that they differ in their opinions about good and bad solutions. Practising lawyers, for instance, are for natural reasons interested primarily in the issues related to the information coverage and the accessibility of the system. Personnel responsible for administration, on the other hand, may want to focus on the consequences of an IT system which can be related to the efficiency of the user organisation as a whole. For law schools and law libraries prize issues may be of primary concern, and so forth. In addition, from the aggregate point of view, issues related to freedom of information, dissemination of knowledge, and free competition may come into focus. To cope with all the different conditions involved in these issues, a general and holistic model is of crucial importance by means of reflecting a broad spectrum of foreseeable points of interest. Such a model should be useful, not only in development and implementation activities, but also when strategic decisions concerning utilisation of IT are to be made.

The fact that the object of this study is so multifaceted, and that one should be able to use the obtained evaluations in many different situations is, however, not the only reason why the elaboration of a general model of evaluation appears to be a good idea. One other motive for this being of vital concern is that if the requirement of generality is not fulfilled, reviewers will have to devote time in each case to the analysis of the kinds of aspects that may have to be addressed. In such processes there is, of course, a risk that the persons engaged in them will have to, metaphorically speaking, invent the wheel again and again. Such a strategy is, for natural reasons, time consuming and in the rapidly changing environment of IT it may be found that the products under scrutiny have already changed by the time the evaluations are completed. At the same time, there is an obvious risk that evaluations performed on an ad hoc basis will generate results which are difficult to compare.

3.2.2 Particularity

Legal IT applications belong to extremely complex matters. Of vital importance here is therefore that a model of evaluation must include very detailed components or, at least, that it must be possible to elaborate it in such a way that it reflects a high level of specification. This may appear as a paradox, but the need to include highly specified components in the model of evaluation is in no way in conflict with the above mentioned criteria of generality. The combination of these two aspects is merely a reflection of the fact that useful theories concerning legal IT applications must be able to reflect a large number of components at various levels of generality.

Particularity is an important factor when computational feasibility is investigated, which means that any theory that should be able to contribute to practical undertakings concerning legal IT applications must be of a very specific kind, and that if the aspects of particularity are not met, there is a risk that the theories will be of little assistance in the development of applications not reflecting any authentic requirements of the legal domain. Such a state of the matter may lead to a situation in which the suggested solutions will have a very small chance of being accepted by the potential users. Particularity is therefore a factor that is closely related to practicability.

Particularity is also a crucial element in the development of process specifications reflecting the legal work process. Careful and extensive elaboration of details is necessary in order to reflect the more subtle aspects concerning various assumptions about the nature of law and legal reasoning. It is further of relevance that in any realistic legal work situation system implementations may have a more or less far reaching influence on the matters of legal substance. A general theory concerning more advanced legal IT-applications must therefore also acknowledge the necessity to develop detailed models of the existing substantial law. This, in turn, makes it necessary to recognise the importance of in depth investigations of legal rule systems, the functions of the legal order, the requirements of potential users, and similar things.

As a consequence, in the long term perspective it seems obvious that a discussion aiming at some contribution to any deeper understanding of the process of legal reasoning, and thus to the development of more adequate support systems, is likely to be dependent on our ability to form even more specific jurisprudential theories – a fact that must naturally be reflected in a more ambitious theory of evaluation.

3.2.3 Flexibility

Generality and particularity are not the only requirements that a feasible model of evaluation must exhibit. IT and law are constantly changing objects and any theory concerned with these matters must take this dynamic aspect into consideration. It is impossible to predict the future pace of development, or to foresee the nature of changes, but the ambition to handle these aspects must nevertheless be set high in order to minimise the risk of not being able to understand and rightly assess new types of solutions.

In practice, this means that useful models of evaluation must be able to manage various forms of changes, e.g. in the form of technical improvements, new forms of services, the ever-growing volumes of legal texts, etc. Managing changes in this context means that the model must be able to include new or elaborate components, keeping the overall structure intact. To accomplish this is necessary if one of the main objectives of this undertaking is to be fulfilled, i.e. the ability to compare various products and services with each other.

As mentioned, the rapid IT-development makes it natural to anticipate continuos changes of a technical nature. To be able to cope with changes of a technical kind is, however, not the only important aspect of flexibility. In the long-term perspective there is little doubt that our present understanding of legal work and legal reasoning will be looked upon as being very primitive. The development of information theory, cognitive science and experiments with so called knowledge based systems make such development quite predictable. A consequence of this is that current theories on evaluation will have to be adjusted in various ways as the understanding of the legal work processes increases.

It is also important to notice that changes of relevance for the assessment of legal IT applications may be initiated by a large number of "external" factors, e.g. sociological, economic, or political factors. Sometimes changes in external factors facilitate development, for instance, by means of providing higher computer readiness, changes in educational policies, investments in computer based rationalisations, etc. On the other hand, external factors may also give rise to problems and provide obstacles of new kinds. It should be noticed furthermore that the occurring changes may be of a very dramatic nature and that the prevailing theories, as well as feasible technical solutions, may have to be rejected as new insights emerge.

A debate in the mass media in Sweden on the elaboration of an existing, nation-wide computer system for social security offices may serve as an example. The debate was related to the issues of privacy, security, and vulnerability in relation to the possible misuse of the intended knowledge-based extension of the system. In this debate various political arguments were submitted but aspects of technology, decision quality, and efficiency were given relatively little attention. The discussion ended with a governmental decision (1992) according to which the project had to be abandoned.[2]

Events like the one just described clearly indicate that flexibility, as well as the ability of incorporating into the theories various types of non-technical and non-legal factors, is a crucial aspect. A consequence of this is that also the models of evaluation must be able to reflect such matters. Likewise it is obvious that there is very little room for dogmatism in the sense that the theories must be open ended to a large extent, and that anyone concerned with evaluation of legal IT products must be prepared to include new factors in the discussions.

3.2.4 Technical Independence

An overview of the IT market and the solutions that have been presented so far make it obvious that a model of evaluation cannot be based on one technical solution only. The situation is just the opposite. It must be possible to relate the model to a large number of various technical solutions that have been presented and, moreover, it must be possible to adjust the model to some extent to the foreseeable elaborations of such solutions.

Any serious attempt to create a model of evaluation must also consider the fact that there exist various types of computer standards, and a large number of products based on different kinds of techniques, e.g. on-line

---

[2] Wahlgren *supra* chapter 1 note 8 at 249.

databases, CD-ROMs, diskette subscriptions, services available via the Internet, and numerous combinations of these subject matters. In addition, a useful model of evaluation should make it possible to compare technical solutions with traditional paper based publications and established information systems, conventional law libraries, etc.

In this context it is relevant to recall that the early attempts to evaluate legal IT applications were frequently concerned with their technical aspects, such as, for example, computer capacities, component specifications and similar things. However, a model developed for the support the legal community and various consumers of law makes such a limited approach less interesting. Undertakings in this field should reflect, instead, the ambition to discuss the relevant subject matters in a non-technical way, so that also potential users without any technical background can understand the components and the conclusions that are reached.

The use of plain, non-technical language is important not only when IT components are discussed. Also legal terms of a more specific or technical nature must be explained or translated into plain language in order to be understandable for system developers and other persons without legal training. Ideally, a model of evaluation should be neutral in the sense that all persons engaged in the development of legal IT applications should be able to appreciate it, regardless of their background. From all this follows that technical independence is a concept with wide implications and that language issues must be given careful attention.

3.2.5 Legal Coherence

Law is in many ways a discipline of a very special kind, and a model intended to facilitate the evaluation of legal IT applications must be able to reflect the characteristics of the legal domain, taking also the nature of the legal material into consideration. The nature of the legal domain makes it thus more or less impossible to use models of evaluation developed for other purposes. For similar reasons, any commercial product or service which does not meet the legal and jurisprudential demands will have little or no chance of attracting users, i.e. if an implemented system falls short of the demands in this respect, it will most certainly meet with problems of acceptance, or it will simply not be used.

When it comes to legal presuppositions a large number of aspects may be taken into consideration, many of which can be taken apart, in turn and analysed in a piecemeal manner. For instance, a legal IT system must handle, to some extent, the fact that, among other things, law is authoritative and fragmented, as well as vague and imprecise. In addition, delicate matters such as principles of equality before the law, the rule of law, authenticity, and the fact that law is becoming increasingly international in nature may have to be reflected in legal applications.

Legal coherence is, however, a concept with broad implications; also aspects related to what may be labelled as the legal culture must be paid attention to. An example of the latter is that it is possible to distinguish professional legal roles of various kinds. This, in turn, is often an incentive for the introduction of legal support systems, e.g. due to the fact that lawyers are normally eager to improve the quality and effectiveness of their work. On the other hand, some phenomena that are encountered when these aspects are investigated may be very difficult to manage from the point if view of system developers. Among other things, it becomes sometimes quite clear that the legal profession is of a conservative nature, and that lawyers may be prepared to adjust their working methods to the changing presuppositions in various degrees. And, as mentioned, some lawyers may even feel that their position as an independent and authoritative decision maker is threatened when the issue of IT support is raised.

To further complicate the matters various objectives concerning legal IT support sometimes clash. For instance, from the layman's perspective, as well as from the jurisprudential point of view, enhanced quality in legal decision-making at a low cost is among the most important aims. Simultaneously, the professional lawyer may want to give priority to system faculties which facilitate the work process by means of supporting work phases which are, for some reason, considered to be less inspiring. In a similar way the freedom of an individual decision-maker within an organisation may be in opposition to the co-operative effort to unify decision-making within the organisation, e.g. in order to minimise the costs of appealed decisions, or strengthen the consistency of the corporate image.

3.2.6 User Adaptability

Perhaps the most difficult aspect to cope with when investigating the feasibility of legal IT-applications is the fact that potential users may be of very different kinds.[3] The law affects all people in various ways, and the users of a legal IT application may consist not only of highly trained legal experts with several years of professional experience behind them and working with intricate legal issues, but also of laymen seeking solutions to various kinds of day-to-day problems, and, of course, anything in between. An example of the latter is provided by a large group of law students who utilise legal information systems for training purposes. An additional important user group is the one comprising various intermediaries, e.g. librarians or undergraduate teachers that have to navigate through the legal material in order to assist others, without being trained lawyers themselves.

From the fact that users are of different kinds does not only follow that various legal areas come into focus. The existence of numerous user groups does also mean that a model of evaluation must be able to reflect situations in which different *aspects* of law become important. In some situations, as e.g. in teaching, pedagogical aspects, such as understandability and simplicity stand out as the most important ones. In other cases, e.g. when a lawyer is preparing for litigation, completeness, authenticity, and the fact that the system is updated may be the most crucial aspects. In still other situations, as in planning sessions, the access to case scenarios and methodological support for calculating may be of primary concern, etc.

Furthermore, it must be observed that various legal domains exhibits varied characteristics. There are, for instance, few similarities between a tax law examination and a civil law investigation due to the fact that the legal material in these two domains is of a very diverse nature. This may also be illustrated by the fact that statutes may play a dominant role in some legal areas, while other areas of law are best labelled as case-based. Of relevance in this respect is also the fact that the predominant solutions may be more or less debatable, and so forth.

In addition, it is often desirable to relate legal IT systems to the sub-phases of the legal decision process, and in the development of a feasible

---

[3] *Cf.*, on this problem from a general point of view, Brümmer *supra* note 1 at chapter 5 section 2.

model of evaluation a number of functional aspects must be taken into consideration. To illustrate it may be observed that in some situations, e.g. in work situations where large numbers of similar cases are to be decided on a routine basis, support for decision formulation and decision administration, may be of primary concern, and in a wider sense it is doubtlessly so that knowledge elicitation, information retrieval, interpretation, and formulation – all of which are the core aspects of legal reasoning – are different activities which are best served by different types of support systems.

3.3 Basic components of Legal Information Systems

3.3.1 Overview

The evaluation model that is developed in this study starts from a decomposition of legal IT applications into three basic objects of study, viz. *information content*, *technical features*, and *organisational issues.* This division originates, in turn, from a tentative definition of legal IT applications and legal information systems described as "collections of technical units, methods, procedures, and eventually also people, organised in order to support computing and communication of legal information." [4] From this follows that the model is intended to cover in principle all types of information systems a lawyer may encounter – from stand alone computer systems to large law libraries,[5] although in this study the focus is set primarily on IT related systems.

The inclusion in the model of *information content aspects* requires no extensive explanation. In a meaningful evaluation of any IT application it is

[4] This description is an elaboration of the standard definition of data processing systems described as a "collection of machine units, methods and procedures, and eventually also people, organised in order to process data." Standardiseringskommissionen i Sverige (ed.), *Informationsteknik – ordlista: Dataordboken*, 1989 at 64 (original in Swedish). An IT application may consist, in turn, of parts which are themselves IT applications.

[5] An earlier and tentative version of this model has been presented in Wahlgren, Peter, *Evaluation of Computerised Legal Networks*, 1995.

necessary to look into a number of issues such as, for example, completeness, authenticity and the quality of the information that is provided.

To illustrate, it may be noticed that information quality is probably one of the most important issues for the future development of the Internet and the World Wide Web, which lately has been said to evolve "into what might be thought of as a chaotic repository of the collective output of the world's digital 'printing processes.' ... The ephemeral mixes everywhere with works of lasting importance."[6] Likewise "the experience of most people ... is not that the Net contains great works and crucial research information. Instead most of what is there is perceived to be of low value".[7] This is also true for much of the legal information that is provided, and this state of the matter being without doubt a reflection of the fact that many of the qualitative "check-points" traditional publishing involved, in the form of reviewers, publishers, distributors, librarians working with acquisitions, etc. have disappeared in the digital environment.[8] Instead, the possibilities to publish information are more or less directly available to anyone with access to a computer and an Internet connection.

Low quality is however not the only thing that makes it necessary to critically evaluate electronically communicated legal information. The importance of trying to find criteria for the evaluation of information quality is also underlined by the fact that digitalisation has made it much more difficult (and sometimes impossible) to check out and confirm authenticity, originality, issuing dates, etc. of digital documents.

At a somewhat more detailed level, i.e. when individualised products are being scrutinised, points of interest would be the ways in which the material is selected, in which historical material is handled, and the extent to which the information has been adjusted in order to meet the requirements of the users of the IT applications in question. Likewise it is highly relevant to investigate the extent to which the potentialities of the computerised media, as we now understand them, are utilised in order to enhance the value of the legal information.

---

[6] Lynch, Clifford, *Searching the Internet*, 1997 at 44.

[7] Stefik, Mark, *Trusted Systems*, 1997 at 68.

[8] *Cf.* Katsh, M. Ethan, *Law in a Digital World*, 1995 at 88.

Also the need to include *technical*, or, to use a somewhat broader term, *methodological features* is obvious. IT applications belong to the phenomena that are by definition completely dependent on technical matters. The basic components, i.e. telecommunications, computers, and computer programs are also complicated matters that can be future decomposed almost infinitely. Thus, the objects of interest include a wide range of complex aspects, such as communication protocols, various search languages, speed and capacities of computers, compatibility of different computer programs in use, etc. In this context also the functions of the applications are investigated. The analysis thus focus on the kind of legal work processes the applications are intended to support, and whether or not they can be considered to be successful from the practical point of view.

The importance of incorporating the *organisational aspects* into the model is indicated by the need to investigate and compare various attributes related to the management and administration of the services. All IT applications depend on some sort of organisation for the performance of various tasks: to build up new and administer the existing databases, keep track of information and communication, handle user support, manage billing and marketing, and so forth. In practice this means that it is necessary to take into account a large number of factors, such as support facilities, prize policies, forms of agreements, availability of the network, stability of the information providers, etc. It is, of course, also relevant to find out whether or not there exist channels through which the users may articulate their views and opinions.[9]

[9] In Sweden it is possible to see a shift of interest into a perspective in which organisational aspects are getting more and more attention. This is reflected, among other things, in the formation of a "Foundation for legal information" in which several organisations and authorities in the legal domain participate. The objective of the foundation is to make sure that comprehensive information about Swedish legal sources and related information becomes available on computer-based media and other technical media. An overriding aim is also to vindicate aspects of legal quality. Thus the foundation devotes its resources to a variety of issues such as free access to legal data, market competition, and the evaluation of legal IT products. *See* Arbetsgruppen för datoriserad rättsinformation, *Sammanträdesprotokoll May 10, 1989.*

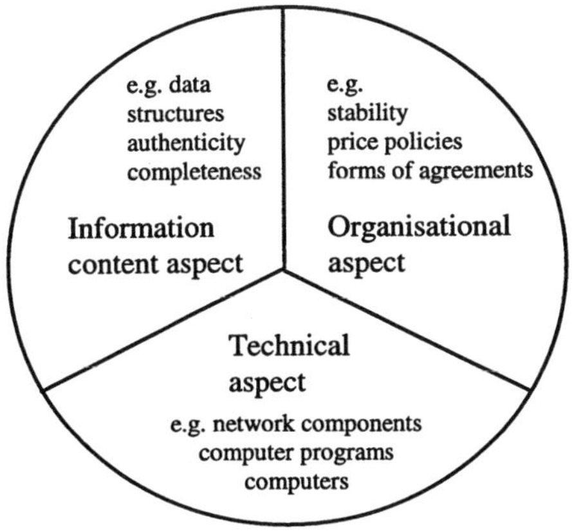

Figure 3.1: Basic components of legal IT applications and legal IT systems.

Each of the aspects mentioned above can be divided in turn, into more detailed subject matters, often in several succeeding phases. For example, the network issues can easily be separated into questions related to standardisation, connectivity, etc. When the stability aspect is investigated, it is relevant, among other things, to look at the legal status of the database producers and the information system hosts. Likewise, when structures related to the information content are scrutinised, the points of interest range from document formatting, utilisation of indexes and editorial notes, the ways in which the information is separated into legal domains, etc.

In this way, systematic particularisation of legal IT applications eventually makes it possible to form elaborate, and sometimes hierarchically organised, check lists reflecting a holistic taxonomy of the basic components. Such compilations provide, in turn, initial steps in the systematic evaluation of legal IT applications and in the following sections the information content, the technical features, and the organisational aspects are addressed in a more extensive way.

3.4 Information Content

Any evaluation of the information content in legal IT applications must be related to the requirements of the users, or potential users. That is simply to say that an investigation on how well the information in a given IT application covers a legal issue, or supports a certain work task, must be related in each case to specific problems, as they are experienced by the users.

From this naturally follows that it is difficult to say something substantial about the actual identity of the information in legal IT applications (i.e. the precise documents, titles of volumes, names of publication series, etc.) which has any bearing on legal information management in a more general sense.

An additional complication lies in the fact that various jurisdictions use different material, and that in all practical investigations concerning the kind of material that ought to be included in a legal IT application, it is necessary to thoroughly analyse the nature of the jurisdiction that is being addressed.

From a general point of view it is nevertheless possible to distinguish various aspects related to the information content, which are crucial to the way in which an information system will be utilised and appreciated. One can also make a distinction between (i) the ideals of jurisprudence as they are reflected at an aggregated, social level, and (ii) information content aspects that are related to the objectives of the user organisations. In addition, it is relevant to relate the nature of the legal material in IT applications to (iii) subject matters that are of primarily importance to the individual user, and in the following sections these requirements are addressed separately.

It should be noted, however, that relations between the requirements that can be detected at the social level, the organisational level, and the user level, as they are outlined in this study, are of an inclusive kind in the sense that features of relevance at the aggregated levels normally also will have an influence over how IT applications will be looked upon from the perspective of the individual user, and vice versa. In this respect the identification of various levels of requirements reflect an ambition to present a categorisation suitable for systematic evaluations. It is not suggested that the requirements that are being discussed in the following can be separated in any conclusive way. On the contrary, useful IT applications in the field of law must reflect various sorts of quality standards and meet user expectations of many different kinds.

3.4.1 Jurisprudential Requirements

3.4.1.1 Introduction

At the social level there is little doubt that there exist what may be labelled a legal framework, i.e. a number of basic standards that all law libraries, as well as legal information managers and serious producers of legal IT applications must take into consideration in the identification and selection of the information that is to be included in the system. These standards may be looked upon as being of a jurisprudential nature in the sense that they differ from the obvious aims and requirements of the individuals working within the legal profession, as well as from the immediate objectives of public authorities, the interests of commercial user organisations, etc. In other words, the standards that may be perceived at this level reflect quality aspects of the legal system, as well as requirements of the society at the aggregated level.

Standards of relevance for the legal system taken as a whole are reflected to some extent in a jurisprudential notion known as *the doctrine of legal sources* – a collection of theories concerning the nature and origin of legal material. The existence of the doctrine of legal sources may indicate, in turn, that the task of evaluating the content of a law library or any other kind of legal information system is a simple undertaking. This is, however, not always true; in its details the doctrine of legal sources is a much debated notion,[10] and in many respects there is a lack of consensus when the more fundamental aspects of the law are being discussed. Likewise, many of the contributions to this theory are of a very theoretical nature – a large part of the discussion has, for instance, been devoted to the ontology of the law.[11]

[10] *See, e.g.*, Strömholm, Stig, *Rätt, rättskällor och rättstillämpning*, 1996, *and* Magnell, Viktor, *Rättskällebegreppet*, 1994.

[11] "We have many different theories about the law or what the law is. These theories are all proper theories, but yet they contradict each other because each one rests on or entails very different sets of presuppositions which reflect very disparate moral, ontological and epistemological beliefs or doctrines. Nearly every general philosophy or philosophical school has implications for legal

When the doctrine of legal sources is examined it becomes furthermore quite clear that the jurisprudential standards vary between different legal jurisdictions. Sometimes it is possible to find far reaching similarities, as e.g. between the legal systems in the Scandinavian countries, while in other cases the differences are of a fundamental kind.

Of relevance is also the fact that the notions which are reflected in the doctrine of legal sources have been almost without exception elaborated before the advent of IT. The guidance they may provide must therefore be adjusted in most cases in order to be meaningful in an IT based setting. To take into consideration is thereby that in a traditional legal information system based on paper documents and books the ability to combine the core material that can be found within the legal sources with other types of information in a dynamic way is restricted, due to practical and technical limitations. As IT makes it possible to compile and manage material in a more or less unrestricted way, however, obstacles of this kind are loosing their importance.

Consequently, highly relevant questions are to what extent is it desirable to complement the traditional legal material? What other types of material should be added to a legal information system based on IT, and where can relevant supplementary information be found?

Theoretical multiplicity, the existence of different traditions in various jurisdictions, and the influence of new technology may thus indicate that the possibilities to make any distinct statement about the kind of material that should be included in jurisprudentially sound IT applications are limited.

On the other hand, from the point of view of the legal information manager, the above-mentioned difficulties need not be perceived as obstacles of a definite kind. In most situations it is not necessary to include all theoretical presuppositions in the perspective. That is simply to say that it is seldom desirable to try to elaborate in practical system developing activities any detailed theory on jurisprudential and social requirements concerning legal information, valid for all jurisdictions and all types of law.

---

theory? Nearly every legal philosophy is a special case of, or application to law of a more general philosophical position?" Smith, J.C., *Review of Wahlgren, Peter, Automation of Legal Reasoning*, JT, 1993-94 at 248.

An important conclusion is furthermore that it is possible to find a consensus on a number of things, despite the existence of various epistemological assumptions, and the various ways in which different jurisdictions clash. It is, for instance, quite obvious that the doctrine of legal sources – or to use a less prestigious term, theoretical jurisprudence – reflects several fundamental presuppositions of relevance for legal information management in a more general sense. It is thus also possible to claim that in a given jurisdiction theoretical jurisprudence will to some extent

- define the kinds of material that should be considered as authoritative,
- provide standards concerning the ways in which this kind of legal material may be amended or omitted,
- describe the hierarchy and relations between different types of legal material, and
- reflect fundamental principles concerning the ways in which access to and dissemination of legal knowledge should be managed.

3.4.1.2 Authoritative Legal Material

In the process of identifying the material, which for various reasons should be considered as authoritative basis for a legal system the most important factor to investigate is probably the historical aspect which will be reflected in turn, as a rule, in the existing institutional and organisational structures, as well as in established processes generating legal rules.[12] To simplify matters further, the core material will be reflected to a large extent in the existing publication series, some of which will be of official character (e.g. law gazettes, case reports issued by the courts, etc.). In addition, in many jurisdictions this material will be complemented with legislative preparatory works, published in official volumes, administrated or issued by the government.

---

[12] *Cf.* Magnell, *supra* note 10.

In the civil law type of jurisdictions, as, for instance, in the Scandinavian countries, the doctrine of legal sources will specify in this way legislation, legislative preparatory works, and case law. Simultaneously, in many common law jurisdictions, case law and acts will supply the most important material, while legislative preparatory materials will be considered to have a less important position. In the jurisdiction of the European Union, in turn, the core materials are divided into primary and secondary materials, the former consisting of treaties (including amendments and alterations), and the latter of regulations, directives, decisions, and so called "soft law", i.e. recommendations, declarations and statements of the European Council or the European Commission. Moreover, in an inventory of the legal sources of the European Union it is also necessary to include the so called legal principles, and decisions from the European Court. In addition, in many practical situations, this material must be related to the legal material of one or more of the member countries, as well as to jurisprudential literature, reflecting the so called legal doctrine, published in monographs, legal periodicals, etc.

At first glance, the fact that the identity of the core legal material must be established in most cases by means of investigating institutional matters and established publication series, indicates that it is actually possible to determine the identity of the elements that should be included in a sound jurisprudential information system, simply by making an inventory of the subject matters that are actually being used. And although the material may seem initially limitless, the existence of various types of jurisdictions makes it clear that the identification process can be broken down into undertakings with manageable volumes of information. The European Union, which is based on quite an intricate doctrine of legal sources, may serve here as a good example. That is to say that although the material is voluminous, it is by no means impossible to distinguish various types of information and to classify and identify the components within each type.

Thus, from this perspective, the task of selecting legal material for the inclusion in legal information systems in order to make it complete with respect to the ideals of a state governed by the law, is one with a rather predictable outcome. The obvious way to start is without doubt by identifying the commonly accepted bulk of legal material, as it is reflected in the existing publications series, and described in general introductions to the legal system.[13]

In Sweden, an illustration of such a delimitation of legally relevant material has recently been submitted by the "IT Commission", a group set up by the Government with the objective of defining strategies and facilitating the availability of IT.[14] The Commission has defined the concept "basic legal information" by means of including into it legislation, rules issued by the public authorities and the municipalities, preparatory documents generated by the parliament and the government, official investigations preceding legislation activities, and all decisions concerning legal issues generated by the national courts as well as the administrative authorities.[15]

As a reaction to this a special Work Group has been set up in order to make suggestions for a modernised information retrieval system for basic legal information. So far the Work Group has listed some twenty legal sources and related material to be included in such a system, viz:

1. Legislation as it is published in the official collection of statutes, Svensk författningssamling (SFS). 2. A register over legislation published within the SFS. 3. Consolidated Acts, (Often the issues of SFS contain only the parts of a certain act that has been changed in some way. Full text versions are provided only when the act is first issued, and consolidated versions only when the changes are of a more fundamental kind. As a consequence, in order to find out the current wording of a certain act it is often necessary to retrieve and combine several numbers of SFS issued at various times. Working with the paper versions of SFS, this is sometimes a very time consuming and cumbersome task.) 4. All earlier versions of each act in consolidated form. (The objective being that it should be possible to retrieve each complete historical wording of an act just by means of specifying a certain date.) 5. The regulations of central public authorities (among other things comprising some 60 official collections of regulations).

---

[13] Bernitz *supra* chapter 1 note 7.

[14] *See*, concerning the background and objectives of the Swedish IT commission, "http://www.it kommissionen.se/itsite/pages/visionma.htm".

[15] IT Kommissionen, *Official Letter to The Government*, The Ministry of Communication, October 8, 1996 at 2-3.

6. The Directives of the Government. 7. A register over State Commissions. 8. The Legislative Motives of the Government. 9. Official reports and investigations (the so called Ds and SOU series). 10. Statements from the Council of Legislation. 11. Government bills. 12. Reports of the Parliamentary Standing Committees. 13. Parliamentary publications (encompassing a large number of various kinds of documents). 14. Cases from all national courts (first instance district courts and county administrative courts excepted). 15. Decisions from central public authorities. 16. Decisions from the Parliamentary Ombudsman, and the Parliamentary Auditors. 17. Swedish International Agreements. 18. Decisions from the European Court of Justice and the European Commission of Human Rights. 19 Municipal legislation. 20 EU-Law.[16]

The definitions provided by the IT Commission and the Work Group are, extensive as they may seem, however, not the only possible ways of delimiting the concept of legal information. To recall in this respect is the fact that the works of the Commission and the Working Group are restricted in the sense that they only discuss the kinds of legal information whose dissemination the state is responsible for. Looked upon from the point of view of the law library, or the legal information manager, however, the concept of legal information may be given an even broader definition.

For one thing, in most cases the internationalisation of the legal domain make it also necessary to include material from various international organisations, which, due to enactments and implementations, have obtained a more or less compulsory status. Examples of organisations which generate material of this kind are The European Union, The Council of Europe, The Organisation for Economic Co-operation and Development (OECD), The United Nations (UN), The World Intellectual Property Organisation, (WIPO), and The World Trade Organisation (WTO). This list can easily be extended by adding numerous regionally as well as globally operating organisations. Likewise various kinds of international treaties and

[16] The Work Group for a new Law Data System (Arbetsgruppen för ett nytt Rättsdatasystem) has so far published two memorandums, viz. *Gruppens överväganden i den första etappen av arbetet* (Preliminary Considerations), February 24, 1997, and *Kravbeskrivning för ett moderniserat Rättsdatasystem* (Specifications) July 3, 1997. *See,* concerning the enumeration above, the latter at 2-6. *Cf. also,* on the delimitation of legal materials in Sweden, SOU 1973:23, *supra,* chapter 2 note 13, *and* several articles concerning "better legal sources" in SvJt 1976 and 1977.

similar material may be of relevance, but here the situation for natural reasons differ between various topics of the law.

Additional starting points for the analysis of requirements of legal information at the aggregate level can be found in the doctrine concerning *the rule of law*, or the concept of *rechtsicherheit*. The rule of law is a widely accepted and much discussed cornerstone of current jurisprudence, and provides also complementary quality standards for how legal information ought to be managed. The concept may be divided into components, such as predictability, objectivity and equality. In this context, predictability means that all material must be available and possible to define in advance, and from this naturally also follows that the material in a legal information system always must be updated. Objectivity means that the material should be of an official character and accurate in nature, and equality indicates, among other things, that the same material must be used irrespective of the place and time when a certain issue is to be decided.

In this context also the principles of *freedom of information, right of access* and *free exchange of information* are of relevance. The principle of freedom of information reflects a desire to ensure public access to the work of the public authorities and the courts. This clearly indicates that also official documents and material that have been generated in individual cases should be looked upon as being parts of the legal material potentially relevant for the inclusion in legal information systems.[17]

The principle of free exchange of information, in turn, is a notion closely related with the old utilitarian and democratic ideals of the informed citizen who is, in all situations, able to make well-balanced decisions based on more or less complete information. Thus, free exchange of information does not only presuppose free access to official material. In an open discussion about legal IT applications the inclusion of other types of legally relevant materials can easily be motivated. It is, for instance, obvious that also jurisprudential literature, legal commentaries of a critical nature, as well as various forms of data, and statistics, etc. become relevant again and again in legal work situations.

Simultaneously, suggestions indicating that only official material should be included in public legal information systems may easily be criticised as

---

[17] *Cf.* however also section 4.3 on legal issues.

being unfair, or as showing censorial indications, due to the fact that it automatically excludes critical commentaries from the private sector which, of course, are crucial for a free debate.

The first simple conclusion that may be drawn from these initial considerations is that the issue of how to identify the relevant legal information from this aggregate point of view cannot only be approached by means of investigating the formal origin of various types of information. Nor does it appear to be a good idea to decide that only officially sanctioned information should be included in a legal information system.

On the contrary, from the jurisprudential perspective it is rather clear that there exist no natural borderline concerning the nature or origin of the material that can be considered to be relevant. Notions like freedom of information and the democratic ideals of a free exchange of information make it possible to motivate the inclusion of a large number of various types of legal information, not just of the officially generated documents.

From this also follows that various kinds of information that may help users with the navigation in the legal domain may be considered. Examples of the latter are compilations or indexes giving information about lawyers, governmental activities and publications, law societies, legal publishers, legal software, technology consultants, management, training, universities and colleges, as well as other legal resources. Information of this kind may in turn consist of names, addresses, general overviews of services and products, pedagogic descriptions of the legislative process, organisational structures, etc.

It must nevertheless be noted that the question concerning the type of material that should be included in a legal information system to some extent has to be looked upon as a political decision. Furthermore it must be observed that the answers that can be given in this respect are closely related to the ways in which the information dissemination within a given jurisdiction or a given state has been organised. That is to say that if an information system has an official status, in the sense that it is set up by the state, the responsibility of the system administrator will be much greater as compared to what can be expected from a system marketed by a private publisher.

Finding any objective grounds for the selection of material that can be included in a legal information system is thus very difficult. It may be suggested to start with, however, that the objective should be to include all types of officially and jurisprudentially relevant information. It may furthermore be argued that, if there are doubts as to any particular piece of information being classified as relevant or not, the primary choice should be to include rather than to exclude that piece of information. The latter standpoint is suggested because all decisions concerning relevancy may be looked upon from various angles, and therefore also decisions concerning omissions may easily be criticised.

Another tentative assumption that may be submitted here is that when traditional legal materials are being scrutinised, from the point of view of the legal system developer it is rather obvious that it is quite difficult trying to change the identity of this information. This is simply due to the fact that historical reasons and institutional structures, which establish what is to be considered as the core legal material, also determine the kinds of material that professional users of legal information systems will expect to be able to find. A failure to include this type of material in a legal information service will therefore easily come under criticism, and any experiment with alternative strategies contains the risk that the service will not be used, or that it will be looked upon as being of doubtful value.

To propose that all types of information can be included in a public legal information system is however not the same thing as to say that all conceivable types of information generated by the authorities should be represented in such a system. A strategy solely reflecting a desire to reach completeness could easily worsen the situation by means of burying the users in large volumes of non-relevant and perhaps also trivial information. To take into consideration is also that the ability to manage material of a non-official nature is, for various practical reasons, limited.

Consequently, the conclusion that all types of legally relevant material can be included in a public information system must be looked upon for several reasons as a matter of principle, reflecting a desire to analyse general requirements of legal information as such. In actual system design there exist several reasonable arguments against the idea that all documents generated by public authorities should be made available.

Looking somewhat more carefully into these matters, it becomes quite obvious that the identification of the commonly accepted legal material that should be included in a public legal information system may not be as easy and self-evident as it may seem at first glance. From this also follows that before any final decision is made about the selection of material to be included in a public information system a number of additional criteria concerning the omission of materials should be investigated.

In this context it may be recalled that according to some legal philosophers there are several factors influencing the character of the legal material actually being used, besides the well-balanced theoretical considerations and democratically ensured institutional reasons. It has furthermore been suggested that some of the factors that have a decisive influence over these matters are of a non-jurisprudential, nature.

3.4.1.3 Publication and Promulgation

For quite a long time it has been argued that one of the most important factors that influence the choice of material that is actually being used within the legal sector is whether or not the material has been published. That is to say that the nature of the legal material that is included in the existing legal information systems may not so much be the consequence of jurisprudential findings, or a true reflection of a distinct doctrine of legal sources, as it may be the result of practical undertakings by the publishers of legal material. The existence of such a decisive "publication factor" may obviously have far-reaching consequences. The extreme scenario would be that in which the publication factor will be used to decide whether or not given material will be used at all, or whether it must remain forever buried in some obscure legal archive – the state of the matter that would naturally, be quite depressing from the jurisprudential point of view.

The awareness of influences of this kind is not new. As recalled by *Richard Susskind* it is a phenomenon described already by *Jeremy Bentham* who wrote in the middle of the nineteenth century that "[case] reports are published by anybody that pleases, and by as many people as please; and when nobody publishes, nobody cares".[18] When discussing current English common (case-) law Susskind analyses this aspect in more detail and arrives at the conclusion that "[t]he decision whether or not to report a case is often commercially inspired rather than through any passion for a coherent

---

[18] As quoted by Susskind *supra* chapter 1 note 13 at 20.

development of common law. Commercial Law publishers, like information retailers, will look to the marketability of the subject matter. So, cases are often reported on the strength of the novelty of the circumstances involved rather than in virtue of their establishing or clarifying important principles or rules of law."[19]

The fact that publication is essential for the actual utilisation of legal information is thus well documented in the jurisprudential literature. Much of the discussion does not concern, however, publication *per se,* but rather *promulgation,* i.e. that part of the law making process which ensures that laws become public. The importance of publication as part of the promulgation process is well known and widely accepted as a essential ingredient of any legal system, motivated by the obvious fact that individuals must have access to legal rules if they are to understand them and be able to obey them.

Promulgation is commonly also dealt with in legal rules about proper legislative proceedings, and in several jurisdictions its importance is reflected in the fact that the rules about the promulgation process can be found in the constitution.[20] As a consequence, in most modern jurisdictions, the legal system in itself secures to some extent the dissemination of legal knowledge. It should be noticed, however, that regulations of this kind have been mostly concerned with the promulgation of laws, and not with other types of legal rules or legal information.

From the fact that promulgation is ensured in most jurisdictions through official measures also follows that the commercial influence over the publication process is limited in various ways, at least when the original legislative material is concerned. The ability of the private sector to decide whether or not some material will be published can therefore be expected to be more relevant when other types of legal information are being analysed. Most noticeable here is the fact that on various occasions it has been suggested that publication strategies (and hence the law publishers) have

---

[19] *Id.* at 21.

[20] *See*, for historical exposés, Blume, Peter, *Fra tale till data*, 1989 at 24-25 and *passim, and,* especially on the Swedish legislative process, Herlitz, Nils, *Om lagstiftning*, 1930 at 373-390. *Cf. also*, on the current Swedish situation, Bernitz, *supra* chapter 1 note 7 at 71-73 and *passim.*

had a considerable influence over the extensive growth of the case law system in the U.S. during the last century.

The importance of publication as a commercial factor deciding whether or not legal material will actually be used must not be exaggerated, however. For one thing, it is obvious that it is not possible to successfully market all types of legal information. Nor can publication be looked upon as an isolated occurrence. In each case there must also exist some sort of demand for the information in question – otherwise the material will simply not be used, despite extensive publication activities. To suggest otherwise would be to suggest that the legal system is easily manipulated.

The truth is perhaps somewhere in between. To claim that publication is of no relevance at all is obviously wrong, and the fact that certain information is selected for publication apparently sets *de facto* standards for the use of legal information in many situations.

An example of the latter is the *Swedish Law Book* – a collection of laws, published annually combined with aggregated references to case law and legislative preparatory material. The Swedish Law Book is compiled and published by a private company (*Norstedts Juridik*) and this product has without doubt had a considerable impact on the legal information usage in Sweden for a long time, although, perhaps, not so much through the selection of laws that it contains, as through the referencing system it provides. A crucial factor is probably also that the Law Book contains so called consolidated legislative texts, i.e. the Acts are regularly updated as the amendments and changes are being published – which is a difference as compared to the official law journal, SFS, which, as mentioned above, in most cases merely provides the parts of the act that have been changed. To put together a complete and updated version of a Swedish act just by means of using the SFS journal can therefore be very time-consuming.

It must nevertheless be assumed that it is actually possible to influence and change the use of legal information. This may be illustrated by the fact that the Swedish Law Book has recently met with a competition from another private company (*Fakta informationsförlag*), that in 1996 presented a compilation of commented legislation, *Karnov*, consisting of three volumes of about 4.000 pages.[21] In this product the legislation has been

[21] Versions of The Law Book and Karnov are also available on CD-ROMs. In 1997 Fakta also started to publish a comprehensive compilation of Acs, *Sveriges lagar.*

complemented with comments by legal experts, and by compilations of case references and indexes.[22] The texts are intended to be updated four times a year and the obvious assumption behind enterprises of this kind, which for natural reasons presuppose considerable investments, is that it is possible to affect the practical use of legislative and jurisprudential material.

A realistic conclusion would probably be here that the publication factor can play a more or less important role in various situations, depending on the type of information in question, and the situation in various jurisdictions. In some cases the publication factor (and thus private enterprises) may wholly determine whether or not certain legal material will be used, while in other cases a decision to omit some information in a private publication will have little or no effect at all, on the type of legal information that is actually used, due to the fact that the legislative system in itself secures the dissemination of the information through promulgation and various forms of more or less official publications.

The fact that this "non-legal" publication factor exists has, nevertheless, far reaching implications, especially in the light of the IT development, which affects in various ways traditional publishing activities. In this respect it becomes obvious that the factual usage of legal sources in a given jurisdiction can be influenced. It is equally clear that IT and digitalisation of information provide new, important opportunities for legal information management, especially for the possibilities to combine various kinds of legal information. From the general point of view there are therefor also reasons to suspect that IT may have the power to change the doctrine of legal sources, at least in the long term perspective.

From this it naturally follows that it is apparent that there exist unique possibilities to modify and complement the material that can be included in legal information systems, as compared to the "pre IT" situation. This provides, of course, not only a great challenge for legal information managers, but also an important opportunity for jurisprudence, as well as for society taken on the whole, to improve the material and the usage of legal information from the qualitative point of view.

---

[22] In order to meet this competition Norstedts has recently presented a series of, domain defined, *Law Book Commentaries*.

3.4.2 Requirements of the Legal Organisation

3.4.2.1 Introduction

As mentioned in the introduction to this chapter, the requirements stipulated for legal information are of an inclusive kind in the sense that the needs of an organisation will reflect to a large extent the accepted jurisprudential standards in its field of operation. In addition, all organisations must be able to satisfy the needs of the individuals working within them. Lawyers, as well as others dealing with legal information in a professional manner, are completely dependent on the access to adequatc and updated material, and if an organisation fails to meet the demands of this kind it may eventually encounter internal problems, as well as problems with recruitment.

It is furthermore noticeable that the quality of information used by a legal organisation must be in line with what is accepted by co-operative organisations, supervisory authorities, customers, etc. Failure in this respect may have the effect that the people involved loose confidence in the organisation, which may lead in turn to loss of authority or, for organisations acting in the commercial sector, to inability to compete.

First and foremost, however, requirements concerning information content, i.e. the *identity* of information, must be related to the objectives of the organisation in question. It is thereby obvious that requirements for legal information will reflect in each particular case the domain in which a certain legal organisation operates. Naturally this also means that the objectives vary a lot. In this respect there are few similarities between organisations working with, e.g., Patent Law, Criminal Law or Administrative Law.

The requirements of a legal organisation will be related, however, not only to the legal domain in which a certain organisation operates. In its more subtle aspects the needs of the organisations will also depend on the kind of situations in which the materials are intended to be used. Questions such as the following may become relevant: is the function of the organisation primarily to provide efficient litigation support, and is it therefore, from the point of view of the legal information managers a question of identifying material to be put into a system supporting such activities? Alternatively, is the task of the organisation development of pedagogical teaching tools for legal education? Or, perhaps, is its overall objective to provide in depth legal knowledge for traditional legal research? From this, *functional* point of view law firms, law schools, unions, public authorities, courts, and other kinds of organisations working with legal information may have little in common.

In this context it may furthermore be noticed that different objectives may also exist among different organisations working in the same legal area. The obvious example here is that the ultimate information profile of an employer's organisation will be quite different from the one of a union, disregarding the fact that they both operate within the domain of labour law. In this respect not only the type of comments and the literature that will be regarded as relevant will vary. Also the selection of cases and the ways the material best ought to be structured will differ.

To complicate matters even more it is apparent that also the internal requirements of an organisation will be of a complex nature. This is simply due to the fact that various user groups may exist also within legal organisations. In this respect different needs may concern not only the identity of information, or the overall functions of the organisation in question. They also indicate that entirely different types of information systems must be developed in order to satisfy various internal objectives. A court, for instance, must be able to adjust the information to judges and administrators, as well as to persons affected by the decisions of the court. Likewise, it must be able to co-operate with prosecutors and lawyers acting before the court. In a similar way a law faculty must not only satisfy the needs of its students and teachers, but also of its researchers, administrators, and so forth.

3.4.2.2 Continuity

In an analysis of legal data quality one of the first things that come into mind is the continuity aspect. This is simply a reflection of the fact that legal material undergoes constant changes in various ways and that in many situations, e.g. during a court process or during negotiations, it may be disastrous not to have access to the appropriate versions of the legal material – or even worse – to be ignorant of changes that may have occurred. Being able to handle the continuity aspect is therefore an extremely important undertaking.

What must be considered is also the fact that the legal material is constantly accumulated. In practical legal work this means that it is often necessary to have access to long series of legal materials, such as statutes, cases, legislative preparatory works, etc. From the changing nature of legal information it also follows that the incoming material must be indexed and stored in such a way that it becomes available in a form that is understandable to the users. At a somewhat more deeper level this entails that new materials must be incorporated into the historical material, and also that older materials must be updated, e.g. by means of adding references to new cases, incorporating changes, amendments, etc.

The continuity aspect, and the ways in which legal information can be managed is naturally also affected by the characteristics of the legal material. It is, for instance, clear that the intricate nature and vastness of legal information will have in many situations the effect that many users will prioritise information system solutions, and publication series which they are accustomed to. From this it also follows that any attempt at making improvements to the information system may be viewed by the user as a change for the worse. This is simply due to the fact that any change will constitute a threat to the more or less established routines – which may have been very cumbersome to master in the first place.

The continuity aspect of legal information sets thereby certain standards for the kind of information systems that will be requested. It is well-known, for instance, that products providing only a few years of materials, or which lack an elaborate reference system, will not be accepted in most cases. The complex nature of legal information thus also entails that new ways of presenting information, and changes in the ways in which the material is indexed may be looked upon with scepticism. In this respect the continuity aspect is something that may be looked upon as a conservative factor.

It is important to underline, however, that the continuity aspect cannot always be used as an argument against changes in legal information systems. The currently turbulent market for legal information makes it quite obvious that a strategy based on the preservation of the status quo would be foredoomed to failure. At present, legal information managers must be able not only to put additional information into established structures, but they must also be prepared to handle completely new types of information products stemming from digitalisation and IT development. Likewise, the ongoing internationalisation makes it obvious that previously established and well known information channels, publication series, etc. must often be combined and complemented in new ways.

In this context it must also be noticed that digitalisation has recently made it possible to work with entirely new components such as hypertext links, flexible data structures, combinations of various media, as well as different forms of material. From this it follows in turn that a legal information manager must not be afraid to try new products, change the information flow, access new services, etc. Likewise, it is quite clear that legal information management must be organised in such a way that materials from many different sources can be combined and reflected in functional structures of a permanent nature.

The conclusion from the above is that continuity in the IT environment presupposes a high degree of flexibility. This may perhaps seem to be a paradox, but this is not really the case. Also from a more practical perspective continuity is an aspect of crucial importance, deciding the ways in which the material ought to be managed from the point if view of the subject matter. It should be noted also that the analysis of these aspects pinpoints the fact that all modifications of legal information systems must be conducted in a careful manner, and that all changes must be described in a way which allows continuity to be preserved.

This in turn sets the focus on the importance of meta information, i.e. the fact that legal information managers must provide the users with overviews as well as the latest news about the ways in which the information system of an organisation is being developed.

3.4.2.3 Authenticity

In most practical legal work situations it is of utmost importance that the available legal material is authentic. The only clearly distinguishable exception is legal education in which hypothetical examples as well as manipulated versions of legal material may provide examples to be used for methodological training, etc.

Authenticity means that information must be presented in its original form, and that no changes, omissions or irrelevant additions have been made. At a more concrete level this entails that for instance statutory material must be provided in such a way that there are no questions whatsoever as to the correctness of the text, e.g. as to whether or not the latest amendments have been incorporated in an adequate manner. Likewise, when various kinds of individual documents are being administrated, components such as dates, or data concerning authors, issuing organisations, etc., must be preserved in their original versions.

First and foremost, authenticity is motivated by the fact that legal information is of an authoritative nature, which makes that the consequences of mistakes based on false premises may be devastating. Legal decisions have frequently serious implications. It is also usual that a large number of administrative authorities is involved in their implementation. Wrongful decisions may thus also be very difficult and time-consuming to alter.

Authenticity is therefore an important factor from the point of view of efficiency. For a legal organisation it is clearly a waste to devote time and energy to the process of altering decisions. Nor is it good for any organisation's corporate image if its decisions are repeatedly revoked by higher instances due to the fact that the information used by the organisation is of a low quality. This state of the matter may also have a negative effect on the morale of the employees of an organisation, and, of course, threaten the position of the responsible legal information manager.

If the organisation in question is a court or a public authority, then also the aspects of equality and predictability of the law have to be considered. In this respect it is of fundamental importance that different courts and authorities should rely on the same authentic versions of the law. Consistency in this respect is a necessary presupposition for the preservation of the authority of any legal system. From this point of view it can thus be also clearly seen that authenticity is a vital component of the rule of law.

Authenticity is, however, of relevance not only to those who become affected by legal decisions. It is also accepted that authenticity may be an important factor for the producers of legal information. In this respect copyright, as well as the so called moral rights of authors impose quite severe restrictions as regards the possibilities of utilising information produced by others, e.g. in an in-house information system of a legal organisation. In this context it may be further observed that the authors' moral rights dictate, among other things, that works shall be preserved in their original form.

It should furthermore be noticed that IT has affected the concept of authenticity in information management in several ways. As compared with the former situation in which traditional, paper-based media dominated, many aspects of authenticity have become much more difficult to handle now. Most obvious is perhaps the fact that in many situations the introduction of IT has made that it is more or less impossible to detect whether or not some material has been changed. From this it also follows that it may be more or less impossible to know whether the available material is in its original form, or whether it is an edited version that is presented.

Another thing to consider is the fact that IT has increased the risks of manipulation in the sense that information in digital form can be much easier altered as compared to materials in traditional legal information systems. This in combination with the widespread use of computers and the increasing number of products and services to choose from has definitely changed the presuppositions for effective evaluation of legal information.

An entirely different issue is that IT has also made it necessary to ensure authenticity of legal information at the deepest level. This is simply due to the introduction of computerised information retrieval, and the so called Boolean search programs which, by means of operating with strings of characters, require strict preservation of the information's authenticity even at the spelling level.

The demand for authenticity does not imply, however, that all forms in changes of legal material should be criticised or looked upon with suspicion. On the contrary, in many situations it will be acceptable – or even desirable – to add certain information to the original material. The intricate nature of legal information makes it often more or less necessary to have access to elaborate reference systems of various kinds, e.g. concerning information about a certain type of material, its origin or publishers, its relations to other kinds of materials, etc. Likewise, the vastness of different kinds of legal information often makes that it is practical to add various kinds of abstracts, keywords, compilations and overviews to the original material.

Nor is it difficult to find examples of situations in which various forms of editing are desirable and beneficial. It is, for instance, quite clear that the so called consolidated versions of acts are often preferable when legislative material is being retrieved, i.e. text versions reflecting the accumulated bulk of changes and amendments of a certain act. The ability to present consolidated acts nevertheless presupposes editing of the original material, which must be sometimes quite extensive. Likewise, when large amounts of case law are to be scrutinised, it is often very useful to have access to abstracts, or content describing headers, in order to get a clear picture of the issues that are dealt with within the various cases. When case law material is managed, it is sometimes also necessary to combine materials from several sources in order to get a meaningful picture of the case. This is simply due to the fact that the higher courts sometimes omit the background descriptions by means of making references to texts that have been used in the decisions of the lower courts.

A further reason why it may be desirable to edit various kinds of legal material is that the intricate nature and the vagueness of the law makes it sometimes necessary to elaborate on local in-house interpretations. This may be necessary, for instance, in order to establish uniform decision-making practice within a certain organisation. Such a routine may be crucial, when the background material consists of case law, for example. The results of such interpretation efforts can be regularly found, for instance, in the forms of loose leaf compilations or computerised support systems within unions, employers organisations, courts, public prosecutor's offices, etc.[23]

Internationalisation of law may likewise make it necessary to translate legal information of various kinds. Translation is, of course, an activity which affects the authenticity of the material, and the nature of law often

[23] In Sweden, for instance, the *National Courts Administration* maintains a number of loose leaf handbooks, developed primarily for the courts, but also in common use of practising lawyers. *See also, The United States Sentencing Commission* at "http://www.ussc.gov/". The Commission "is an independent agency in the judicial branch of government. Its principal purpose is to establish sentencing policies and practices for the federal courts, including detailed guidelines prescribing the appropriate form and severity of punishment for offenders convicted of federal crimes." The commission has developed a number of computer programs, which have become widely used.

implies that a rather elaborate methodology is being adapted.[24] To observe in this context is furthermore that it is sometimes necessary to have access to and work with versions of legal documents in different languages. This may commonly occur within the European Community, where documents are being published in different languages at various times.

Thus, it is quite clear that in many situations various forms of legal information editing may be highly desirable. Likewise, when customised legal information systems are being developed within specific organisations, advanced reference systems, high quality abstracts, and similar features are without doubt components that may increase the usefulness of the original piece of legal information.

In consequence, when trying to summarise the aspect of authenticity, one can draw the conclusion that the requirements of authenticity certainly do not suggest that changes of any kind cannot be accepted. On the contrary, an analysis of this aspect shows that when commercial legal information systems are scrutinised from the point of view of legal data quality it is quite clear that amendments, e.g. in the form of editorial notes, and similar features are among the most important things to investigate. Likewise, in many situations various kinds of abstracts, reference systems, and indexes may be very valuable.

On the other hand, the authenticity aspect focus our attention on the fact that if alterations of some kind are made, it is of utmost importance that they are made explicit. Likewise, it is obvious that it in many situations it is of crucial importance to be able to reconstruct and retrieve the original versions of the legal material. In this respect the rule of law and its various implications makes it important to remember that it is always the original official material that must constitute the ultimate source in legal work.

As a general conclusion it may be said that in situations in which authenticity is an important factor, it may be a good strategy to seek information as near its source as possible. This simply reflecting the fact that all kinds of the so called value added services, as well as commercial information systems based on edited forms of official public information may include risks in the sense that the material may have been wrongfully

---

[24] *See, e.g.,* Vogel, Hans-Heinrich, *Juridiska översättningar*, 1988, *and* Delegationen för översättning av EG:s regelverk: *Anvisningar för översättningsarbetet*, 1995.

altered in various ways. This naturally also sets the focus on the importance of data quality declarations.

These conclusions suggest, in turn, that the best strategy for an organisation focusing on the quality of legal data, and trying to be as efficient as possible with regard to legal information management, is to combine the original versions of legal material with more customised versions so that both authenticity and efficiency can be ensured.

3.4.2.4 Completeness

In an analysis of data quality and legal information it is also necessary to mention the aspect of completeness, or as it is sometimes referred to, the aspect of coverage. The latter is a technical term used to denote the proportion of all relevant documents present in a data base or an information system.[25]

When this aspect is scrutinised it can be concluded right from the start that within the legal sector there is a general agreement that a legal information system or a data base should have as high coverage as possible, or, in other words, that it is normally expected that information provided by a legal information system should be as complete as possible.

The aim for completeness can be explained and motivated in several ways. It must be observed, however, that in the legal context completeness can mean several things. At the most general level completeness is necessary in the sense that all legal sources must be available if legal work should be possible to complete in a professional manner. This, in turn, being a reflection of the fact that all legal investigations should strive for completeness in the sense that all relevant sources should be scrutinised.

The standpoint that lawyers should seek complete information can be traced back to the principle of *ignoranta juris non excusa,* meaning that ignorance can never excuse the inability to adjust one's activities to the requirements of the law. This fact implies, of course, that if some information if left out from the legal information system, this may have a

[25] *See, e.g.*, Bing, Jon & Harvold, Tryggve, *Legal Decisions and Information Systems*, 1977 at 163-69 and *passim.*

devastating effect on the work processes and the decisions that are being made. And if a law library or a legal information system lacks crucial information, this is also a strong argument against its use.

The ideal of completeness can also be looked upon, however, as a reflection of the rule of law. This is again a consequence of the authoritative nature of the law and the fact that official legal decision-making conducted by courts and public authorities must be based on the same material, disregarding where and when the decision-making process is taking place. In this respect the ideals of jurisprudence, such as freedom of information, and various other principles related to the rule of law, underline the fact that it must be possible to retrieve all kinds of legal information in order to be able to check previous solutions, authoritative interpretations, etc.

From a more practical point of view it must be admitted, however, that one cannot expect that any legal information system should include all the conceivable legal sources. The growing amount of legal information, the internationalisation, limited economic resources, and practical problems concerning availability, are some examples of factors which make all attempts to accomplish completeness problematic, if not impossible. From this it also follows that in many situations trying to collect all kinds of relevant materials is just not feasible.

Practical problems cannot, however, overshadow the fact that the goal of legal information managers must be in many cases to provide as complete information as possible. Thus, in all discussions of legal information system development it becomes necessary to bridge this gap between what is ideal and what is practicable. This sets, in turn, the focus on the necessity of law libraries and legal information managers to combine various legal information systems, i.e. instead of trying to construct legal information systems with complete coverage, it is obvious that it is a better strategy in most cases to learn how various kinds of legal sources and information products can be combined.

A further consequence of this is that there is no doubt that the ability of legal information managers and law libraries to combine, and present in adequate ways, information obtained from various sources will become one of the most important and challenging tasks of the future. Considered at a somewhat more specific level this presupposes the ability to reshape, readjust, and integrate information coming from different legal sources.

The above makes it also obvious that law libraries and legal information managers must constantly survey the market in order to be able to recognise new services and products, which may improve their internal information systems. This, in turn, sets the focus on the ability of the law library to supply its users with news reports, to highlight adjustments of the existing legal information systems, and to provide pedagogical overviews when new solutions are being discussed.

Practical problems stemming from the ideal of completeness can be approached, however, not only by means of combining various legal information systems and presenting new sets of material in a pedagogic way. Such a strategy may solve some problems, but it is quite clear that the vastness and the changing nature of the legal material imply that also other approaches must be tested. It is therefore not far fetched to suggest that in many cases it may be wise to shift from the still predominating *just in case strategy* to a *just in time approach*. This means that instead of trying to collect and store as much material as possible, it is in many situations better to try to elaborate the access methods in order to be able to locate and retrieve as complete versions of various kinds of materials as efficiently as possible. Such a strategy also suggests a shift towards the idea that law libraries should be looked upon in the first place as methodological resources, and not primarily as huge collections of physical material.

It must be noticed, however, that a shift to a just in time approach cannot be achieved overnight. It is, for instance, obvious that a reorientation of this kind will demand vast investments in education, not only of the users but also of the personnel of a library, and also the elaboration of various new routines. It is also quite clear that a new way of approach to the vastness of legal information cannot mean that former ways of handling legal information can be immediately abandoned. On the contrary, in order to satisfy the requirements of a legal organisation, the legal information manager or a law library must be prepared also in the future to collect and store large quantities of legal information on a just in case basis. This will be simply due to the fact that many users will expect to be able to retrieve material of their own in their local library in the way in which they are used to. Likewise, due to the continuity aspect, and because some material may be so frequently requested that it would be most practical to have constant access to it, it will be necessary in many cases to continue to collect hard copies of the material. From this also follows that the shift towards a more methodological strategy must be performed parallel to the upholding of a number of established routines. Likewise, it is clear that changes of a more profound nature can only be accomplished in a long term perspective.

Trying to achieve completeness is, however, not only of relevance when legal information is analysed at the general level. The ideal of completeness can also be related to any type of material that can be of relevance in legal work, i.e. legislative material, jurisprudential literature, court cases, etc. The principles of equality before the law and predictability thus also imply that there can be no question of whether or not a certain act, a case decision, or a jurisprudential comment has been excluded from a legal information system because its producer has come to the conclusion that it shows a relatively low importance, or because it lacks the circumstances of spectacularity. In this respect the aspect of completeness stands out as a rule of formality, stating that if a certain category of legal information has been selected for the inclusion in a legal information system, the user of the system must be able to rely on the fact that every one of the instances belonging to that category has been included.

It this context it may be noticed, however, that sometimes a conflict of interest may appear between the ideals of the users and commercial considerations. This is simply because data base producers and commercial publishers may want to give priority to frequently requested information, and for economic reasons may want to exclude rarely requested documents, e.g. court cases decided before a certain date. From the point of view of the users of legal information, on the other hand, it is quite clear that completeness means that a legal information system should provide as complete a series as possible of the selected type of information. The decision whether or not a certain piece of information is useful should be left to the end users, and it should not be based on a subjective (and perhaps non-legal) interpretation of the producer of the database, or the publisher of a hard copy product.

At this somewhat more specific level it should also be observed that completeness may relate to the fact that various legal sources and publication series are more or less intimately interrelated. Illustrations are provided by various kinds of legislative preparatory works which may have to be combined in order to reflect all aspects of a certain legal issue.

Likewise, it may be necessary to combine various court decisions (e.g. from the supreme court as well as from the appeal courts) in order to obtain a complete picture of the case law of a given legal domain. Or, to put it differently, from the complexity of legal information it often follows that various kinds of publication series and types of information may have to be combined in order to cover a legal source from the point of view of the subject matter.

Based on the fact that various kinds of legal material are normally interrelated, it may also be argued that different kinds of reference systems should be considered as necessary parts of a complete information system. This is simply caused by the fact that various forms of indexes may be more or less crucial for the effective identification and retrieval of interrelated legal materials. An example of this is that statutes may have to be accompanied by references to legislative preparatory materials, which are necessary for their adequate interpretation and application. For similar reasons case law series may have to be combined with subject matter indexes, various forms of edited abstracts, etc. The extreme form of this argument is to say that without the various forms of meta information, such as references (original or edited), indexes, etc., showing how various kinds of legal documents interrelate, legal information is not complete in the sense that it can be more or less impossible to use.

In addition to the discussion about the completeness of legal material as such, and its completeness when the need to cover various legal sources is concerned, completeness can also be addressed at a third level. That is simply to say that completeness is also relevant for the way in which legal information is treated at the document level. From this point of view the concept of completeness is closely related to the previously addressed authenticity aspect, implying that all items in a legal information system must be complete. If completeness cannot be guaranteed the users risk missing some aspect of the information that may be of relevance.

At the document level it is thus necessary to ensure that also components such as background descriptions, and various kinds of formal data are preserved. Depending on the context and the type of information system it may also be necessary, however, to add some kind of data to the documents, e.g. concerning the length of a certain text in terms of the number of lines or words, information as to whether or not a document has been edited or changed in any way due to its integration into the system, data about different versions, or references to other interrelated material in order to satisfy the requirements of completeness.

From the point of view of the legal organisation the desirable kind of "meta information" may also be of a somewhat technical nature. In this respect it may be natural, for instance, to accumulate statistical information about the usage of a legal information system. In some situations it may also be interesting to log and keep records, showing to what extent various legal sources are being used, who has been working with a certain types of information, how searches are being conducted, how frequent they are, etc. And although various aspects concerning the employees' privacy can be affected by an arrangement of this kind, it is quite clear that information about user behaviour may be very valuable in order to understand how the resources within a certain organisation ought be allocated. Data about system performance and system use is naturally also of crucial importance for further development of any information system.

If one tries to summarise the reasons why completeness is such a crucial factor in legal information management it is quite clear that, besides the aspects related to the rule of law implying that legal research processes should be as broad as possible, an important incitement is constituted in the fact that it is more or less impossible to decide the relevance of some piece of legal information in advance. That is to say that it is simply impossible to know when and in what situations a piece of legal information may become relevant. A lawyer must be prepared to acknowledge the relevance of all types of information, and an advanced legal information system or a law library must be able to adjust itself to these premises and be prepared to satisfy a large variety of more or less unpredictable requirements.

At the same time it must be admitted that sometimes it is impossible to handle all types of legal information. Information overload is in many situations a practical problem, not only in the form of difficulties with storing but also with regard to efficient retrieval. This, in turn, sets the focus on the means of filing, and adequate ways of making omissions and giving priority. As a consequence, several arguments which can be used in order to exclude certain materials from legal information systems will be addressed. Before this is done, however, the requirements of legal information from the point of view of the individual lawyer will be discussed.

3.4.3 Requirements of the Individual Lawyer

3.4.3.1 Introduction

From the perspective of the individual lawyer there is little doubt that legal information is a very complex matter and that the requirements will vary depending on the situation in which the lawyer finds himself. This is not only to say that various kinds of legal problems may require different forms of legal information. It is also suggested that the need for legal information varies during the different phases of the problem solving process.

To start with, it must be observed that all discussions about requirements of individual lawyers must consider the close relationship between the form and the substance of law, and the fact that text is the fundamental communication medium. It is, however, also apparent that successful legal argumentation presupposes that the notions conceived during the identification of a legal problem can be transformed into explicit terms in order to activate external information systems, (e.g. the employment of a subject index in a legal library requires the conscious use of one or several index terms.)

Likewise, in order to conceive and retrieve relevant legal information, several, previously identified concepts may have to be related to each other. An inspection of the established pieces of legal knowledge may thereby indicate that additional information may have to be retrieved. Legal information retrieval is thus a process that may have to be activated repeatedly, and often with different objectives in mind. The ability to identify the relevant point of law and decide when all the relevant items of legal knowledge have been established is of critical importance here, as any mistake during this phase may be fatal to the outcome of the decision. Most lawyers are well aware of this and recognise the fact that law-search is one of the most crucial aspects of the legal work process.[26]

---

[26] An IRI-survey covering different categories of lawyers indicated that law-search was the most desirable activity for rationalisation in legal work. Wahlgren, Peter, *ADB, telekommunikationer och juridiskt arbete*, 1983 at 58. Although this study is rather old now, it is obvious that the internationalisation and the growing bulk of legal information has in no way diminished the difficulties related to efficient legal information retrieval.

As concerns the identity of legal information that is being requested, various users and user groups will without doubt have different needs. In a similar way it is obvious that requirements concerning the best ways of combining and presenting the information will also vary. It is, for instance, clear that the needs of a legal expert preparing for litigation will differ when compared to a layman's needs, seeking advice on how to proceed in a legal dispute. In this respect it is possible to distinguish to some extent groups of users with similar needs, e.g. immigrants, handicapped, laymen, experts, teachers, and so forth. From the point of view of the legal information manager, however, the complications in this respect may become rather difficult to handle, at least if the ambition is to provide something more than a rough compilation of basic legal material. This, of course, due to the fact that a good understanding of the requirements of a certain group may require extensive analysis.

It must furthermore be observed that there is an on-going discussion about *the nature of knowledge* that can be extracted from legal sources. That is to say that apart form the obvious fact that legal documents and legal texts of various kinds must be looked upon as core elements, complementary and alternative legal structures are also discussed – issues which are of crucial importance in the age of IT.

One frequently debated issue in this context is whether or not it is possible to extract legal rules from legal information, or whether additional components must be included in order to conceptualise rules. It has thereby been stressed that, in addition to knowledge that may be found in legal sources, lawyers must also consider knowledge of a subjective nature. Some legal philosophers have also argued that the material that can be found in legal sources is to be understood primarily as the part forming (transformable) components for consideration in legal work, constituting merely *raw-material* so to say.[27]

It is also clear that as an examination of this kind is being elaborated, the requirements that are identified are becoming more and more diversified,

[27] *Cf.*, on categorisation of legal knowledge, Susskind, Richard, *Expert Systems in Law*, 1987 at 56-57, who suggests a demarcation between *academic legal knowledge* ''law-formulations together with legal commentaries on these materials ... 'the repositories of law''' and *experimental legal knowledge* ''knowledge of the day-to-day practical administration of the law".

and that ultimately each individual will have different opinions about the kind of information that should be included in a legal information system.

In addition it must be noted that the previously mentioned normative framework is also highly relevant at the individual level. That is to say that in their decision making and other kinds of daily activities lawyers are normally bound to follow a large number of administrative and methodological rules (to be explained) concerning the ways in which the work processes ought to be conducted. To complicate matters further different rules of this kind are used in different legal areas.

From all this it follows that it is very difficult to elaborate upon the identity of substantial law in such a way that individual requirements can be described in any detail, without the description becoming at the same time of rather limited interest.

Hence, in the following sections a somewhat different approach is shown in which the focus is set on the various *forms* of legal knowledge that can be identified by studying the legal work process. The assumption is here that such an approach may help to identify the kind of functions and information structures that should be given priority in order to satisfy the requirements of the users. It is also assumed that an analysis focusing on forms of legal knowledge can be more easily kept on a more general level, being also able to identify various desirable ways in which legal information could be managed in the law libraries of the future.[28]

[28] The categorisation of legal knowledge reflected in sections 3.4.3.2 - 3.4.3.6 has been previously outlined in Wahlgren, *supra* chapter 1 note 8 at 176-87.

3.4.3.2 Legal Documents

Looking at legal information retrieval in an unprejudiced way makes it obvious that the way in which legal knowledge may be approached depends intimately on how the law is represented. In this respect there is little doubt that legal knowledge appears mainly in written form – and that lawyers must concentrate in practice on the investigation of legal documents. From this it follows in turn that in practice the search for legal information is closely related to document retrieval.

Search for legal documents is thus a normal, but often cumbersome task, showing a number of well-known characteristics and distinguished by frequently reappearing problems. The most common difficulty is perhaps the previously mentioned fact that the amount of material related to a certain issue may be immense. This means that lawyers are very dependent on search aids, and that the outcome of a search process is related to some extent to practical skills of various kinds, concerning e.g. the physical operation of retrieval facilities, familiarity with law library organisation, legal subject indexes, etc.

It should furthermore be remembered that legal documents appear in many shapes, and that because of this various kinds of documents must be often investigated and related to each other before a legal issue can be identified. Identification of the relevant documents often poses a problem in this respect since knowledge of legal publications series and other kinds of secondary structures, e.g. document organisation in various kinds of in-house files, court files, individualised agreements, etc. is important for effective legal information retrieval. It should also be noticed that extracting large numbers of documents from various sources may be a cumbersome task. Searching for legal documents may therefore create not only problems of an intellectual nature, but also physical arrangements, distance and other tangible aspects may be of relevance as regards the ability to complete the process in an efficient manner.

In spite of these complications, the first trivial conclusion must state, nevertheless, that legal documents are natural components, or that they at least constitute the necessary points of departure in the design of legal information systems for the future. This is, of course, also clearly reflected in the existing legal information systems, computer-based or not, in which documents are almost without exception the only objects of concern.

A further consequence of this is that it is rather obvious that legal information systems – within their different fields of interest – should seek to give access to as many relevant documents as possible. Likewise, it is quite clear that the documents should be arranged, linked, and classified in such a way as to be accessible to as many users, or categories of users, as possible. From the need to combine various legal documents it also follows that elaboration of meta information of various kinds, i.e. information about the information within a certain system, must be given considerable attention.

3.4.3.3 Legal Texts

Looking somewhat closer at the requirements of the individual lawyer it becomes obvious, however, that the final aim of legal information retrieval can seldom be to read a document from the beginning to the end, or to find a document *per se*. For instance, in statutes it is usually a few specific sections that provide the relevant knowledge for a specific problem, in case material a lawyer may devote his initial interest to final statements, in a legal handbook it may be sufficient to read a paragraph or a chapter, and so forth. Hence, in authentic search situations the objective of legal information retrieval is to identify various subdivisions of legal documents.

Effective text-browsing, in turn, presupposes familiarity with the ways in which the material is organised in various legal documents, e.g. the awareness that final statements in appealed court decisions are to be found after the description of the circumstances, that subject indexes in law reports may appear in the latest issue of each volume, etc. A professional search for text paragraphs is also related to the understanding of document organisation at a general (i.e. non-legal) level. Knowledge of the latter kind is often used, no doubt, in an unconscious way. Nonetheless, it must be assumed that general knowledge concerning document organisation will be employed in a procedural manner. That is simply to say that it is reasonable to assume that the inspection of e.g. titles, tables of contents, summaries, headlines, etc., in legal documents is often conducted in a similar way.

Also, at this level of organisation, it is obvious that material from various legal sources may have to be combined. A certain issue may have been discussed and described in many different texts originating from various sources. In other words, lawyers must normally inspect and juxtapose several interrelated texts. From this it follows in turn that lawyers must be able to utilise reference systems of various kinds (footnotes, literature references, and name indexes, and so forth).

Just how important this ability to combine texts from various sources is can be illustrated by a well known decision of the Swedish Supreme Court (NJA 1957 s 621). In this case a practising lawyer was found guilty of malpractice because he failed to observe a text passage in a book of jurisprudence well-known among lawyers, issued some 30 years earlier, where, among other things, a supreme court decision from 1904 was analysed. It should be observed that no explicit references to these texts were given in the law editions that were in common use at the time.

A closer look at references to interrelated legal texts reveals that they can be of several different kinds. A noticeable difference exist, for instance, between original and edited references. Original references are included in the text by the author or the publishing authority. This is, for instance, the case where explicit references to other materials are imbedded in the text in various ways, e.g. in the form of footnotes, indexes, etc. Edited references, on the other hand, have been added to the text by, for example, an editor, information manager, or a system designer. Also edited references can be of different kinds. They may reflect relations to other materials that have been implicitly referred to in the texts (a work of jurisprudence may give references to "case law" which, in turn, may mention "preparatory works", etc.) Edited references may however also interconnect texts which initially had little or no relationship to each other. They may also be utilised when material is being accumulated, as when case decisions are being published. Each kind of reference may be essential for effective legal information retrieval, and in the legal sector many information products more or less depend on elaborate sets of references. It is even possible to claim that elaborate referencing systems often constitute the most easily distinguishable "value adding component" in legal information products.

In this respect the consequences for legal information management are clearly distinguishable. The importance of texts and text structures in legal work indicates that a most important objective of legal information management will be to elaborate and, if possible, combine various legal sources functionally and in such a way that the requirements of individual users can be meet in the best way. This means that various kind of referencing systems may have to be developed and integrated into legal information systems so that the different texts and text paragraphs can easily be combined. In practice, it may thus also be necessary to initiate more or less technical activities, such as hypertext linking, database maintenance, etc.

As concerns the implementation of effective referencing systems various approaches may be of relevance. In this respect there is a continuum between the very simple linking of explicit, original references, and the development of more ambitious projects, which may presuppose the elaboration of edited referencing systems, manual indexing, and cumbersome construction of intricate hypertext structures. The latter kind of editing is obviously more problematic as it does not only presuppose extensive knowledge of legal sources in various legal fields, but it also depends on the availability of considerable resources. This is simply due to the fact that the material may be very voluminous, and because the aspect of continuity often indicate that some sort of established organisation is necessary in order to handle changes and amendments of the material over time.

3.4.3.4 Legal Concepts

An in-depth analysis of legal information retrieval from the point of view of the lawyer must go beyond the text-representation level. Another crucial observation therefore indicates that a search for legal components in authentic situations is domain-related. From this follows, in turn, that any subject matter that is perceived by a lawyer in a given work situation may eventually provide the first association to a legally relevant concept. This implies that an essential condition for the ability to initiate search processes effectively is possessing immediate access to a rich spectrum of *legal concepts*. In a discussion of legal information retrieval it must be observed, however, that each activated legal concept may have a decisive influence on the successive sequences of the search process. This follows from the basic function of legal concepts, which is to tie elements to each other in a legally relevant way.[29]

Sometimes this connecting function of a legal concept may be highly technical. This is, for instance, the case when a legal concept is to provide links to explicit legal definitions appearing in legal rules of substantive nature, e.g. *data intrusion* is a legal concept used in order to communicate information about certain related elements (prerequisites), such as unauthorised access or change, data files, electronic data processing, and so forth. The concept is of a technical nature since in an instance of rule application each prerequisite has to be established in an indisputable way. If any component is lacking, then data intrusion is not an adequate term.

Legal concepts may be, however, less technical. That is to say, legal concepts need not be of any immediate relevance to rule application. The main function of a concept may be to provide a convenient, general label in order to facilitate communication about a number of related legal concepts.[30] *Information Technology Law* for instance, is a concept interrelating a great number of legal concepts dealing with different kinds of activities.

The observation that concept structures play a crucial role in legal thought processes may seem trivial and obvious. It is, however, important to observe that conceptual structures constitute the fundamental corpus of legal knowledge, and that various kinds of legal concepts are basic building blocks in all fields of the law. Legal concepts appear in almost innumerable versions and, depending on the domain, form together more or less elaborate structures. The clarification of the meaning of legal concepts and their relations to each other are the major objectives of continental (dogmatic) jurisprudence. In consequence, in all detailed discussions concerning the design of legal information systems it must be accepted that legal concept structures are vital for the understanding of how to retrieve the relevant legal knowledge.

---

[29] This technical aspect of legal concepts has been extensively discussed by Lars Lindahl who submits that ''The connecting function of a legal-technical concept is a special case of a general phenomenon ... On the whole, it is even possible to claim that the connecting function is a presupposition of a *concept*.'' Lindahl, Lars, *Definitioner, begreppsanalys och mellanbegrepp i juridiken*, 1985 at 43 (original text in Swedish).

[30] *Cf.* Frändberg, Åke, *Till frågan om de juridiska begreppens systematik*, 1985 at 84, who distinguishes between legal concepts with a systematising function (*systematiserande R-begrepp*) and a function of constituting rule elements (*regelkonstituenter*).

From this point of view it is, however, also apparent that different individuals will give priority to different concepts, as well as different conceptual structures. From this it follows, in turn, that because the requirements vary among different users, the ultimate legal information system aiming to serve more than one user would be the one that would be able to present the legal information in various ways.

A further consequence of this is that an effective legal information system should reflect as many adequate legal concept structures as possible, and also that the same type of legal knowledge, e.g. an act or a legislative preparatory work, may have to be represented so that it can be accessed in several ways.

It thus becomes apparent that major undertakings for legal information managers should be to try to identify the various user groups, and try to understand the levels of abstraction that these groups would prefer to work with. Such an analysis will indicate, for instance, that laymen and undergraduate schools will request legal information at a non-technical, pedagogical level.[31] Expert lawyers, on the other hand, will request in many situations very detailed legal information, giving high priority to precise definitions of requisites, extensive references to related materials, and similar aspects. The legal information manager will thus have to be able to customise legal information systems, so that they can meet the requirements of individual lawyers, or groups of lawyers, providing this kind of detailed knowledge.

3.4.3.5 Legal Rules

In continental jurisprudence the notion of legal rules is a commonly accepted one. It is furthermore quite common to describe the legal reasoning process as a process of rule application. Although not entirely uncontroversial, it may be argued that legal rules are a rather effective means of describing and understanding the law.[32]

---

[31] *Cf.* Gunnarsson, Britt-Louise, *Lagtexters begriplighet*, 1982.

[32] *See*, for a more extensive discussion, Wahlgren *supra* chapter 1 note 8 at 146, 266-70.

In this context it must be noted, however, that some legal philosophers have strongly emphasised the incorrectness of perceiving the legal system as a collection of predefined rules. The debate whether or not legal decision making ought to be understood as a rule-based process of deduction has been rather persistent. The discussions include both descriptive and prescriptive arguments. Likewise, numerous discussions of advantages and disadvantages – have been submitted.

As mentioned before, the primary objective of all processes of legal information retrieval is to find a legal description that matches the current case. In legal rules, descriptions appear as antecedents or consequents and in their information retrieval lawyers may aim for either kind. Aiming for descriptions in the form of antecedents is perhaps most common, but sometimes the primary objective is to scrutinise descriptions of consequents. The latter is, for instance, the case when hypothetical scenarios are to be evaluated during planning sessions.

It is important, however, to observe that it is often inadvisable to terminate the process of search as soon as one, seemingly relevant description has been found. In order to get something out of a legal description the lawyer must be able to find the corresponding antecedent or consequent. In other words, the objective of legal information retrieval is to find a *complete legal rule*, and not only an isolated description.

Additional complications may arise from the fact that a consequent description in one rule is also frequently an element of an antecedent description of another rule. Lawyers must therefore often sift through hierarchically ordered chains of rules.

The relations between conditional elements in legal rules are sometimes easily spotted, e.g. when the complete rule is expressed in a single text section. The process of relating the elements of legal rules to each other may pose problems, however, for several reasons. One difficulty is that the interrelated conditional elements of a rule often appear in different parts of a legal text, e.g. a statute.[33]

The difficulty may consist not only in being able to find the interrelated conditional elements of legal rules. It may also be cumbersome to comprise

[33] In theoretical contributions the phenomenon of dispersed rule elements is sometimes explained by means of indicating a demarcation between rules and rule expressions. *See, e.g.*, Peczenik, Aleksander, *Rättsnormer*, 1987 at 9 (''norms'' and ''norm expressions'').

complete antecedent and consequent descriptions. That is to say, that in order to perceive a complete description of a legally relevant situation it may be necessary to investigate more supplementary material. A vague definition in a statute may, for instance, have to be combined with an illustration of a prerequisite in a case-report or in an amended regulation. In jurisprudence this is commonly referred to as *legal rule fragmentation.*[34] Thus, inter-related rule-fragments may be dispersed in a limited area of law but from time to time it may be necessary to investigate seemingly remote areas for guidance on some aspect.

3.4.3.6 Legal Rule Systems

A further investigation of the legal information retrieval process shows that within substantive law, rule fragments are not the only structures that have to be extracted. Lawyers must also pay attention to other kinds of relations. One important legal structure that must be considered reflects legal rule systems. It means here that legal rules may be complete *per se* but in spite of this in practical work it may be necessary to handle them in combination with other kinds of legal rules.

The operative function of various kinds of legal rules may be illustrated by the fact that alleged criminal acts must be examined in accordance with the rules of the penal code. The examination is guided, in turn, by rules determining the ways in which evidence is to be evaluated. Simultaneously, rules on how sentencing ought to be performed must be taken into consideration. In addition, to be able to fully understand the penal code and the criminal procedure it may also be necessary to consider the rules of formality, governing the way in which the court proceeding ought to be managed. The latter type of rules is in turn closely related to rules on how judges are appointed, how jury members are selected, etc. In other words, the rules of substantive law (dealing with the original legal problems) must be related to various kinds of methodological rules, and formal rules (regulating the way in which rules of substantive law may be applied).

[34] *See*, generally on rule fragmentation, Sundby, Nils Kristian, *Om normer,* 1974 at 387, *and* Eckhoff, Torstein, *Rettskildelære*, 1971 at 44-51.

Within analytical jurisprudence several suggestions concerning classification of rules have been submitted. Perhaps the most well-known division between different kinds of rules is the one introduced by *H. L. A. Hart*, who has presented a model based on the concept that rules exist at two different levels, and that they are divided into *primary* and *secondary rules*.

Thus the secondary rules may said to be at a different level than the primary rules, for they are all *about* such rules; in the sense that while primary rules are concerned with actions that individuals must or must not do, the secondary rules are concerned with the primary rules themselves. They specify the ways in which the primary rules may be conclusively ascertained, introduced, eliminated, varied, and in which their violation conclusively may be determined.[35]

Hart divided the secondary rules further into: *rules of recognition* (deciding criteria for the validity of other kinds of legal rules), *rules of adjudication* (defining a procedure for identifying the individuals and the procedures to be followed when primary rules have been set aside), and *rules of change* (defining procedures for the change of primary rules).[36]

The notion of a secondary system has also been accepted by *Carlos E. Alchourrón* and *Eugenio Bulygin* who recognise two groups of rules within the secondary system: "We have given the name of secondary system or judge system to the set of norms regulating the actions of judges as such. These norms may be divided into two groups: (i) those that determine in what conditions the judges may judge and what types of question they may resolve (norms of competence); and (ii) those that establish obligations and prohibitions for the judges".[37]

A related, but rather controversial sub-division of entities in law is the distinction between rules and principles, suggested by *Ronald Dworkin*. Principles are proposed here to serve as a complement to rules denoting a set of "standards that do not function as rules'' and are to be adhered to "because it is a requirement of justice or fairness or some other dimension of morality.''[38]

---

[35] Hart H.L.A., *The Concept of Law*, 1961 at 92.

[36] *Id.* at 92-96.

[37] Alchourrón, Carlos E. & Bulygin, Eugenio, *Normative Systems*, 1971 at 151.

[38] Dworkin, Ronald, *Taking Rights Seriously*, 1977 at 22.

Submissions stressing various kinds of rule systems have been also proposed by a number of Scandinavian legal philosophers, e.g. by *Alf Ross* who recognises three different rules of competence (regulating *personal competence, procedural competence, and substantial competence*);[39] by *Tore Strömberg* who makes a distinction between *rules of conduct* (describing patterns of activities), *rules of qualification* (defining legally relevant qualities), and *rules of competence* (defining legally relevant competencies);[40] by *Aleksander Peczenik* who, among other things, separates between *constituting norms* and *regulating norms*.[41] and by several others.[42]

Categorisations of various kinds of legal rules have not been elaborated upon here. In this context it may be sufficient to conclude that in legal information retrieval lawyers must be able to perceive and extract rule-systems. Extending the meaning of the terminology concerning rule fragments, it may be therefore appropriate to say that lawyers must pay attention to various forms of *law fragmentation*, and, consequently, that legal information managers should accept and be able to handle various kinds of rule systems.

3.4.4 Information overload

3.4.4.1 Introduction

In the legal sector information overload is probably the most common reason for the application of selection processes. The fact that legal material sometimes takes on gigantic proportions is quite well known, frequently leading up to the conclusion that certain material should be omitted from the information systems, whereas other material must be prioritised.

---

[39] Ross, Alf, *Directives and Norms*, 1968 at 96.

[40] Competence in Scandinavian jurisprudence has been extensively commented on by Strömberg Tore, *Rättsordningens byggstenar*, 1988 *passim*.

[41] Peczenik, *supra* note 33 at 15-32.

[42] *See, e.g.*, Sundby *supra* note 34 at 190-306, Eckhoff, Torstein & Sundby, Nils Kristian, *Rettssystemer*, 1976 at 128, and Jareborg, Nils, *Värderingar*, 1975 at 87-97.

Problems with information overload may be experienced not only by the users of information systems, but also by their producers. This is simply to say that at some point the task of collecting, updating and managing of information will become so cumbersome that the only realistic way to handle the situation will be to make a selection, omitting some of the material.

In a similar manner, the user may perceive problems with information overload as a practical obstacle. Difficulties may occur, for instance, when the databases contain too many documents so that the search tools are no longer able to distinguish the relevant from the irrelevant, or when the databases in an information system or a library are so numerous that it is no longer is possible to recognise the relevant ones. Difficulties of the latter kind may appear also, of course, due to the fact that information services and products become so numerous that it is difficult to choose between them – a situation which presently can be observed at the Internet.[43]

Information overload may be handled to some extent by means of making the search tools more effective, or by means of extending the storing capacities of the information system.[44] Likewise, a number of problems may be approached by means of forming meta indexes of various kinds.[45] In this respect the question of how to select legal information for the inclusion in information systems is very much the issue of the available resources, technical investments, etc. On the other hand, it must be admitted that many practical problems with information overload may lose their importance if the material is decomposed into smaller, more manageable portions. In such undertakings, a number of starting points exist, e.g. definitions of jurisdictions, document series, types of publications, subject-matter domains, issuing organisations, etc.

---

[43] *See, e.g.*, "http://www.ilrg.com/"which lists some 3.100 legal web-sites.

[44] The LEXIS®-NEXIS® services contain more than 18.300 sources (13.500 news and business sources, and 4,800 legal sources). More than 9.5 million documents are added each week to the more than 1.3 billion documents online. *See* "http://www.lexis-nexis.com/lncc/".

[45] *See*, for such initiatives, the previously mentioned, *The Global Legal Information Network, GLIN*, at "http://lcweb2.loc.gov/glin/glinhome.html", *and The European Legislative Virtual Library, ELVIL*, "http://www.sub.su.se/elvil.htm". *See also*, for theoretical contributions, Chiang, Win-Shin, S. & Price, Kathleen, *International Access to Legislative Information: A Preliminary Investigation*, 1992, *and* Blumer, Thomas, J, Bolis, Monica & Hyde, Janice, *International Access to Legislative Information: Vol. II, Collection, Storage, Retrieval and Delivery of Public Information*, 1994.

As the material grows, however, the demands for active legal information management will increase and the ability to provide high quality IT products will ultimately depend not only on available technical and economic resources, but equally important will be the producer's understanding of how to index the material and how to make adequate, jurisprudentially sound selections. In such undertakings a number of aspects should be taken into consideration and in the following sections some of them will be discussed in more detail.

3.4.4.2 Lack of Substance

In many situations information may be excluded from a legal information system because it is repetitive. The user of any information system wants to be able to retrieve information that will add some kind of substance to a certain issue. Conversely, if some information does not contribute anything new there is usually no reasons to include that material. A typical example here would be, of course, large volumes of court decisions on similar issues and with identical outcomes. In the design of data bases for such areas of the law it is obviously enough to select illustrative examples of such cases and combine them with information about their frequencies.

In this respect the *Council of Europe* has issued recommendations according to which court decisions may be excluded from legal information retrieval systems "if the grounds on which they are based are stated according to a standard formula or formula clause".[46] The general principle being that "in [legal] sections where a selection is made, this must be objective, ... and the selected decisions must be generally representative of the jurisprudence in the sector in question."[47] Moreover, it has been suggested that when decisions expresses a "constant practice" the decisions should be "represented in such a way as to reflect the main principles of the jurisprudence in the field concerned. On the other hand, this should not tend to impede a possible evaluation of case law. Consequently, the legal

[46] Council of Europe, *The selection, processing, presentation and archiving of court decisions in legal information retrieval systems*, 1996 at 10.

[47] *Id.* at 7.

information systems should, at adequate intervals, store decisions that confirm or reverse a 'firm practice' of the courts. Appropriate indications could be given, for example by adding annotations confirming or changing the practice."[48]

Although case law is a typical example when this aspect is discussed, material containing recurring information may also be found in legislative preparatory works as well, as in works of dogmatic jurisprudence, e.g. in voluminous background descriptions which occur sometimes in several documents in order to supplement various arguments or lines of reasoning. In an electronic information system, however, there is obviously no need to include more than one version of such material. The need to combine various versions of similar material can be satisfied instead by an elaborate system of references. Difficulties connected with such a solution stem from the fact that the material in question must be edited in a comprehensive way, which is very time consuming and often also presupposes legal expertise.

3.4.4.3 Relevance of the Subject-matter

Unnecessary repetition of information is not the only criteria for the exclusion of certain material from a legal information system. Another argument for the exclusion of material from such systems may be that for reasons of systematisation the material in question ought to be included in a different information system, e.g. because it belongs to a different jurisdiction, or because it concerns a different topic.

"Selection by fields of law is a useful way of limiting the amount of information available for retrieval when establishing systems designed for special groups of users. --- This could be done by storing all decisions given by one or several types of specialised courts, for example fiscal courts, criminal courts, etc."[49]

The issue of how to classify information based on the relevance of the subject matter is, however, in many situations a very delicate one. That is to

[48] *Id.* at 10.

[49] *Id.* at 9.

say that any selection based on the relevance of the subject matter presupposes categorisation of the material, which may not always be easy to do objectively. It is, for instance, obvious that a certain piece of information may become relevant in another situation and that the ways in which legal materials are evaluated and looked upon change over time. In the design of legal information systems consideration must therefore be also taken of the fact that the development of the law may be impossible to predict and that sometimes analogies and principles from one area of the law may become highly relevant also in other situations.

In a discussion about the subject matter's relevance, it must be noticed furthermore that different fields of law can be defined in different ways. This means in turn that material may be classified in various ways, depending on where and by whom the classification is made.

The difficulties of a decision in this respect make it possible to argue that information systems should be as neutral as possible and that selection of material depending on the subject matter's relevance should be in principle avoided. It may even be suggested that the important thing is that all material is made available and that a decision as to whether, and in which situations a certain piece of information is to be considered as relevant or not should be left to the user to decide for himself.

On the other hand, selections based on the relevance of the subject-matter are in most situations crucial for reaching practical solutions. Perhaps the most common way of defining the subject matter's relevance is to explicitly select those categories of cases that a certain court or a certain authority has the power to try and decide. Such material may then be extended by means of including legislation, jurisprudential literature and other kinds of information concerning those categories. The result of such a compilation may then reflect a jurisprudential notion known as *subject-matter jurisdiction*.[50] Examples of this are Tax Law, Labour Law, etc. From the point of view of a professional lawyer, categorisation by subject matter is without doubt a very practical way of organising legal information. Legal

[50] *See, e.g.*, for an illustration of various kinds of subject matter jurisdictions in the International Court of Justice, Shabtai, Rosenne, *The World Court*, 1995 at 81-111. Principles of subject matter jurisdiction also determine the competence of various kinds of courts (e.g. criminal courts and administrative courts) that may be found within a certain country or a certain territory.

information systems reflecting subject-matter categorisations are therefore easily accepted as a rule.

At the same time, when the volume of information is vast and when information originates from many different countries, it is easy to overlook important material as well as to identify the material which can be excluded. Selections based on the identification of subject-matter jurisdictions may therefore result in very large collections of material, so that in order to reach manageable solutions further categorisations may have to be done. Moreover, it must be observed that the relevant considerations may be constantly changing in the sense that new subject-matter categories, such as e.g. Gene Technology Law, International Environmental Law, etc., may come into focus, while the previously established legal topics may lose their importance.

Categorisation by subject matter is, however, not the only possible way of separating material. Jurisdictions, as well as legal materials may be defined in various ways. That is to say that in addition to subject matter defined areas of the law there also exist other kinds of categorisations, which may be used as starting points in the design of legal information systems. Jurisdictions may be, for instance, looked upon as being of a *territorial* nature, i.e. it may simply be postulated that cases occurring within a certain territory are the ones that should be considered to be relevant. And, in a system based on these principles, the strategy is simply to include all the material of relevance for the legal system of that territory. In practice, a large number of national legal information systems are examples of such undertakings.

In addition, a decision about the inclusion of a certain case can be influenced by the fact that a person is physically present in, or has some relations to, a certain territory (e.g. by means of citizenship, marriage, habitation, etc.). This is often referred to as *personal jurisdiction*.[51] Categorisations of a similar kind may be used in order to develop effective information tools for certain groups of persons or organisations. Selections of this kind may be relevant, for instance, when the information system, or databases within a certain information system have been designed for

[51] *See, e.g.,* on territorial and personal jurisdiction Eek, Hilding, *Folkrätten*, 1987 *and,* on the relations between various principles of jurisdictional competence, Brownlie, Ian, *Principles of Public International Law*, 1990.

different purposes or various user groups. Legal information systems designed for the support of, e.g. tax planning, developed for accountants, real estate brokers, lawyers specialising in Labour Law, etc., are illustrations of products reflecting this type of categorisation of legal material

To make things even more complicated, the organisational principles of various jurisdictions may sometimes clash. This may make that the development of information systems reflecting various jurisdictions may be very complicated in some cases. In territorially-defined jurisdictions, for instance, only material generated by organs within a certain country may have to be considered as relevant. Some users may therefore find any extraterritorial materials to be irrelevant and superfluous. On the other hand, in subject-matter-defined jurisdictions, materials from various countries may have to be considered, e.g. due to international treaties, common legislation, etc. and if some materials are omitted, users may find the information system incomplete. Another matter to consider is the fact that a court's right to decide on certain legal issues may presuppose the existence of both subject-matter jurisdiction and personal jurisdiction.

Finally, it must be mentioned that the ongoing internationalisation and globalisation of the legal sector has changed many established presuppositions concerning the categorisation of legal material. It thereby appears that the subject-matter-defined jurisdictions may gain importance while territorially-defined jurisdictions are more frequently looked upon as of secondary importance. Likewise, it appears that specialised, personally defined legal information systems, aiming e.g. to support various kinds of legal professionals, or types of companies, will become more common. This may, however, vary a good deal depending on the area of law, which is why in each specific situation the relevant conditions must be thoroughly investigated. This obviously indicates, in turn, that flexibility and the ability to adjust to changes will become increasingly important for the providers of legal IT products.

The difficulties in this respect should not be looked upon, however, as definite obstacles. That is to say that although a selection process based on subject-matter jurisdictions presupposes active selection and systematisation, there is a large number of components, that may be used as a starting point for the decision on the relevance of certain legal information. To notice is also that in most situations, selections based on subject-matter relevance probably are the most efficient and commonly accepted ways of achieving manageable solutions.

3.4.4.4 Formal and Hierarchical Relevance

At some point in the scrutiny of legal information it becomes obvious that some portions of the legal material have such a low degree of relevance that it will be natural to exclude them. This is due to the simple fact that much legal information must be looked upon as being of a hierarchical nature.

Relations of this kind are most easily noticeable, of course, when case law is investigated. Materials coming from higher courts are normally more relevant for inclusion than those generated by the lower courts. Hierarchical relations exist also, however, between other forms of legal information, for example between the constitution, the common legislation, rules and recommendations issued by public authorities, etc. There is normally also a hierarchical difference between works of jurisprudence, e.g. developed for educational purposes, legal handbooks, and academic dissertations.

It must furthermore be noted that various legal sources found within a given territorial jurisdiction may exhibit different relations, depending on the area of the law. Case law may for instance be the primary source in Criminal Law, but at the same time may be of marginal interest in Procedural Law.

Sometimes hierarchical relations between various kinds of legal material form a patchwork in that certain powers may be delegated to lower instances or other authorities. In this respect the conditions may vary between different jurisdictions and between various legal areas. Delegation of authority may also be very specific, i.e. it may concern legal issues of a very special kind. In Sweden, for instance, penalties following road traffic offences are decided by the courts, while the question of the revocation of the offender's driving license is decided by an official authority, despite the fact that the underlying offence is the same. From this it naturally also follows that selections of this kind must be performed very carefully and that sometimes a decision to include or to omit a certain kind of material must be followed by a decision about related matters. The problems in this respect must not be exaggerated, however, in most cases formal rules exist, defining how various kinds of interconnected materials are related.

It must be remembered that decisions of the lower courts must not be lost sight of. These decisions may be highly relevant, for instance, due to the fact that they concern matters which have not been tried by the higher courts. The same may be true for decisions made by public authorities. In many areas of law hierarchical selection is, nevertheless, a practical way of delimiting the bulk of legal material. Hierarchical selection is also acknowledged by the Council of Europe as being a "useful way of limiting the amount of information available for retrieval."[52]

3.4.4.5 Obsolescence

Another reason that often motivates the exclusion of material from a legal information system is its obsolescence, that is when the material has become too old and therefore obsolete. The Council of Europe has expressed this in the following way: "[c]onsideration should be given to avoiding complicating the use of the system by the accumulation of a growing amount of obsolete information".[53]

Legal material may become obsolete for several reasons, e.g. due to new legislation, technical development in a given domain, or changes concerning the ways in which the courts decide on a certain issue. To decide about the exclusion of given material is, however, a delicate matter, and it is not possible to conclude that material can be omitted from a legal information system only because legislation has changed. Legal material that is no longer valid in a formal sense may be relevant in legal work processes for other reasons, so that before any final decision is made concerning whether or not old material should be excluded several aspects should be investigated.

One obvious reason to keep available their earlier versions of legal material in legal information systems is that old material may provide solutions which may be relevant to legal actions taken before the rules were changed.

---

[52] Council of Europe, *supra* note 46 at 9.

[53] *Id.* at 8.

In various areas of law, e.g. in Real Estate Legislation or Inheritance Law, these aspects may be more or less permanently present in the sense that the older versions of legislation may have to be referred to more or less constantly.

It must also be remembered that new legislation is normally based on earlier laws, and that arguments concerning vital details, central concepts, etc., are frequently relevant also after changes in the legislation. Moreover, it is widely accepted that arguments that can be found in historical material are often of a high quality and that the value of a legal discourse has nothing to do with the fact that the legislation may have changed in some respect. In this context it may be useful to recall that there is seldom any reason to reinvent the wheel, and that it is sometimes practical to use previous investigations in decisions about the outcome of an argument, despite the fact that some aspect of the legislation involved may have changed. This suggests, in turn, that more often than not there are reasons to keep the historical legal material available in a legal information system for a long time.

In addition, in practical work situations aspects of efficiency must also be considered. Knowing that previous solutions or arguments of high quality have been documented, it is often a good idea to start one's investigation by making an inventory of available information on the subject matter in question, e.g. in the form of court decisions. To have access to a large volume of previously collected information may be therefore extremely valuable. Although this must, of course, not overshadow the fact that time often may be a very useful aspect when legal data bases are going to be divided.

3.5 Technical Aspects

3.5.1 Introduction

In a discussion of technical requirements which can be related to legal IT applications various approaches are possible. In many situations it is natural to look upon technical matters as consisting of computers and other kinds of tangible equipment (hardware), as well as computer programs (software), and telecommunications. Each aspect may then be decomposed and analysed, eventually in several successive stages. In such an approach it is therefore natural to set up standards for each component in terms of capacities, size, speed, etc.

A somewhat different approach is to start from the needs of the users and the requirements of the legal sector. An approach of this kind is more in line with the initial ambition of this study, viz. to depart from the analysis of a legal work situation and then draw conclusions about technical requirements. The focus will then be set to a large extent on functional aspects, such as simplicity, flexibility, user friendliness, etc., the underlying assumption being that it is the legal sector that should eventually determine the standards of IT, and not the other way around.

A third way of investigating technical matters is to try to combine knowledge of various technical potentialities and legal requirements in order to be able to say something more profound about the desirable future of legal information systems as integrated phenomena. This task is more demanding but also more interesting as it is likely to be able to reflect more advanced solutions. In such an approach it is also suggested that both technical and jurisprudential components can be adjusted so that they can work together efficiently.

In the following sections all the three approaches mentioned above are reflected in various degrees. This simply illustrates the fact that also technical components can be described at various levels of abstraction. It is also important to remember, however, that conflicting perspectives and various kinds of priorities may be present when technical matters are scrutinised.

It is obvious, for instance, that demands which can be related to various technical aspects vary depending on the user situation and the tasks that are to be performed. In this respect the requirements differ little from the requirements concerning the information content. For example, a lawyer preparing for litigation will have different needs and expectations concerning the speed and reliability of telecommunications that he must use as compared to those of e.g. a law school class studying the criminal system.

Likewise, when the focus is set on interfaces, a recent British study reports that "lawyers criticised the interface of LEXIS, particularly its look and feel on the screen, its inability to provide you with page numbers of paper reports, the difficulty of moving from page to page, the production of too many irrelevant references and the awkwardness of its downloading as well as the poor quality of printout."[54] A few lines further down it was however submitted that "academics who used LEXIS found it perfectly satisfactory for their needs". In this context it was also underlined that one should remember that "[academics] pay much less, do not have to produce printouts in court and generally use LEXIS to find appropriate references rather than to read on screen."[55]

In this respect it is also noticeable that the varying degrees of computer literacy among the users will affect the formulation of technical requirements. This fact is reflected in the conclusion of the above-mentioned study in which it is suggested that "[t]he keyword search engine of systems such as LEXIS has achieved general acceptance, but *this is partly because users have not generally used alternative search and navigation techniques.*"[56]

Apart from the fact that the users may hold different opinions and expectations when analysing technical solutions, it is furthermore important to keep in mind that different technical solutions may coexist or provide satisfactory solutions of different kinds. From this it also follows that various technical standards may sometimes compete with each other. It may, for instance, turn out that a CD-ROM solution is able to provide more search facilities than an on-line database. Despite this it may be concluded that the latter is preferable, e.g. because it can be more frequently updated, and in an evaluation of technical solutions, the examples of this kind may easily be extended.

---

[54] Paliwala *supra* chapter 2 note 16.

[55] *Id.*

[56] *Id.* (italics added).

In a similar way the advantages of commercially developed products may have to be compared with the, perhaps less advanced but well-understood and fully integrated, facilities provided by existing in-house systems. Applications of the latter kind may have been developed in close co-operation with the users and contain information which has been accumulating during a long time. From this it follows that also psychological and social factors must be considered when technical aspects are being evaluated, a fact that will be further elaborated in Chapter 5.

3.5.2 Component Standards

When basic technical components are discussed, the requirements of the legal sector do not differ much from the needs that can be related to administrative and intellectual work in other domains. This is simply to say that individual users will expect to have access to modern, well-functioning equipment. Matters that are likely to be given high priority are thereby access to computers with enough processing and storing capacity to make possible simultaneous use and switching between several programs, CD-ROM disk drives, Internet connection, and features such as interoperability and portability of data and programs between various systems, etc. To try to specify aspects of this kind even further, e.g. by means of making suggestions concerning the number of MB, MHz, and Kilobits per second[57] that various components should be able to handle, is not meaningful, however. Nor is it possible to discuss the identity of the programs that would be preferable. In this respect the products and the related requirements are constantly changing, and are likely to do so also in the future.

When IT components for the legal sector are discussed, one additional aspect of importance is, of course, the fact that systems should provide adequate and updated software. At present, this entails that everyone will expect to find some version of "Windows", or a comparable graphic interface based on the elaborate use of icons. Likewise, simple to use cut and

[57] MB, MHz, and Kilobits per second are common units for measuring storing, processing, and data transfer capacities.

paste standards, links, and clickable buttons should be looked upon as standard components.

Another factor to consider in an evaluation of software for the legal sector is whether the various programs and the utilised hardware equipment are able to function together in a friction free manner. In this respect compatibility between various components has been a considerable problem in the design and updating of the IT-systems for a long time now. The difficulties originating from various software standards and the existence of different operating systems constitute, however, a diminishing problem as computers become continuously more and more powerful and the different systems are closing in on each other. It should be noticed, however, that although the technical means for interoperability between various standards are well developed, the practical difficulties that have to be overcome in order to accomplish this may be considerable.

When software components are discussed it is furthermore important to mention that in many cases simplicity is an important factor to consider. In this respect it should be noticed that in recent years many software applications intended for administrative "office-work" have become increasingly complicated to use, due to the fact that more and more functions have been included. In several cases this leads to a situation in which computer programs have to be abandoned, or alternatively, where especially trained system administrators have to be employed. The latter may, of course, be more or less impossible for small and medium-size companies due to the cost involved. The main problem here is that too much time has to be spent on trying to find the relevant functions and understand how the program should best be operated. Many computer programs have simply become too confusing for most users to handle in an efficient way. This problem is emphasised not only by the number of products that an individual user has to handle, but also by the increasing complexity resulting from the development of internal and external networks.

As concerns telecommunications the frequently requested facilities include being able to work together with others in such a way that data and programs can be accessed simultaneously from various working places, as well as possibilities of individual employees to work from home. It is also natural that in most cases technical reliability with respect to the ability of access to various systems stands out as an important aspect. Likewise, around-the-clock availability of products, and, if interruptions do occur, secure back-up facilities, together with more or less immediate assistance, are things that are likely to be requested by the end users in the legal sector. In addition, access to standard communications protocols and high-speed data transfer must be taken into consideration.

In connection with technical standards something should also be said about printing facilities. Many lawyers find this to be of high priority and the ability to produce high quality printouts is frequently mentioned as one of the most important aspects when introduction of new computer systems is being discussed. As usual, however, also in this respect the demands vary between various jurisdictions and various positions of the lawyers.

On the one hand, there are the ideals of perfection in style and lay-out, which make it necessary for the system administrator to provide advanced printout facilities. Demands concerning high quality in print-outs presupposes, in turn, access to modern word-processing facilities. Likewise, high quality is not possible here without access to knowledge about document formatting standards and similar matters.

On the other hand, in many cases the need for high-quality printouts may be less urgent. This is for instance the case when an in-house library system for the management of library references is used. In such a system the primary function of printouts may be to function as an aid to memory during the time when the lawyer is trying to retrieve a text from the library. Between these extremes a continuum of requirements can be found, relating e.g. to the production of in-house memorandums, informal reports, official correspondence, authoritative decisions, administrative regulations, etc.

When technical matters concerning equipment are discussed, it may also be appropriate to mention that it is often suggested that 17“ or 19“ screens are preferable since they facilitate the presentation and comparison of a number of texts and cases by means of allowing to have several windows open at the same time.

As regards the evaluation of software and technical components it is furthermore important to investigate how manuals and other kinds of information about a specific IT system are structured and presented. This is important not only because it is this material which determines whether a given system will be easily understood and how it will be utilised, but also because it has a direct effect on the ways in which educational activities must be arranged.

If the manuals are easily comprehensible, complete and correct they can be used in their original form, if not, it will be necessary to adjust or rewrite them. As an illustration of the latter it may be mentioned that at Stockholm University's Law School, an elaborate written instruction on how various kinds of legal software should be operated is produced each year. This has been found necessary not only because of the varying quality of the different original manuals, but also in order to obtain standardised terminology and a pedagogical acceptable structure of the material.[58]

In this context it may also be recalled that new technical standards come up more or less continuously. One recent such line of development is the introduction of the so called network computer, NC. A NC is a small, low cost computer based on the use of internal and external networks. A NC is equipped with a minimal RAM and lacks local mass-memory storage. It is nevertheless capable of supporting Web-browsing, electronic mail, word processing, database searches, etc. This is accomplished by means of receiving all data and software from a server over the network. In addition, all software upgrades, backups, and maintenance are done centrally from the network server. Thus the users do not need to worry about upgrading their software, backing up files, or protection against viruses.

Since all software and data are stored in one central server the users may access their data from any NC, disregarding where it is placed geographically. Security and identification are accomplished through a so called NC Card. Each user is provided with a unique NC Card, very much like a bank card, and is furthermore equipped with a PIN-code. The card can be inserted into any NC, and when used in combination with the PIN code it will provide secure access to the network server.

Apart from the cost aspect the development of NC has been explicitly motivated by the fact that many conventional IT systems have become all too complex due to excessive functionality. In this respect the NC can be seen as a reaction against the development of increasingly elaborate systems. An important assumption in this context stipulates that most users

---

[58] *See, e.g.*, The Swedish Law and Informatics Research Institute, *Studiematerial i rättsteknik*, 1996.

use only a small fraction of features in the existing applications, and that the applications designed for the network computer provide the features that people actually use. In consequence, it has been suggested that the NC applications are simple and intuitive. It is furthermore suggested that the fact that the software is administrated in a centralised way may eliminate the need for huge manuals.[59]

Thus, the utilisation of NCs, in turn, presupposes access to and the development of software standards of an entirely new kind. That is to say that the computer programs intended for applications of this kind must not only be easy to download and install more or less automatically, but that it must also be possible to demodulate them and integrate them with each other in order to satisfy the demands of different users. In this respect the effective utilisation of NCs presupposes also naturally access to web-based technology that can distribute and automatically install a variety of portable applications. It is furthermore assumed that software applications must be able to operate with common interfaces and standard presentation formats, etc. From the technical point of view this also implies standardised information structures and widely acceptable features concerning information mark-up standards and communication protocols for the exchange of information via servers over the Internet.

Whether or not NCs and the accompanying new software standards will be accepted remains, however, to be seen. From the functional point of view the concept of the NC appears to be to a large extent a rediscovery of the user terminals common in the 1980s. As concerns legal applications it may be recalled in this context that in the early days of the LEXIS the users were provided with an especially designed (bright red) terminal providing functional keys for "next case", "previous case", etc. Equipment of this kind is rare today, and it is not obvious that similar features may be again easily accepted by the users. Although, it is obvious that in many situations, e.g. in education, public libraries, etc., the cost aspect may turn out to be an important factor facilitating a broader introduction.

Several problems can nevertheless be anticipated. For instance, it appears quite clear that it will become more difficult to compete with NCs as

---

[59] *See,* for further (commercial) information about NCs, "http://www.nc.ihost.com/", *and* "http:/ /www.nc.com/nc. html#what".

computer literacy increases, and the Internet develops further. That is simply to say that also the general Internet development may eventually lead to more and more user-friendly, intuitive applications, as well as a further development of "pick-up and plug-in programs", making it possible to download and distribute software in more and more efficient ways. Another widely discussed question is whether NCs will reach a "critical mass" in the sense that its users become so numerous that the producers of hardware and software find it worthwhile to develop new components.

Nevertheless, disregarding whether or not NCs will become a common feature in the design of future IT systems, the concept has set the focus on the fact that computers should be more easy to use and administer. This is in itself a considerable contribution.

3.5.3 Functional Aspects

IT can also be approached from the functional level, where a variety of conclusions concerning desirable system performance can be drawn from the analysis of the nature of legal work and material.

One natural starting point is thereby the enormous quantity of legal information. This, in combination with the previously mentioned aim of completeness, immediately sets the focus on storing capacities. A desirable standard for a legal IT-system is thereby quite clear: the system should provide facilities for the incorporation of the maximum of (potentially) relevant information. In practice, this means that an IT system which is intended to be used as an aid in legal work cannot be limited with respect to the volume of the material that it can handle.

In this context mention may be made of the so called *arm's-length-law* and its influence on legal information retrieval. The general assumption here is that the likelihood that a lawyer will actually refer to a certain piece of legal information is related to the distance between the lawyer and the place where the information is stored. Not surprisingly, the arm's-length-law suggests that information that is easily accessible – i.e. which is located at arm's-length – will be utilised more often than information which is located further away, e.g. in a library across the hall, or even worse, in another part of the town.

It must be noted, however, that the concept of distance in the arm's-length-law is a metaphor, i.e. it contains not only physical distance, but also aspects such as lack of search tools, fragmentation of the information, or slow access methods.

The arm's-length-law has been elaborated on by *Peter Seipel* who has suggested three zones in which information can be located, vis-à-vis the individual lawyer, namely the immediate *near-zone,* the *home-zone,* and the *remote zone.*[60] In the traditional, paper based information system materials that can be found in the *near-zone* are books and documents which can be found very close to the lawyer, e.g. on his or her desk. The *home-zone* encompasses, among other places, the internal archives and the library of the organisation where the lawyer is active. In the *remote-zone,* entities such as public libraries, materials that can be found in the archives of public authorities, etc., constitute typical examples.

Thus, from the legal information manager's point of view, the objective should be to place as much information as possible in the near-zone, or, at least in the home-zone of the end users. In practice this means that a legal IT-system should provide smooth access to as many relevant databases and legal information sources as possible, via the Internet and other media, such as CD-ROMs, etc. This includes not only traditional legal documents in full text, but also library references and other kinds of information. In this respect it is obvious that in many ways IT drastically change the possibilities to utilise and access legal information in daily work. A computer on the desk with access to the Internet, as well as other external and internal databases can easily be compared to having access to a large library with innumerable volumes of various kinds of material.

The fact that legal material is so extensive, taking such disparate forms also imposes certain demands on its presentation techniques. It is, for instance, apparent that insufficient access to functions which can provide overviews of the available material may easily become a problem. Examples of this can frequently be observed, e.g., when inexperienced users are confronted with the 1.3 billion of documents provided by the LEXIS-NEXIS service,[61] or when law students encounter the large variety of

---

[60] Seipel, Peter, *Juridik och IT*, 1997 at 102-05.

[61] *See, supra* note 44, *and* " http://www.lexis-nexis.com/lncc/".

services providing EU material via the Internet. From the end users' point of view it is thereby important to stress the fact that the introductory facilities used by the system in order to provide presentations and overviews should appear in forms that are easily understood.

The need to relate the encountered information to the established concepts also entails that in many situations traditional library techniques should be reflected to some extent in the digital context. To be more precise, this means that one should be able to use features such as alphabetical listing of authors, titles as well as topical catalogues, and perhaps even shelf list metaphors via the computer screen. Of crucial importance here is furthermore the ability of the system to provide various kinds of overviews, handle graphical presentation techniques, etc. In this respect IT give access to many previously unavailable ways of material presentation, of which hierarchical menus, the use of icons, and various forms of clickable link structures are some of the most important ones.

It should also be noticed, however, that the accumulation of material made possible by the technique may cause numerous administrative and practical difficulties. It is, for instance, clear that information stored on a large number of CD-ROMs is difficult to handle and that the use of external CD-ROM bases may require access to additional technical equipment if it is to be efficiently utilised. Practical problems may, of course, also appear when users have to manage several on line products in order to reach the relevant documents, which are based, for example, on different search programs, passwords, and different systems of abbreviations. This, in turn, sets again the focus on sorting functions, graphical interfaces and the possibilities for the users to customise the way in which information is presented. For the same reason it becomes obvious that various kind of online solutions which are not adjusted to the Internet will encounter difficulties. Examples of the latter may be so called 3270 protocols and various forms of standards adjusted to some special computer system.

Another factor that immediately comes to mind when functional aspects of legal information systems are discussed is that the need for continuity imposes certain demands on the updating of the information. From the technical point of view the requirements concerning continuos updating naturally also presuppose access to reliable telecommunications, and high quality backup facilities and service. When this aspect is scrutinised, it becomes also obvious that for certain types of legal information on-line data bases have considerable advantages over CD-ROMs and other forms of traditionally distributed information, simply due to the fact that the on-line databases can be updated, in principle, on a continuos basis. From the users' point of view this may mean, for example, that it would be desirable with various forms of news reporting, and for the material in which they are interested in and which has been recently added (e.g. last day/week/ month) to be highlighted. A further consequence of this is that the performance and functions of the software utilised by the information providers become crucial.

When computerised systems for the legal sector are being evaluated it is therefore also of special interest to investigate information retrieval (IR) and other forms of search programs. In this respect it is clear that components such as Boolean operators, allowing for (and, or, not) combination of keywords, as well as left-hand side and right hand side truncation should be standard features. Likewise, it should be possible to search for documents through the utilisation of particular subject fields, and for documents generated within a particular time period. In addition, it should be possible to perform various kinds of the so called proximity searches allowing for the search of words and phrases within a certain distance from each other. It is also desirable that it should be possible to utilise various kinds of automatically generated and editorially produced indexes, hierarchically and chronologically ordered menus, etc.[62]

It is furthermore important, of course, that the retrieved information can be presented in various ways. In other words, the users should be able to switch from one presentation format to one other, adjusting the presentation to their needs, e.g. by means of highlighting headlines, abstracts, rulings, etc. Moreover, various kinds of sorting functions which make it possible to arrange the retrieved documents in accordance with various parameters, for example, type of publication, issuing dates, authors, and the relative weight of the number of found key words or similar features, should be included.

---

[62] It should be noticed that some standards of this kind actually have been implemented and are being utilized, e.g. on the Internet. One such standard is the ANSI Z39.50, which among other things makes it possible to search many databases simultaneously. From the end users point of view, however, much still remains to be done in this area.

In addition, possibilities to search and move around within the retrieved documents should be looked upon as standard features. It is therefore quite clear that emphasis should be placed on the ease of operation, i.e. the electronic versions should also provide ways of moving around which replicate the things that can be done in paper reports. Important features include thereby, among other things, being able to move directly to a specified page, go page by page, or jump between text paragraphs which are defined in various ways. This is a function which presupposes not only access to "page numbers" or similar notions, but also various kinds of "meta" information in order to prevent the users from losing their orientation.

It is also relevant to mention that many legal documents are of such a kind that users would often have a reason to go to the last line of a given report or case at once. Thus, the ability to move rapidly to various points in a given text is a frequently requested feature. This can be accomplished in several ways, for instance through clickable headlines or menus at the beginning of the document which give direct access to a number of specific points in the texts. A useful feature is, of course, also being able to jump to successive occurrences of search terms present in a given document.

It should also be kept in mind that the advantages of hypertext can be extremely useful when functional aspects of legal material are being handled. Hypertext and the use of links can be used not only in order to predefine "jumps" between various parts of a text. Hypertext links can also make it possible to switch between various documents, e.g. provide the ability to move directly to a case referred to in a judgement by simply clicking on a headline or a marked keyword.

In this context it is furthermore important to mention that it is highly desirable that the users be provided with a means to add their own links to the databases, and retrace their own search paths. They should also have access to facilities which make it possible for them to complement the material, e.g. with their own comments, personal documents, in-house interpretations, etc. Thus, from the point of view of the users it is important that they are able to adjust the material and develop their own structures with respect to the storing and presentation of the material.

Finally, something should be said about the potential features that should be incorporated into the more advanced search systems for lawyers. Some of them have been discussed and tested for a long time now, but as yet very few of them have gone beyond the experimental stages.

One obviously highly desirable function is thereby natural language processing with respect to user queries. Such a function would be highly useful in the sense that it would make it possible for the users to pose questions without being limited by any formal syntax. In the long-time perspective it may also be assumed that natural language processing could facilitate access to legal information for a wider range of users. This could be done by means of diminishing the importance of mastering a more or less technical legal language when a certain system is used. In this respect natural language processing also appears to be an important component of the so called conceptual search – an elaboration of the IR technique for the legal domain that has been frequently discussed and urgently requested for quite a long time.[63]

An additional feature which is frequently mentioned as one of the crucial objectives in the development of more advanced IR systems is the integration of legal thesauruses. This could be very useful not only because it could facilitate the use of the systems for non-experts. Thesauruses are also crucial in the development of more or less autonomous functions for the translation of legal terms from one language to another.[64]

3.5.4 Advanced Legal IT-systems

a) From texts to more elaborate structures. Existing IT systems for law have been developed, with few exceptions, for the handling of texts and documents. The fact that almost all the existing legal materials appear in the form of texts and documents is, of course, no surprise at all, and from the commercial system developer's point of view it is quite clear that users favour evolutionary development rather than a sudden and radical departure from paper systems. An important factor is naturally also that texts and documents remain unchallenged as forms of legal representation. Intensive as they are, neither the theoretical development, nor practical undertakings

[63] An early example is provided by Hafner, Carole D, *An Information Retrieval System Based on a Computer Model of Legal Knowledge*, University of Michigan, 1978.

[64] *See, e.g.*, ELVIL, *supra* note 45.

with advanced IT applications, have yet generated any true alternatives for practical work.[65]

The analysis of the nature of legal material outlined in the previous sections makes it quite clear, however, that several additional types of systems could be introduced into the legal domain. In this respect the fact that the legal material can also be seen as consisting of, among other things, concept or object structures, rules, and rule systems, indicates that the so called decision support systems and expert systems could be used. Likewise, combinations of various representation techniques are likely to be appreciated by the users – the fact which has been anticipated in several research projects for quite some time now.[66]

Thus, an overall conclusion is that it is desirable that the multilayered nature of legal information should be reflected to a larger extent in the future development of more advanced IT solutions. From the users' point of view this is simply a consequence of the fact that the systems should provide as rich and multifaceted information as possible. In practice, this means that the applications should be able to handle not only texts and documents, but that they should also be able to provide facilities enabling the users to shift between different types of concept structures, interactive, rule-based knowledge bases, and various forms of customised information. From the system developer's point of view this entails, furthermore, that IT-systems which are able to combine features such as IR, rule based representations, interactive dialogues, hypertext, and various forms of graphics should be given high priority.

b) From general to customised systems. The technical development makes it apparent that it is possible to create smaller and more detailed IT-systems. Such development is not only likely to be the consequence of the perceived combination of different types of representation forms indicated in the previous sections. In this respect it is also important, of course, that the technique becomes continuously cheaper and more accessible.

---

[65] The scarcity of practical applications based on alternative forms of representations, that have been brought into day-to-day use has recently been illustrated in a student survey conducted at IRI. *See* Baur, Jürgen, *Legal Decision Support Systems – Implemented Systems,* 1996 at 33.

[66] Illustrations of how such combinations can be worked out are given in Wahlgren, *supra* chapter 1 note 8.

An additional factor indicating that the more individualised solutions are likely to become more predominant is the obvious fact that the legal market for legal information is limited. This, in turn, makes it possible to predict that features which will enable the users to elaborate and customise the information will become an important means of competition on the market. It is also noticeable in this context that a development towards more focused, in-depth oriented legal IT applications can presently be observed in the fact that a large number of smaller systems, better adjusted to the needs of certain groups of users, e.g. lawyers working with tax law or employment law, etc., are presently being introduced and marketed.

Another potential consequence of this is that in the foreseeable future, in addition to the import of technical means of a more user friendly kind, development of new forms of representation may make it possible to design and implement into the IT systems customised knowledge structures reflecting the requirements of individual lawyers. This development may eventually lead to a situation in which it will become possible to develop truly customised systems.

It is also noticeable in this respect that a continued development towards more detailed information structures and an accompanying elaborate design of individualised support systems can easily be motivated – at least when looked upon from the users' point of view. This is simply a consequence of the fact that from the users' perspective many existing commercial systems which provide very broad and general information are quite poorly adjusted to the actual requirements of the individual lawyer.

In other words, this means that very few, if any, practising lawyers have a need for information systems covering all the domains of the law. On the contrary, almost all lawyers are active in one or just a few areas of law; a lawyer working in e.g. employment law has normally little or no interest in the development of criminal law. Likewise, most tax lawyers are probably totally indifferent to the latest changes in, for instance, copyright law, and, of course, even less enthusiastic about paying for getting access to that kind of information. From this it follows that the ultimate support system for an individual lawyer is seldom the one providing a broad range of information, but more often the one which gives access to as much detailed information as possible about a limited topic.

If one analyses this aspect somewhat closer it becomes quite apparent that most professional lawyers working within a given field of law are dependent on their own expertise and individual knowledge. From this, in turn, one can draw the conclusion that it should be possible to customise all advanced support systems in the sense that the users should be able to add their own information and comments, and restructure the material in order to satisfy their own requirements.

The fact that the material and the systems should be possible to customise does not mean, of course, that official and general information can be omitted from legal IT-applications. On the contrary, the material originating from official legal sources will always make up a crucial component of legal IT products, and in this respect it is important to underline the fact that elaboration of more individualised solutions can by no means be looked upon as an alternative to more general systems. Instead, individual systems should be regarded as complements to other types of legal information systems. It should also be noticed in this context, of course, that different parts of a conventional legal IT-system providing broad information can be utilised by different users. General systems can also, naturally, be combined with more specialised products and it is furthermore possible to elaborate general systems so that the users can recast the information, utilise individualised search templates, etc.

The development of more detailed, customised systems should not be looked upon, however, solely as a consequence of more elaborate representation forms and accompanying technical features. Also other forms of technical means affecting the ways in which lawyers may customise their own search profiles can be anticipated. In this respect the development of the so called "push technology" and related features may become relevant, making it possible to distribute material in accordance to specifications, which have been elicited automatically from logged search profiles of individual lawyers, or from points of interests which have been consciously articulated by the users in other ways. Overlooking this development it also becomes clear that various information-tailoring services can be anticipated, that is to say services providing information reflecting the interest of the users according to parameters which have in some way been indicated by them. Such systems can not only provide the users with updated information within their respective fields of interest, but they can also highlight news, and constantly monitor changes.[67]

c) From IR to integrated functions. As the IT development continues, it is obvious that various functions and facilities are becoming more and more integrated. From the point of view of the lawyer utilising IT in order to search for information this means that he can expect the conventional IR systems to be elaborated and supplemented in such a way as to be able to assist him in several aspects of legal work. Examples of complementary functions would be access to interactive dialogues in order to identify legal problems more easily, support for interpretation, formulation assistance, communication facilities, etc. At a somewhat deeper level this may include predefined "easy-to-use" search templates, access to legal concept structures and definitions, professional on-line assistance in legal news observation, expert analysis & commentaries, reference checks, and so forth.

Likewise, it is possible to anticipate a wider use of on-line conferencing systems and discussion groups, libraries providing electronic versions of legal forms, chat sites, on-line consultation and calculation, interactive help with writing, etc.[68] In addition, on-line services can provide access to conceptual services, such as manual document search, references and formal evaluations, as well as check lists for case processing, etc. Several facilities of this kind have already been presented and what can be expected in the future is that they will be more firmly integrated into better composed and more elaborate products.

It is, of course, important to remember in this context also that all the legal information systems are likely to be integrated into common administrative IT systems as well as practical work processes. From this, in turn, it follows that a number of factors – of which many are not necessarily of a legal nature – have to be adjusted to and integrated into the systems and vice versa. This is, of course, a great challenge for the legal profession when

---

[67] Early examples of this have already been presented, although as yet not only focusing on legal information. *See, e.g.*, LEXIS®-NEXIS® InfoTailor™ at "http://www.lexis-nexis.com/lncc/products.html".

[68] *See, e.g.*, for references to web-sites illustrating the above, *supra* chapter 2 notes 21-28. For an example of a document formulating assistance, see also LEXform which can "be used to remove all the formatting (page numbers, level information, leaders), change the length of the lines, and add the path and filename of the final formatted document to the top of the first page" at "http://www.lexis-nexis.com/lncc/custserv/html/wintech/lexform.html".

even the ways in which the work is done can be expected to change in more or less fundamental ways.

d) Towards standardisation. In an analysis of the future development of advanced legal IT applications it is naturally also interesting to discuss various forms of standardisation. The relevance of standardisation is apparent in many ways. From the user's point of view, for instance, it is obvious that it would be good to have more uniform interfaces for legal IT applications in order to facilitate efficient use by making it easier to shift between various products. More specifically, this implies that the design of such elements as legally relevant icons, menus, as well as unification of other forms of graphical elements should be given a proper attention in the development of future applications.

Development of more uniform interfaces is quite easy to motivate. For one thing, it is clear that many current interface solutions are difficult to understand and thus also difficult to remember. As concerns icons and graphical elements this is without doubt caused to a large extent by the fact that there are no commonly accepted components, so that the existing solutions differ too much. The fact that many solutions are poorly adaptable to the requirements of the legal profession makes it quite obvious, in turn, that a number of improvements can be accomplished by means of further analysis of useful legal concepts, graphical representation forms, cognitive aspects, etc.

The interface component, draws our attention, in turn, to a number of aspects related to the behaviour of software indicated for use in legal work. A survey of current legal IT-systems shows that also these aspects vary a lot. In the long run there can be little doubt, however, that the development of standardised criteria for the performance of various kinds of software intended for legal work must be considered as an urgent task for the legal profession and the legal domain. This is simply because customised legal software will become an increasingly crucial component of legal work.

This means in practice that the utilisation of the so called Boolean search operators, truncation, highlighting, reference checks, proximity searches, presentation formats, browsing, thesauruses, and similar facilities should be given considerable attention. In this context it is also apparent that it is desirable to find more uniform standards for such things as performance of electronic mailing systems, litigation support systems, communication facilities, design and monitoring of legal chat systems, security and cryptation, etc.

In this way also the characteristics and behaviour of the so called search engines and other kinds of common, "non-legal" computer programs come into focus. The present situation is obviously not the most efficient one and the kind of "de-facto" standards that users must adapt leave a lot to desire – a comprehensive search of the Internet, for instance, is quite time-consuming and complicated in that e.g. various versions of Boolean commands have to be used. In addition, a large portion of information that has been tracked down will turn out to be outdated, while a lot of newly issued information may not be found at all. The overall objective here is, of course, to seek for solutions that will facilitate shifts between various legal sources, search engines, and material distributed by different legal institutions, i.e. situations which become more and more frequent due to the internationalisation and the merging of various jurisdictions, among other things.

Admittedly these aspects have been given considerable attention for quite some time. In this context it is, for instance, relevant to mention a long-time project concerning the development of a Common Command Language (CCL) for computer-based IR[69] and, as a more recent example, the above indicated ELVIL project.[70] It is also noticeable, of course, that these aspects are not easy influenced by individual users or producers. Difficulties in this respect cannot be used, however, as arguments against future attempts towards more uniform and efficient solutions. From the legal information managers' point of view it is obvious that these aspects should be given considerable attention.

Closely related to the unification of interface and software aspects is the question of legal document standards, i.e. the ways in which layout and various components, such as titles, headlines, paragraphs, references, etc. are being handled. Document standards are important, among other things, for the efficient use of hypertext and for the management of relations between documents of different origin.

---

[69] *See* "http://www2.echo.lu/echo/ccl/en/ccl.html".

[70] *See supra* chapter 2 note 17.

Document standards are also important presuppositions for the formation of searchable fields within texts. They are furthermore necessary for customised and uniform presentations. Efficient uniform handling of document standards presupposes, in turn, access to various forms of mark-up languages as well as the so called document type definitions (DTDs), and similar components.

A mark-up language consists of a number of standardised components that can be used in order to enable a computer program to identify various types of data (or document) elements, such as headlines, graphics, etc. Two important standards are SGML (Standard Generalised Markup Language) and HTML (HyperText Mark-up Language).[71]

Aspects related to standardisation of documents will without doubt grow in importance with continued development. In this respect it is also possible to foresee a growing demand for further development of more precise and elaborate systems of standardisation, This is paradoxical to some extent, however, since mark-up systems cannot be too comprehensive, due to the fact that they become too complex and thus also too expensive to handle.

As a consequence, the development into more and more comprehensive systems has recently led to the presentation of a more limited, Extensible Mark-up Language (XML), which is a simplified version of SGML. XML was first presented at the end of 1996[72], and to make any definite speculations about its future development, as well as of similar initiatives, is, of course, difficult. What is possible to foresee, however, is that these aspects will become more and more urgent. It is also possible to predict that with time, the need for standardisation will be also felt with respect to other forms of legal information, e.g. of the kind mentioned in section 3.4.3 above, such as. rules, rule systems, legal concepts, etc. In this way it may eventually become also possible to develop standards for more advanced applications, such as legal expert systems, and legal DSSs. The latter may be important, among other things, for the integration of various systems into more complex and general applications. It is naturally also interesting to try to develop quality checks for the performance of such systems.

---

[71] *See, e.g.*, "http://www.sil.org/SGML/sgml.html#toc-general".

[72] *See* Arbetsgruppen, *supra* note 16 supplement 4, *Arbetsgruppens rapport om standarder för ett moderniserat rättsdatasystem.*

A related example of an attempt to achieve more standardised solutions that can be mentioned in this context is the Governmental Information Locator Service (GILS) – a U.S. project attempting to develop a kind of a uniform electronic card catalogue system for federal information.

GILS posts consist of descriptions of information sources, e.g. printed bibliographies, catalogues, manuals, indexes, CD-ROMs, databases, web-sites, and even individuals with specialised knowledge in some topic. GILS is a distributed system in which each producer of information is responsible for the content of the descriptions of the information sources. A GILS record can also contain references to other GILS units. A collection of rules (attribute sets) for the description of information make it possible to conduct structured searches,[73] and standards of this kind can also provide various forms of document meta data necessary for the efficient use of information.

A somewhat parallel development, in the sense that it is based on the indexing of information, is the one that has been undertaken by operators active on the Internet. Several search engine owners have initiated comprehensive projects with quality checks and categorisations of web-sites.[74] Another thing that may need to be more or less urgently revised from the point of view of standardisation is the use of different languages, various systems of prefixes and abbreviations, as well as standards concerning the arrangement and updating of links, etc.[75]

---

[73] The GILS project has met, however, with a lot of criticism, and its future is still uncertain. *See* "http://www.access.gpo.gov/su_docs/gils/gils-eval/html/toc.html".

[74] *See* Lynch, *supra* note 6, *and* Resnick, Paul, *Filtering Information on the Internet*, 1997 at 54-56. As a recent commercial (non-legal) example of an indexing service, see "http:// www.4Internet.com /"advertised as "the fastest and easiest way to use the Internet. Our researchers have spent thousands of hours searching the web in order to bring you the best of the Web in all the categories listed below."

[75] *See*, for general overviews, *e.g.*, Oudet, Bruno, *Multilingualism on the Internet*, 1997 at 67-68, and Hearst, Marti A., *Interfaces for Searching the Web*, 1997 at 60-64.

3.6 *Organisational Issues*

Inclusion of organisational issues in an evaluation of legal IT applications is important for several reasons. Initially, it must be observed, however, that the term "organisational issues" is a broad concept. It can be related not only to the suppliers of legal information products, but also to the future development of law libraries, as well as other organisations working with legal information. In this context the internal organisation of law libraries and other organisations using legal information is not, however, the primary object of concern. Instead, the following sections focus on issues which may be relevant to investigate when suppliers of "externally developed" IT-products are evaluated.

3.6.1 Stability

To start with, it is obvious that all choices concerning information providers and IT presuppose some sort of investment of the user organisation, e.g. in education, hardware and software, or in reorganisation of work processes. This in turn makes it necessary to investigate the *stability* of the suppliers of legal information in order to evaluate various alternatives. The overall objective here is naturally trying to find out whether a certain information supplier can be expected to be a reliable supplier over time. In order to investigate this several factors may have to be looked into. Previous undertakings by the producer of a certain information service, the scope of the ongoing activities, and the general acceptance by the market of the organisation behind the product are just a few examples which may give indications as to whether a certain service appears to be of a well-established or permanent type.

A complementary strategy that can be used in the evaluation of organisational issues is by investigating the *future plans* of various legal information producers. The future plans of an information supplier may not only give indications as to whether a certain product or service may develop in a direction which is in line with the development of the user organisation, but explicit future plans may also make it possible to evaluate the long term prospects of the service as such.

Although future plans may appear to be the best way of testing the stability of a certain legal IT producer, it must be noticed that explicit plans about the future are not always easy to get at. The ambitions of a certain organisation may be hidden to outsiders for various reasons, e.g. due to competitive and strategic motives. Another reason why it may be difficult to find explicit descriptions of future activities may be that the management of a certain organisation have come to the conclusion that it is not wise to make all too specific plans, e.g. due to the fact that IT development is too rapid, and that the best, long-term strategy is to have an open-minded attitude towards the future. In this respect detailed plans about the future development of a certain legal information service may remain tacit in that they are only reflected in the overall commercial objectives of the company, such as growth or demands on returns from investments. In addition, it must be observed that the way in which a new product is accepted by the market may determine the future of the organisation behind it, and this, in turn, may be more or less impossible to predict, let alone make any detailed plans for.

It should be furthermore kept in mind that a critical attitude may be advisable when plans concerning future activities are actually being made explicit. That is simply to say that all plans about the future should be thoroughly analysed in terms of their credibility, realism, the underlying basic assumptions, etc. From all this follows that difficulties related to the analysis of future plans of legal information suppliers are quite considerable.

An aspect closely related to stability is furthermore the *size* of the organisation providing the service. The general assumption is that a larger organisation will have more resources, and thus that it will also be better prepared to overcome difficulties. This is in many situations true and, without doubt, access to considerable resources is sometimes necessary, e.g. in order to solve upcoming technical problems, update and maintain large information bases, give efficient support to marketing, educate users, etc.

On the other hand, in many cases size may be a factor of diminishing importance, as technical development makes it possible also for smaller organisations to develop new competitive products and services. Efficient and consistent use of IT can well compensate for not having access to a large organisation. From this follows that also small and less well-established organisations should be given serious attention, and that a big size of an organisations does by no means provide a guarantee for the ability of that organisation to produce more advanced or efficient solutions. In this context it may be noticed that for several reasons also large organisations may encounter difficulties. Large organisations may be hampered, for instance, by bureaucracy or by too long a distance between decision makers and various user groups. It is also noticeable that the very size of the organisation may reflect and cement more or less outdated ways of perceiving legal information management and the related issues. This is simply because IT has made obsolete many of the factors which previously made that size was an important parameter for the development of legal information products.

Apart from size, it is obvious that the *economy* of the supplying organisation is an important factor to consider in the evaluation of the kind of services that the end user or a law library should invest in. Economic resources constitute to a large extent a decisive factor with regard to the possibility of maintaining and developing high quality products and services over time. It is also clearly noticeable that this factor becomes increasingly important as the producers of legal information become more and more aware of the value of their work and as the prize of legal information increases.

It may be important to notice, however, that financial resources constitute by no means a guarantee for the long-term survival of a legal information service. Examples of the opposite can easily be found, and there are many different reasons for this, e.g. on the Swedish legal IT market various established information producers and publishing firms have merged together or have been bought up by foreign investors.[76] It must therefore be kept in mind that well-functioning products and services may sometimes be overtaken by competitors. In the relatively short history of IT and law this has also lead in some cases to the situation in which well-established and useful services have been closed down or transformed in order to be integrated into a new context.[77] From this it follows that although

[76] *See* Konkurrensverket, Beslut June 26, 1995, *Wolters Kluwer Sverige ABs förvärv av samtliga aktier i Juristförlaget JF AB.*

[77] *See, e.g.,* Paliwala *supra* chapter 2 note 16 "After 1979 LEXIS became available to lawyers in England with Butterworths Telepublishing Limited as the UK licensees. At about the same time, the STATUS project became the basis for the development of a home-grown on-line system known as EUROLEX. The possibility of a competitive market in information retrieval systems

considerable funding and access to financial resources may give indications about the future development of individual information services, it is by no means a sufficient indicator of the long term survival of legal information suppliers.

In this context it must also be noticed that technical development makes it possible to initiate projects without considerable investments. This, in combination with the fact that legislative and other kinds of core legal information are freely available in many jurisdictions (or that they are available at a low cost), makes it possible to establish services and launch products with the help of quite limited resources. However, it must be observed that this may eventually lead to a more intensive competition between various organisations active on the legal market, making financial resources crucial for long-term survival once again. It must nevertheless be acknowledged that the market for legal IT-related products and services shows presently a lot of turbulence, which means that when a commercial vendor of legal IT products is evaluated, one should routinely look for indications of instability, e.g. by means of investigating official debt registers, and similar sources. Likewise, it may be wise to try to find out how well a legal information system has been received by the market, since this will obviously be a good indication of how the service is likely to develop over time.

ended when Butterworths Telepublishing acquired EUROLEX resulting in an effective monopoly over legal information retrieval systems."

3.6.2 Competence

In an evaluation of the legal IT market one should furthermore investigate the *competence* of the organisations behind various services and products. Competence is an aspect which may be decomposed, in turn, into legal competence, technical competence, and competence concerning legal information management.

The *legal competence* of an organisation providing the service is, of course, a necessary component for several reasons. As illustrated in the previous sections, it is not only crucial to have a deep knowledge of the nature of legal information in order to understand how services should be developed and implemented. Legal competence is also necessary in order to understand the functions of the law and the legal work situations which are to be supported by IT products and services.

More precisely this means that a good understanding of the doctrine of legal sources and of the legally acceptable ways of making references, knowledge of legal work processes, insights into democratic and legislative processes, and other related issues, are necessary presuppositions for long-term survival on the legal IT market. Likewise, it is necessary to have a good idea about the background of the potential user groups, the characteristics of various legal professions, etc., in order to understand the kind of information that a certain legal information service should include.

Access to legal competence is, however, not enough. All serious examples of product development for the legal market must also be related to a good understanding of the potentialities connected with IT development. At present, this is more or less a full time job. The steady stream of new kinds of products and novel technical solutions appears to be forever growing, and it is obvious that development of products and services with any chance of survival on the market presupposes *technical competence* among the producers, reflected in, among other things, proficiency in computer and information science, programming techniques, telecommunications, man-machine interactions, and a number of similar aspects.

Technical competence is, of course, also essential in the sense that it is the necessary condition for getting any service or product actually working. It should be noticed, however, that an organisation working with legal IT products must not be too one-sided in its technical orientation, or, to put it differently, that pure technical competence must be complemented with practical skills so that various technical solutions can be implemented in a user-friendly way. Likewise, on the legal market it is necessary for the organisation to be able to market and explain technical solutions in a non-technical manner that would be understandable to potential customers without any special interest in IT.

It should be further noticed in this context that technical competence of various kinds, e.g. concerning communication methods, can be gained, to some extent, from others, so that all kinds of technical skills need not be present in one organisation. In certain situations it may even be preferable to utilise services provided by others. Such an arrangement may make a given organisation less vulnerable and more flexible, due to the fact that technical competence can more easily be replaced or extended. Organisational solutions based on a combination of contributors of legal and technical competence may also leave more scope for efficient back-up facilities through agreements with several organisations, making it thus possible to minimise the risk of technical interruptions. Solutions of the latter kind presuppose, nevertheless, administrative talent among those who are to co-ordinate the services, and from the end users' point of view it is, of course, important to have only one, easily identified, counterpart, so that discussions about the responsibility for malfunctioning components can be avoided.

In addition, it must be remembered that any experiment involving new technique is combined with risks, secondary effects, and costs. New technical solutions may require, for instance, investments in user education, reorganisation of work tasks, as well as the updating of previous, already working IT solutions, computers, programs, and communication facilities. These effects cannot frequently be disregarded since they may lead to problems in the implementation phase. In extreme cases established presuppositions of this kind may even make, in turn, that projects have to be abandoned. In such situations, and especially where various solutions appear to be more or less equally good from the qualitative point of view, one frequently recommended way of avoiding unnecessary problems is to stick to well-known suppliers with whom one already has an established and well-functioning relationship. The general assumption here is that even if their solution may appear initially as not the least expensive one, in many cases the choice will prove nevertheless to be the correct one, since the secondary costs related to hidden effects will probably be lower.

From this it also follows that in some situations it may be wise not to initiate too drastic changes in legal information management, or at least to implement the changes step by step in order to avoid serious difficulties with user education, user acceptance, etc. In support of this view a recent Swedish article referring to several international studies can be mentioned, claiming that five out of six large IT projects fail, and that they often do so due to the fact that too advanced technical solutions have been implemented.[78] From the point of view of the legal information manager, it is thus important not to let oneself be too impressed by references to the latest technical innovations or visionary descriptions of the future. That is to say that technical competence of the organisation behind a given legal service must also be in line with what is expected by the user organisation and what can be actually used by it.

In consequence of the above, although legal and technical competence are vital components, the most crucial aspect to be investigated in an evaluation of an organisation supplying legal IT support is probably *legal information management as a form of combined competence.* In this context this means that it is critically important to be able to make use of IT in legal work within the framework of the accepted standards of legal information.

This means that the personnel of an organisation developing IT-related services for the legal domain must be able to understand the specific problems encountered in it. It is thereby possible to look upon the development of legal products and services as a chain in which a large number of various skills must be combined together and activated. That is to say that more advanced electronic products for the legal market can only be realised through the combined effort of persons possessing different kinds of competence. What is needed here is thus a combination of special knowledge of legal structures (text and document representations must be complemented with other forms of information), technical proficiency in the marking of legal documents (legal texts must be able to function in various situations for different users), previous experience from system development and analysis of legal work activities (electronic products must

[78] Borgström, Håkan, *Nitlotter för miljarder*, Ny Teknik 21/97 at 21-23.

be adjusted to the work process of the legal domain), and skill in graphical design for multimedia (the presentations and the interaction must be user-friendly and easy to understand). It is also possible to foresee that the traditional knowledge of the substantive aspects of law will have to be complemented with knowledge about different user situations and functions of law – the latter simply in order to understand the kind of products and services that should be reasonably developed.[79]

3.6.3 Flexibility

Apart from the obvious fact that an organisation providing IT-related services for the legal sector must be proficient in both legal and technical matters, as well as being able to combine the two, it is also clear that *flexibility* of organisations producing IT related services is an important aspect of the survival on the legal information market. This is simply to say that the fact that an organisation is proficient in a current technology is no guarantee for the future. The crucial aspect is instead whether an organisation is able to adjust its products and services to changing pre-suppositions of various kinds, so that it can meet the demands of various groups of users over time. Users' demand have been reflected so far by, for example, the need to make on-line data base services available through the Internet, integrate the products and services into constantly changing administrative frameworks, and adjust the information to the CD-ROM media – the latter, for instance, by means of marking the material in order to make it possible to effectively utilise hyperlinks and various new forms of search programs, etc.[80]

As far as flexibility is concerned it must be noted, however, that changes in legal information products need not always be combined with improvements of a qualitative nature. That is to say that from the point of view of the producer it is normally desirable to diversify and alter the products and

[79] In Sweden, at least three large IT projects in the legal domain have met with vast problems recently, obviously caused by the lack of combined competence in this respect. *See* Bergström, *supra* chapter 2 note 16, Nilsson, *supra* chapter 2 note 16, *and* Lunneborg, Rolf, *Fogdarnas nya system fick dumpas*, Svenska dagbladet 1997-04-23, *and* Sundström, Margaretha, *Fogden överger problembarn*, 1997.

[80] *Cf. supra* section 3.5.4 on the need for standards, etc.

services more or less constantly for commercial reasons, i.e. simply in order to sell more. For the same reason a producer may find it interesting to let various products overlap, or to combine several products with each other, e.g. several CD-ROM products containing related information, or an electronic journal available on-line with its paper version, so that the users become obliged to buy two versions instead of one. Alternatively, the users may have to subscribe to publications issued as a series, despite the fact that the individual volumes address completely different legal areas. In this respect there exists a potential conflict of interests between the producers and the users of legal information products. Although it must be remembered that publication in the form of series must not always be looked upon as something bad. From the general point of view it should be noticed that such a strategy may well have the effect that also less frequently requested material becomes available.

It should also be pointed out in this context that any changes in a legal information system may bring about difficulties for the users, due to the fact that it becomes necessary to adapt to new routines, and that well known components have to be abandoned. On top of it all, secondary effects relating to the users must be taken into consideration, such as, for example, user education, adaptation of the new technique, or updating of related information. From this in turn it follows that organisations providing the services must be prepared to educate the users, adjust the products in various ways, and be able to integrate new material into established jurisprudential structures.

From the point of view of the users it is also obvious that the their needs to handle various objectives and different kinds of demands undergo changes over the time. The users must thus be constantly able to influence the development of the information system. As a consequence, the existence of a user organisation, or some other form of established ways of receiving feedback from the users are important components in the evaluation of the legal information suppliers.

3.6.4 Service

In an evaluation of the organisational aspects of legal information suppliers it is relevant to investigate components which may be labelled as service-mindness, and which are related to the working relations and the users' daily contacts with the personnel of the organisation behind the product. Important to investigate here is, for instance, the ability of the organisation in question to handle the conflicting perspectives and meet criticism coming from the users.

The factors of relevance in this respect are, among other things availability and skill in explaining complicated matters in a practical way, using simple, everyday language. Crucial aspects of a friction-free co-operation over time are thereby service resources, promptness in giving personal assistance, and other forms of user support. As a consequence, when various information suppliers are being compared, it may be a good idea to look for the existence of components such as help desk, newsletters, organised forms of user education, etc., which may indicate the degree of service that a certain organisation is likely to provide. Of importance for the user here is of course also the ability to work out customised solutions that would influence and perhaps also reduce the price of various solutions. The latter could be of interest for users that for some reason only are interested in parts of a certain product.

A difficulty in this respect is, however, the fact that components related to various levels of service are obviously difficult to measure and evaluate in advance, i.e. before a service or product has been supplied. Many of the relevant aspects must be studied over time, and one may be able to form an opinion about some crucial aspects perhaps only when problems have actually occurred.

One way to find out whether or not a certain organisation appears to be reliable in this respect may be to try to get information through contacts with other users, who are willing to share their experiences. Or, if information of this kind cannot be found, one may try to get hold of reviews of various kinds before a given product is put into daily use.

Thus, a practical strategy for getting an overview of the available solutions is naturally also by asking for reference projects and names of current customers that may be contacted and interviewed. Here, not only customers that can describe a long term relationship with the producer of a legal service should be approached, but also users that have recently bought or implemented a solution originating from the organisation that is being scrutinised. In this context it is furthermore relevant to investigate the formal terms that a certain organisation relies on when licensing issues and other forms of usage are being discussed. These may be labelled with the collective name of contracting issues.

In its details such issues differ, depending on the type of product that is to be negotiated, i.e. to a large extent the various characteristics of e.g. CD-ROM licenses, on-line database or electronic "e-journal" subscriptions, and other forms of on-line services presuppose different regulations. Likewise, it is obvious that, for example, the procurement of computers, computer programs, and subscriptions to telecommunications services must be dealt with in different ways.

Looking at contracting issues from the general point of view, however, it is possible to find certain common aspects which are relevant in most long-term relationships. If one concentrates on contracting issues especially associated with IT, it is then necessary to investigate, among other things, the conditions related to licensing, product specifications, payment terms, time aspects (delivery and access to services), liability, and means of solving conflicts (*Cf.* also section 4.7 *infra*).

3.7 Summary

The decomposition of legal information systems into three main aspects, combined with an extensive discussion of the components of each aspect, like the one outlined above, provide feasible grounds for the evaluation of various suggested solutions. Although it must be admitted that it is not a sufficient way of reaching specific conclusions about the functionality or the pro and cons of various legal IT-solutions.

A systematic evaluation, it may be argued, must also reflect more explicitly the various user requirements that can be related to the systems. In addition, it is desirable that different requirements should be possible to relate to various system components in a straightforward way. The reason behind this is simply that various user groups (or potential user groups) will give priority to different things, and, consequently, that the development of a more adequate system specification also presupposes the ability to reflect the demands of various user categories.

One way of accomplishing a more comprehensive solution is thereby to combine various identified user categories with the legal information systems aspects in the form of matrices that can be used as check lists. The aspects of information content, technical issues and organisational matters can thus be reflected as in figure 2.

2 a Aspects of Information Content

Examples of User Categories – Requirements

Issues of relevance:	End user: Lawyer	End user: Management	End user: Administrator	Client/ Customer	Co-operating organisations
Coverage Relevance Completeness Continuity Authenticity Origin of material Selection criteria Intended use Omissions					
Indexing References Indexes TOCs					
Data organisation Data structures (formal, hierarchical, procedural, time related) Legal sources Documents Texts Concepts Rules Rule systems Combinations Interoperability De facto standards					
Managing Editing Updating News reporting Filing					
User friendliness Meta info. System info. Software info. Abbreviations Commands Languages Manuals					
Contracting issues Content Specification Customisation Price policy					
etc.					

2 b Technical Aspects

Examples of User Categories – Requirements

Issues of relevance:	End user: Lawyer	End user: Management	End user: Administrator	Client/ Customer	Co-operating organisations
Hardware Computers CPU standard Capacity Storing etc. Printers Quality Speed Capacity etc. Servers Functions Capacity Storing etc.					
Software Functions Compatibility De facto standards Adjustments Commands Interfaces Versions etc.					
Communications Standards Speed Capacity Configuration etc.					
Contracting issues Licensing Updating Education					
etc.					

2 c Organisational Issues

Examples of User Categories – Requirements

Issues of relevance:	End user: Lawyer	End user: Management	End user: Administrator	Client/ Customer	Co-operating organisations
Stability Legal status Size Market acceptance Future plans					
Resources Economy Personnel Back up					
Competence Legal Technical Combined References available?					
Service Availability User support User information Additional services					
Flexibility User organisation Speed in updating Customised solutions Price policies					
Contracting issues Licensing Copyright Liability Price policies					
etc.					

Figures 2 a-c: Examples of matrices for the evaluation of legal information systems. Each matrix can easily be expanded as to reflect more or less detailed levels of the various components. Likewise, the categories of users and requirements that may be affected by a legal information system can easily be adjusted as to fit into a certain type of organisation. For instance, if the information system that is being evaluated is to be implemented in a teaching organisation, the user groups will contain teachers and administrators, and the customer category will be replaced by students. When a court system is discussed various forms of jurisprudential and formal requirements concerning the information content may come into focus, and so forth. An illustration of the expansion of technical IR components is given in Figure 3 below.[81]

[81] *See*, for a similar approach on the evaluation of legal websites, BGIC, *supra* note 1.

3 Technical Aspects

Information Retrieval Components

Examples of User Categories – Requirements

Issues of relevance:	End user: Lawyer	End user: Management	End user: Administrator	Client/ Customer	Co-operating organisations
Search functions Type of commands Short forms Truncation facilities Designated search Forms Free text search Proximity search Highlighting Prefixes Time aspects Combinations Refinements Retracing Query reuse Thesauruses etc.					
Hypertext Type of links (Original/edited) Relevance of links Completeness Logical aspects Retracing Flexibility etc.					
Presentations Graphics Icons Fonts Search results Relevance ranking Relevance feedback Short forms Overviews Indexing Abstracts Sorting Use of colours Meta information etc.					
Capacities Speed Storing etc.					

Regular use of matrices has several advantages, among which is the possibility of identification of the legal information system's various aspects that are likely to come into focus when different types of requirements are discussed. Likewise, various types of standards can be worked out as the various user categories articulate their requirements.

Matrices are also easy to understand, they can be used by all the categories affected by an information system, and they are easy to expand and adjust to various situations. When a comprehensive system is being analysed it may be reasonable, for instance, to combine some 20-30 matrices reflecting system requirements and functions of various kinds.

Admittedly, an approach based on matrices has also its disadvantages. It is, for instance, clear that a number of combinations ("cells") in a matrix, like the matrices illustrated above, will have little or no relevance. Likewise, matrices may be cumbersome to develop and they are not always easy to survey. Moreover, it must be remembered that the forming of matrices is merely a way of obtaining a structure for the aspects that may have to be included in an analysis. In order to actually evaluate a specific legal information system it may be also necessary to investigate how the systems function in realistic situations and how well they are appreciated by the groups affected by them. Hence, as a parallel approach, a large number of activities may be used, e.g: observations, interviews, user surveys, and other forms of sociological methods. In addition, when legal requirements at a higher level must be identified, more theoretical or jurisprudential analyses may have to be performed. It should also be observed, of course, that in order to be used in system specifications the various requirements may sometimes have to be translated into more technical terms.

4 Legal Issues

4.1 *Introduction*

In a future oriented study on law libraries and legal information management, it is apparent that it is crucial to identify legal issues and discuss needs of regulations following as natural consequences of the accelerating IT development. Illustrations of this are also reflected in an enhanced interest in the legal issues related to e.g. copyright, freedom of information, the responsibility of the state to give access to and disperse official information in a digital form, privacy and administrative rules of various kinds. In the following sections a few of these issues are addressed in some detail.

4.1.1 No Rules

Initially, however, in this context it should be noted that it has been suggested on occasion that several of the areas touched upon in this study should remain unregulated or unaffected by the law. Such arguments have been especially frequent with regard to the Internet, and in several so called discussion lists ideas concerning "legal free zones", and autonomous, non governmental regulation by the parties involved have been presented.[1] In

---

[1] *See, e.g.,* for overviews and further references, *Center for Democracy and Technology,* "http://www.cdt.org/" (April 1997), *and, Blue ribbon Campaign for online freedom of speech, press and association,* (July 1997) "http://www.eff.org/blueribbon.html".

some cases such notions have also been combined with arguments suggesting that public networks should not be commercialised.

Underlying such attitudes is the natural desire to avoid unnecessary administrative hassle and bureaucracy. As the development continues, however, arguments indicating that some subject matters should be left unattended by the law become increasingly difficult to motivate. Commercial actors have already made their mark on the Internet and from the legal perspective it is rather easy to foresee difficulties if the emerging problems are not attended to in a professional manner. There are also numerous arguments making it rather obvious that a lack of regulatory system is not a realistic alternative.

The existence of a working rule system is for instance a necessary presupposition for further development of public networks and the services they provide. Access to a working legal system is also an important security device and therefore a critical component in the continued development of products and services. This is simply because investments are difficult to motivate if their consequences and possible failure cannot be controlled or disregarded to some extent.

Here it is also relevant to recall that the Internet often has been related with criminality – a fact which has frequently been reported on other media.[2] This is an additional fact which makes it obvious that the law cannot be put aside. The necessity to introduce a certain amount of regulation may be made explicit in this context by the fact that criminal activities may also affect persons that have little or no connection with the services provided via IT or telecommunications. In this perspective, to suggest that all acts performed with the assistance of public networks and telecommunications should remain unattended by the legal system is, of course, unrealistic. Instead, it is rather clear that the discussion about legal free zones, and similar notions must be looked upon as a short-sighted and already obsolete solution.

---

[2] *See, e.g.,* for an overview and a discussion, Olsson, Anders R., *IT och det fria ordet – myten om storebror*, 1996 at 107-27 *and, passim.*

4.2 *Intellectual Property Law*

From the point of view of the legal information manager as well as of end users, the most apparent legal feature affecting a free and efficient use of IT is without doubt intellectual property law, and especially the legislation concerning copyright. This is true not only for the legal sector, but also for almost any other domain. This does not mean, of course, that intellectual property law must be looked upon as something bad. On the contrary, intellectual property law is a necessary instrument with which to protect the economic and moral rights of authors and creators. If authors had no possibility of protecting their creations, and getting financial remuneration for it, fewer works would be made available since very few authors would find it meaningful to publish or make their work available in some other way if it could be immediately copied and redistributed by others. In this respect intellectual property rights are often said to contribute to economic and social development in the sense that they encourage fair trading and promote creativity.

Looking at the function of intellectual property law from some distance it is difficult to see how any further fruitful development of IT could be possible without some kind of protection. For many reason it seems obvious that some sort of economic protection is necessary as regards investments in information products. And, as time goes on, this aspect is likely to become even more important, as the resources that are needed for the creation of competitive products and services will become more extensive.

Intellectual property law is a relatively recent legal construction, being at the same time an extensively international phenomenon, due partly to the formation of the *World Intellectual Property Organisation* (WIPO)[3] which goes back to the late nineteenth century. At present, however, intellectual property must be looked upon as an established legal institution governed by various important international conventions and regulated by several EC directives. Among these should be mentioned the *Bern Convention* for the protection of literary and artistic works from 1886,[4] *The Paris Convention*

---

[3] "http://www.wipo.int/eng/index.htm".

[4] *See*, for the full text, including several amendments, *The Berne Convention for the Protection of Literary and Artistic Works Paris Act of July 24, 1971, as amended on September 28, 1979* "http://www.wipo.int/eng/iplex/index.htm".

for the protection of industrial property from 1883,[5] *The Rome Convention* for the protection of performers, producers of phonograms and broadcasting organisations from 1961,[6] and the recent 1995 TRIPS (Trade Related Aspects of Intellectual Property Rights) Agreement.[7] of the *World Trade Organisation*[8].

The directives relevant to intellectual property issued by the EU, include the 1991 Council Directive on the legal protection of computer programs,[9] the 1991 Council Directive on rental right and lending right and on certain rights related to copyright in the field of intellectual property,[10] the 1993 Council Directive on the co-ordination of certain rules concerning copyright and rights related to copyright applicable to satellite broadcasting and cable transmission,[11] the 1993 Council Directive harmonizing the term of protection of copyright and certain related rights,[12] and the 1996 Council Directive on the legal protection of databases.[13] In addition, several other international conventions and agreements exist.

---

[5] *Paris Convention for the Protection of Industrial Property of March 20, 1883*, "http://www.wipo.int/eng/iplex/wo_par0_.htm".

[6] *International Convention for the Protection of Performers, Producers of Phonograms and Broadcasting Organisations, Done at Rome on October 26, 1961* "http://www.wipo.int/eng/iplex/-wo_rom0_.htm".

[7] *Agreement on Trade-Related Aspects of Intellectual Property Rights* (TRIPS) "http://www.wto.org/wto/intellec/1-ipcon.htm".

[8] "http://www.wto.org/".

[9] *Council Directive 91/250/EEC of 14 May 1991 on the Legal Protection of Computer Programs*, OJ no. L 122, 17/05/91 p. 42.

[10] *Council Directive 92/100/EEC of 19 November 1992 on the Rental Right and Lending Right and on Certain Rights Related to Copyright in the Field of Intellectual Property*, OJ no. L 346, 27/11/92 p. 61.

[11] *Council Directive 93/83/EEC of 27 September 1993 on the Coordination of Certain Rules Concerning Copyright Applicable to Satellite Broadcasting and Cable Retransmission*, OJ no. L 248, 06/10/93 p. 15.

[12] *Council Directive 93/98/EEC of 29 October 1993 harmonizing the term of protection of copyright and certain related rights*, OJ no. L 290 , 24/11/93 p. 9.

[13] *Directive 96/9/EC of the European Parliament and of the Council of 11 March 1996 on the protection of databases*, OJ no. L 77 27/3/96 p. 20.

Although, the details of the legislation concerning intellectual property differ somewhat in various jurisdictions, the above-mentioned conventions and directives have made that intellectual property regulations in many countries are basically of a similar kind. Generally, intellectual property rights can be divided into two main branches: industrial property rights, i.e. rights concerning patents, trademarks, industrial design and unfair competition, and copyright with the so called neighbouring rights. In Sweden these issues are regulated primarily by the Patents Act,[14] The Trademarks Act,[15] The Act on Marketing Practices,[16] and The Copyright Act.[17]

International conventions and national laws are normally maintained by public authorities but intellectual property rights are also protected and supervised by the so called reproduction rights organisations, i.e. organisations that administer and protect the interests of its members, (members can consist of individual creators, such as e.g. writers and composers). Of crucial practical importance is also that copyright is meticulously observed by publishers and other kinds of companies trading in intellectual property rights. As a consequence, in practical situations official legislation is normally supplemented with various forms of agreements between the parties involved.

In principle, all aspects of intellectual property rights are of relevance for IT development. The fact that works can be stored and distributed in a digital form makes no difference in this respect – the laws of the physical world apply also to digital storage and distribution. What is protected by copyright is the expression of an idea, not the idea itself, or a theory behind a certain work.

Noticeable is also that the laws governing intellectual property are quite precise. As concerns copyright, the basic premise stipulated is that it is the creator (the artist, the author, etc.), or the person to whom the rights have

---

[14] In Swedish, *Patentlag* (1967:837).

[15] In Swedish, *Varumärkeslag* (1960:644).

[16] In Swedish, *Marknadsföringslag* (1995:450).

[17] In Swedish, *Lag (1960:729) om upphovsrätt till litterära och konstnärliga verk*, in the following referred to as URL.

been transferred, that has the right to decide when a certain work is to be published, and to what extent it should be distributed. In this way "it is the owner of a copyrighted work that has the exclusive right to reproduce it, prepare derivative works based upon it, distribute copy by sale or other transfer of ownership, to perform and display it publicly, and to authorise others to do so."[18] From this it also follows that it is not allowed to make copies of original works without the permission of the author, or someone to whom the copyright has been transferred.

Special rules apply to situations in which a work is the result of a joint effort, or when a work has been produced by someone who is to be considered as an employee. According to Swedish legislation work is protected by copyright for seventy years, from the time of the death of the creator. It is also important to notice here that various forms of exceptions exist, delimiting the exclusive right of the creator. One such important limitation is that "fair use", or personal (non commercial) use of copyrighted works, is permitted, although it must be noted that computer programs and digital databases are not included in this exemption (section 12 URL). Likewise, various exceptions relate to educational purposes and libraries. Swedish copyright law explicitly states, for instance, that archives and libraries have the right to make copies of works for lending purposes among other things (section 16 URL). The only type of work that is excluded from this exception concerns computer programs – an exemption that excludes in many cases also digital information on CD-ROMs, since such products contain often, in addition to e.g. databases, computer programs.

When a copy of a work has been legally sold, the original rights concerning transfer of that copy expires. In the copyright terminology it is said that these rights have been "exhausted". According to this "the first sale doctrine" the copy can then freely be sold, lent, or otherwise transferred further. It is important to notice here nevertheless that also in this case copies of computer programs in machine readable form are to some extent excepted from this general rule (section 19 par 2 p 2 URL) From this exemption follows that, e.g. a library cannot make computer programs freely available to its customers. If a library wants to lend computer programs, or otherwise make them available to its customers in some other

---

[18] Rosenoer, Jonathan, *CyberLaw: The Law of the Internet*, 1996 at 1.

way, the library must reach an agreement with the rightholders of the programs in each single case.

Violation of copyright is punishable by the law and most copyright laws include such sanctions as fines, imprisonment and an obligation to compensate rightholders for economic losses. In addition, contracts between actors on the information market contain as a rule liability clauses that can be activated in cases of violation. On the other hand, information providers disseminating information originating from external sources often try to delimit their responsibility in this respect.

Copyright is obtained automatically when a work is published or when it is otherwise made public. No special form of registration or any other kind of administrative undertaking is necessary. Registration is, however needed to some extent in order to obtain copyright protection in the USA.[19] In the USA, as well as in other jurisdictions, it is still also common (but not always necessary) to mark works with a copyright sign (©) combined with the name of the author and the year in which the work was originally made public.

It is important to note that most of the basic concepts in this legal field were developed long before computers and electronic transmission of digital information were invented. From this it also follows that legal regulation has been under a lot of strain during the recent decades, and that changes and amendments have been – and still are – numerous. A fact that is clearly illustrated by the exemptions concerning computer programs mentioned above. It is also quite clear that the legal system has often had difficulties in keeping up with the pace of the technological development. In this respect, new phenomena, e.g. those appearing on the Internet, frequently give rise to confusion, creating the need for legal analogies and creative interpretation.

As an example, in this context mention can be made of a recent case decided by the *Swedish Supreme Court*, concerning liability for the transfer and distribution of illegal copies of digital information by means of IT. An owner of a so called Bulletin Board System (BBS) was then freed from accusations concerning illegal copying or complicity of such crimes

---

[19] *Id.* at 3.

committed by the users of the BBS.[20] Although the decision has been much discussed and also initiated activities form the legislator.

The strain experienced by the legal system as regards intellectual property rights is not only due to the fact that new technical solutions are presented more or less continuously. Complications arise also from the fact that information is becoming a crucial aspect in many fields of society, and that the use of IT is more widespread. Technical means for the processing and communication of information, that some years ago were available to only a few selected ones, are presently within the reach of anyone with access to a computer and a modem. Activities such a mass-copying and world-wide distribution, which only a short while ago demanded vast resources and took days to complete, can now be accomplished almost immediately with a few key strokes, e.g. in a computer room of an undergraduate school.

Technological development does not only mean that the number of violations of intellectual property rights has grown drastically. It also means that the severity of the injuries that can follow from the misuse of the technology has increased. In addition, internationalisation and the speed with which communication and data processing can be completed, have made it much more difficult to deal with these violations. Various forms of illegal operations are also a very common phenomenon. As concerns computer programs it has been estimated that some forty per cent of the copies in use stem from illegal copying.[21] The fact that the illegal handling of information in digital form represents immense economic values has recently also been made a top political issue between China and the USA.[22] This incident reflects the fact that intellectual property rights are becoming one the most important objects of international trade.

In addition to problems concerning copyright which are caused by the mass-handling of information and the speed of the capacity of the techno-

---

[20] NJA 1996 s 79.

[21] Business Software Alliance, *Press Release*, May 7, 1997.

[22] In May, 1996, the United States announced the publication of a $3 billion preliminary retaliation list targeting Chinese exports to the United States. The cause of the US action was China's failure to enforce satisfactorily its commitments under the February 1995 agreement on intellectual property rights (IPR) protection. *See*, "http://www.usia.gov/regional/ea/prcipr/prcipr.htm".

logy, it is also obvious that the digital technique makes it often very difficult, or even impossible, to detect more subtle violations, such as changes, omission and amendments. When a document, a text, a picture, or some other form of work is altered in a non-digital environment the changes can almost always be detected in some way, or if not, a considerable effort is necessary to accomplish an alteration, e.g. to rewrite a text in order to hide the changes, which is in many cases simply impractical. In a digital environment, however, all types of works can be manipulated without leaving any trace of the changes whatsoever. A copy of the original digital work becomes identical with the original.

Manipulations of this kind are, however, not unregulated. Besides being violations of the economic rights of their authors, they sometimes also constitute violations of the part of the copyright known as the Moral Rights, which consists among other things of the right of the author not to have his work altered, and to have his name mentioned when the work is published or made otherwise public. At a somewhat more detailed level this means that every author of a given work can claim the right of paternity (section 3 URL), i.e. that the name of the author should be stated to the extent and manners required by proper usage. The latter being a concept whose exact meaning depends on the type of work and the concrete situation. Likewise, any author can claim the right of integrity. This right relates to alterations when the work is copied, alterations to original works, and the use of unaltered works in an unworthy context.

Intellectual property is not only protected by copyright. Digitalisation and the Internet have generated issues and problems which have made it necessary to activate also other rule systems. Many of these rules have existed for quite a long time, and just like the copyright legislation they have been developed in order to handle various issues in a pre-IT context. IT has thus made it necessary to look upon several rule systems from a new perspective.[23] Many examples of the above can be mentioned, some of which are actually not older than a year or two. The rapid pace of development makes it also quite clear that issues of this kind are likely to appear at an ever-increasing pace also in the future.

---

[23] *See*, for an overview of Swedish legislation, Lindberg, Agne & Westman, Daniel, *Praktisk IT-rätt*, 1997.

1. One current issue which has been much discussed is the extent to which the use of the so called hypertext links on the Internet should be considered as a violation of intellectual property rights. Hypertext-links, i.e. the possibility to instantly jump between different pages of information, located perhaps thousands of miles apart, just by means of clicking on a word, a picture, or some other element, and without using any search words or other kinds of complicated functions, are of course one of the most outstanding features of the Internet. The typical situation here is that information providers use links in order to connect information on the same topic, produced by others. If this is done explicitly, there are probably seldom or never any problems, provided that the linked-to information does not violate any copyright claims. That is simply to say that if someone has made information available on the Internet, it must also be assumed that this information should be open for others to see.[24]

Legal issues may arise, however, when web site owners try to gain economically by means of utilising information provided by others. This can be accomplished in several ways. One way of doing it is by means of using so called frames.[25] The use of frames, or framing, is a technique which, among other things, enables producers of web sites to incorporate remote sites, or information stemming from remote sites, into their own context. Viewers may thus be able to look through one site to another. This can be done without terminating the connection with the linking site. In this way producers of web sites can incorporate entire web sites produced by others, or parts of such sites, and providing them with their own advertising, logos and promotions. Theoretically, this can be done in such a way that the viewers remain unaware of the fact that the provided information originates from someone else.

---

[24] Rosenoer *supra* note 18 at 10, "Because World Wide Web is, in essence, a protocol that exists only to link sites to each other, it is hard to see how anyone could claim the right to restrict site access only to those receiving specific permission to do so." *But see*, Tysver, Daniel, A., *Ticketmaster v. Microsoft Dispute* at "http://www.bitlaw.com/hot/ticketmaster.html", 1997, who reports an emerging legal dispute between two US companies, *Ticketmaster* and *Microsoft*, concerning this issue. *See*, generally on legal issues concerning links, Bechthold, Stefan *The Link Controversy Page* at "http://www.jura.uni-tuebingen.de/~s-bes1/lcp.html", 1997.

[25] Frames were originally presented as a feature of hypertext mark-up language (HTML) available for use in so called web-browsers such as *Netscape Navigator* and *Microsoft Internet Explorer*. It was introduced as a HTML extension in 1996. *See, e.g.*, Poler, Ellen, *Frames and License Agreements*, "http://www.collegehill.com/ilp-news/poler1.html", 1997.

A related technique is inlining, i.e. linking documents through graphical elements which are visible on the screen as part of Web documents, but which originate from a different source, that can be located anywhere on the Internet. In this area an ever-increasing number of variations and combinations of different technical solutions can be observed. Noticeable is however that sometimes applications of this type of technology may become very annoying for the user, especially when the computer starts to download large volumes of information which has not been explicitly requested.

As concerns these latter types of linking, rules concerning protection of company names, trademarks, and unfair competition, may easily be violated. In addition, since many web site owners are dependent on revenues from advertising, framing can also give rise to economic losses for them if their information is utilised by others out of its original context. It is also easy to predict legal disputes concerning various ways of a more or less automatic use of codes from remote web sites in order to capture effects of different kinds. As to this date, however, very few disputes of this kind have been formally settled in public.[26]

2. Another recently much debated issue concerns the use of company names on the Internet, and especially the possibilities to register Internet addresses containing names and trademarks consisting of alphanumerical characters, such as words, acronyms and labels. For some time the routines for registering domain names in the so called ".com (commercial) domain" made it possible for anyone to register any name or trademark, disregarding whether or not this meant violation of someone else's right. The registering organisations administered the applications in the order of their submission, making no comparisons with official registers concerning names or trademarks. This was utilised quite extensively by less serious actors, who applied and got registration for a large number of well-known and well-established company names. Names and trademarks could thus be imbedded in Internet addresses which had no connection with the official rightholders.

In effect anyone searching on the Internet for a trademark or a company could end up at a site that had no relation whatsoever to the company or the product in question. In some cases attempts have also been made to sell the

---

[26] *See,* Gentzschein, Anna, *Internet Links: Legal Implications*, 1997.

right to use a name on the Internet to the companies in whose name it had been originally registered (sometimes referred to as "Domain Name Grabbing" or "Domain Napping").

When this is being written very few cases concerning these matters have been settled in public. As concerns name giving of addresses on the Internet, however, the emerging problems have lead to the adaptation of more elaborate rules and a more conscious practice among the name giving organisations.[27]

3. Copyright issues of a new kind have also emerged with regard to the concept of multimedia on the Internet and CD-ROMs. The crucial issue is here the extent to which it should be possible to obtain protection for the collection or combination of various kinds of information, e.g. texts, pictures, video, graphics, sound, etc., when none or few of the original contributions are the result of any original creative effort of the compiler. In other words, the critical question is to what extent it is possible and desirable to give protection to something which consists basically of a new combination of previously published material. And, conversely, to what extent it should be possible to use the works of others for the formation of such products.

In this respect various solutions have been discussed and suggested. To start with, it is quite clear that the copyright legislation acknowledge protection for the so called composite works, i.e. combinations of works or parts of works which become new literary or artistic works. From this also follows that a multimedia product which utilises materials obtained from others can obtain protection as a work in its own right, disregarding the fact that each component of such a product may be protected as a work of it own (section 5 URL). Of relevance in this context is furthermore the fact that according to the copyright legislation anyone is free to quote from other works, as long as it is done in a reasonable manner (section 22 URL).

As concerns databases in the form of multimedia or of a more conventional kind an EC directive has recently been issued.[28] The directive explicitly states, among other things, that databases should obtain protection

---

[27] *See*, "http://141.161.67.230/piet/internic/recent/", *and* for a review on the Swedish situation, Lundberg, Johan, *Internet: Domännamn & svensk rätt*, 1997.

[28] *Supra* note 13.

for a period of fifteen years provided that they represent a substantial investment (article 7). This is referred to in the directive as a *sui generis* right (right of its own) for databases, and it is now up to the various member states to implement this rule into their national legislation.

The extent to which the legislation has to be altered in order to be in line with the EC directive differs between the various EU countries in accordance with differences in the details of the legislation of the different countries. In Sweden for example, the copyright legislation has acknowledged a similar rule for a long time now, the rule being known as catalogue protection, which means that any considerable large compilation (i.e. a product in which a large number of particulars have been summarised) obtains protection for the limited period of ten years (section 49 URL).[29]

In addition, translations and other results of information processing can obtain protection, provided that those contributions represent certain quality. Protection can thus be given to the transformation of a work from one media to another (section 4 URL). Clearly stated is also that computer programs, which are often imbedded as crucial parts of multimedia products, can be the object of copyright (section 1 URL).

Protection can furthermore be obtained for a database containing official materials, provided that some kind of non trivial feature has been added to the information. For example, it is quite clear that it is possible to obtain copyright protection for an elaborated cross reference system,[30] a certain layout, or a pedagogic presentation of the material. Likewise various means of abstracting, and perhaps even headlining court decisions can obtain protection,[31] as works of their own or as derivative works. Whether or not hypertext links *per se* or the design of such components are protected by the copyright legislation remains, however, to be clarified.

---

[29] *See,* Ds 1996:71, *Rättsligt skydd för databaser, and,* Jensen, Eva, *Myndigheternas databaser: ensamrätt och tillgänglighet* 1997.

[30] The most well known case of this is probably *West Publishing Co.* v. *Mead Data Central Inc.* in which West's method of arranging legal decisions was given copyright protection. *See,* 479 US 1070, 107, S.Ct. 962 (1987).

[31] In Sweden there is presently an ongoing legal dispute between two publishers, *Norstedts* and *InfoDirect,* concerning the right to utilise case headlines generated by Supreme Court judges.

As concerns products on CD-ROMs and other kinds of electronic products that are distributed outside the Internet, it must be remembered that a lawful transfer presupposes some sort of an agreement between the producer and the user. It is also clear that one of the most crucial components of such an agreements is often the regulation of copyright and the right of the user to further utilise the information.

From all this it also follows that the forms of regulating the ways in which information may be used – in digital as well as in traditional contexts are in most cases quite well established. Likewise, it is quite clear that many, and perhaps most, new forms of information products, disregarding whether they are labelled as multimedia or whether they are to be regarded as illustrations of true Cyberspace products, are likely to obtain some sort of legal protection against free copying and further unauthorised use.

This is, however, not the same thing as to say that all problems with unauthorised copying have been solved. Complications may arise due for numerous reasons. Among other things, a number of issues have emerged, for example, in connection with the interpretation of various new forms of licenses that have appeared on the digital market. Besides previously established forms of contracts, depending normally on the number of users that a certain product has been licensed for, several new forms have been introduced, such as "shrink wrap" and "web wrap" licenses. Shrink wrap is a form of an agreements that is distributed together with the package of products, e.g. CD-ROMs, combined with a message that the buyer/licensee accepts the terms of the contract as soon as he or she breaks the seal of the package.

The so called web wrap licences represent a similar construction. Before or after a user has downloaded a certain material from the Internet, a number of terms are presented, combined with a message stating that the user is said to accept the terms if he or she installs or otherwise uses the material (alternatively acceptance may be related to the clicking of a button on the screen). For obvious reasons the terms of such contracts can be difficult, or even impossible, to analyse before any decision concerning, e.g. a subscription or a purchase can be made. Sometimes also the legal consequences of such contracts may be questionable. For example, according to the Swedish legal doctrine of contracts, all terms of an agreement must be available to the parties for inspection at the time the agreement is being settled. This presupposition makes the legality of many forms of shrink and wrap licenses highly questionable. A further conclusion from this is therefore that legal competence is often needed when products are acquired, and this, in turn, sets the focus on the elaboration of access policies among the users and distributors of information.

As concerns information available on the Internet and the World Wide Web it is furthermore noticeable that for some time there has been a discussion going on concerning the existence of the so called implied licenses. "The World Wide Web's history, custom, and practice, as well as the reasonable expectations of the public – particularly now that there exist Web sites that require a password and user ID to enter – all support the existence of ... an implied license for Web site visitors."[32] To what extent such a license can be utilised, if it exists at all, is, however, still unclear. The answers will depend, no doubt, in each case on the context and the type of information in question. Possible interpretations range from rights to see, link to, quote from, frame, copy, and produce derivative works.

The extensive use of technology, the limitless possibilities if copying and distributing materials, as well as the fact that digital material is easily manipulated, are the arguments which are often used in order to suggest that copyright is becoming outdated. In discussions about the future it has also been therefore submitted that copyright in its present form provides an unnecessary obstacle to the free flow of information and that alternatives should be worked out.

The question of the feasibility of the copyright system in the digital environment has thus lead to the initiation of a number of experiments with other forms of solutions aiming to secure the protection of intellectual work. Likewise, various ways of administering the rights of creators have evolved. As concerns the latter several trends are clearly visible, one being the growing importance of the so called reproduction rights organisations, (RROs), formed in order to protect the interests of some special group of creators. As compared to individuals RROs can develop more efficient routines in order to control the extent to which the works of the associated members are being utilised and, thanks to the combined strength of their

[32] Rosenoer *supra* note 18 at 10.

members, they are also in a much better position to negotiate with publishers and distributors, for example.

Another, more pragmatic way of meeting the digital challenge is to shift to various forms of "pay in advance systems" and accept the fact that once the information is made public in digital form it is no longer realistic to try to control it. Pay in advance policies can be utilised at several points of the chain in which information is produced, for example, by authors, publishers, or data base producers. This development has lead, in turn, to a growing market for various intermediaries, specialising in acquiring and distributing information on a pure commercial basis.

In addition, various technical solutions are being contemplated. For example, one solution has showed that it is possible to mark information and digital documents by means of adding small programs that are able to detect when they are manipulated, and react each time they are being copied. Such small-scale programs can be made in order to identify the computers they are being transferred to. It will thus be also possible to digitally authorise computers so that they are able to identify the kind of programs that they should accept. Here, various kinds of solutions are possible, e.g. to let a digital work destroy itself after a certain time, after a certain number of copies have been made, or after incidents of unacceptable transfer on the Internet. Sometimes this technology is referred to as *trusted systems*, and it entails a wide range of forms ranging from "trusted readers for digital books, trusted players for playing audio and video recordings, trusted printers for making copies that contain labels ('watermarks') that denote copyright status, and trusted servers that sell digital works on the Internet."[33] In this context it is naturally also relevant to recall that numerous projects aiming to develop various forms of encryption facilities have been initiated.

Moreover, experiments with various types of security levels are being conducted. "The most valuable digital properties might be protected by systems that detect any tampering, set off alarms and erase the information inside. And an intermediate level, a trusted system would block a nonexpert attack with a simple password scheme. And a lower security level, it would

---

[33] Stefik, Mark, *Trusted Systems*, 1997, at 69.

offer few obstacles to infringers but would mark digital works so that their source could be traced."[34]

As concerns protection of digital information, various forms of physical measures can naturally be also utilised. Parts of information that is vital for a certain application available on the Internet (such as, e.g., a certain program) can be distributed, for instance, in forms that are easier to control, such as on CD-ROMs, or – if it is a password – by ordinary mail. In such a way the vital functions for the efficient utilisation of a database can be distributed to those who pay the fees, disregarding the fact that the bulk of the information is distributed electronically and that it is perhaps also freely accessible via the Internet.

4.3 Freedom of information

4.3.1 Introduction

Not all kinds of material are protected by intellectual property law. As concerns law much basic information is excepted from copyright. A consequence of the fact that in many countries legislation, as well as other kinds of official materials generated by public authorities and courts are free from copyright claims. This is for instance the situation in Sweden were legislation, legislative preparatory materials as well as court decisions are considered to be official information which is available for free, or at a low non-profit cost.

As illustrated in section 3.4.1.2 above, it is in a discussion about the elaboration of legal information systems quite interesting to broaden the perspective and also be open for a development in which a large variety of additional public information, generated within the authorities will become interesting to include in such systems. From this in turn also follows that it is relevant to make an inventory of the legislation surrounding this kind of information.

The suggestion that a legal information system should include all kinds of legally relevant materials can easily be looked upon as being of a

[34] *Op cit. Cf., also,* the EC IMPRIMATUR project, at "http://www.imprimatur.alcs.co.uk/", 1997.

controversial nature. Especially the inclusion of official documents and investigations preceding legislation may be questioned, and in several jurisdictions such an order is just not conceivable. In this respect the principle of freedom of information is interpreted in various ways and in several jurisdictions it is simply not acknowledged as valid at all.

In Sweden, nevertheless, the fundamental rules concerning access to public information are given in the Freedom of the Press Act (FPA),[35] which is part of the Constitution, and is thus governed by special rules regarding the ways in which it can be changed. The main principle is that official documents are of a public nature. That is to say that all Swedish subjects shall have free access to such documents (The right-of-access principle). The principle is explicitly motivated by the ambition to encourage free interchange of opinions and the enlightenment of the public (Chapter 2, Art 1 FPA).

By means of promoting a free exchange of ideas and a general information flow, the right-of-access principle is considered to be a guarantee of the legality of action of the authorities. This by means of securing an important control function in that the public can examine all background documentation concerning current discussions and various forms of administrative and legal actions taken by the authorities.

The ideas expressed in the Swedish right-of-access principle can be traced back to the mid-eighteenth century and the principle is considered to be a cornerstone of the Swedish Constitution. In this context it may be noted that much of the public debate preceding the Swedish application for a membership in the European Union was based on uncertainty as to whether or not one would be able to uphold this principle in the future. The Swedish government has thereby stated that Sweden's participation in the final negotiations concerning the *95/46/EC Directive on the Protection of Individuals with Regard to the Processing of Personal Data and the Free Movement of such Data*, made it possible for Swedish viewpoints to be taken into consideration.[36] An implicit reference to the inclusion of Recital

[35] In Swedish *Tryckfrihetsförordning* (TF).

[36] "In the work with the [95/46/EC] Directive, Sweden has acted firmly in order to reach solutions which are not in opposition to the Swedish right-of-access principle or other aspects of the Constitution. The Swedish efforts in this area have been successful." *Regeringens direktiv till Datalagskommittén* (Dir. 1995:91), (Original in Swedish). *Cf,* The 95/46/EC *Directive on the Protection of Individuals with Regard to the Processing of Personal Data and the Free Movement*

72 of the Directive which reads in the following way: "[w]hereas this Directive allows the principle of public access to official documents to be taken into account when implementing the principles set out in this Directive."

In principle, all documents kept by public authorities are official documents, disregarding whether they have been received from some other or whether they have been drawn up by the authority, and regardless of their content. Exemptions are drafts and preliminary versions of documents which become official documents when they receive their final formulation. Further exceptions include memorandums and other kinds of notes drawn up in order to prepare oral presentations, which obtain the status of official documents only if they are filed after the matter to which they refer has been decided.

The FPA gives quite explicit definitions concerning the various concepts used. "Documents", for instance, are described as "any written matter, picture, or record which can be read, listened to, or otherwise comprehended only by means of technical aids", which means that databases and other mechanical or electronic records are subsumed under this category (Chapter 2, Art 3 FPA).

An official document must be available to anyone who wants to consult it, usually in the original, and in principle upon request. It is also important that any private individual has the right to obtain a copy of such documents.[37] As for documents which can be read, listened to, or otherwise comprehended only by means of technical aids they "shall be considered to be kept by a public authority, if [they are] available to the authority in such a form that it can be read or listened to, or otherwise rendered comprehensible."

The principle of free access to official documents can only be restricted if it is necessary with regard to

---

of such Data, 1995 OJ of 23 November 1995 No L. 281 p. 31 (also available at "http://www2.echo.lu/legal/en/dataprot/directiv/directiv.html").

[37] Although the authorities have the right to demand a non profit fixed fee for the production of copies.

- the security of the Realm or its relations with a foreign state or an international organisation;
- the central finance policy, monetary policy, or foreign exchange policy of the Realm;
- the inspection, control or other supervisory activities of a public authority;
- the interest of preventing or prosecuting crimes;
- the public economic interest;
- the protection of the personal integrity [privacy] or economic circumstances of private subjects; or
- the preservation of animals or plant species." (Chapter 2, Art 2 FPA)

Restrictions with references to the above mentioned aspects shall be explicitly stated in a special act, – The Official Secrecy Act (OSA),[38] – or in other acts which refer to the OSA. Detailed provisions concerning administrative matters with regard to secrecy appear in the Secrecy Ordinance.[39]

Of relevance in this respect is furthermore that the FPA make exceptions for "record [which can be read, listened to, or otherwise comprehended only by means of technical aids] which forms part of a register of persons, if by law, or statutory order, or by a special decision taken by virtue of law, the authority is not entitled to prepare such a transcription. Register of persons shall be understood to mean any register, list, or other record containing information which concerns a private subject and which can be related back to that private subject" – a limitation implicitly referring to the Swedish Data Protection Act[40] (Chapter 2, Art 3 FPA). The right-of-access is limited

[38] In Swedish *Sekretesslag* (1980:100), reprinted (1992:1474).

[39] In Swedish *Sekretessförordning* (1980:657), reprinted (1994:1030).

[40] In Swedish *Datalag* (1973:289), reprinted (1992:446).

in this respect also in the sense that a public authority has no obligation to make available a record for electronic data processing in any other form than as a print out.

Applications for access to official documents shall be made to the public authority which keeps the documents and the application shall be promptly examined by the same authority. In some cases, however, viz. if a document is of "key importance for the security of the Realm" it may be prescribed that the application should be examined by a particular authority, and in such cases the application must be submitted at once to the competent authority. It is also important to mention that it is explicitly stated that "no public authority may inquire into a person's identity on account of his request for access to an official document, or inquire as to the purpose of his request", insofar as such inquiry is necessary in order to enable the authority to ascertain whether or not any obstacle exists to prevent the release of the document (Chapter 2, Art 14 FPA).

As concerns the interchange of documents between public authorities, the basic principle is that public authorities should assist each other in this respect. This principle is reflected, e.g., in a special Act concerning the administrative organisation and work of public authorities (Art 6 The Public Administration Act)[41] and in Chapter 14 of the OSA.

Of relevance in this context is also The Archives Act[42] which extends the right of public access in time by means of ensuring that official documents are preserved in official archives.

4.3.2 The Official Secrecy Act

Detailed rules regarding the duty to observe secrecy and restrictions against making official documents available are given in the OSA. The provisions given in the OSA limit the right of access to official documents provided for in the FPA. The structure of the OSA reflects the above mentioned points 1-7 in the FPA and each point is elaborated on in a special chapter devoted to

---

[41] In Swedish *Förvaltningslag* (1986:223).

[42] In Swedish *Arkivlag* (1990:782).

it. The OSA provides quite detailed regulations concerning the type of data that should be protected. The question of whether or not secrecy shall apply in any individual case should be answered with regard to the risk of various forms of harm that may be caused, or other forms of negative effects which may be experienced by the individuals.

The OSA thus define restrictions concerning disclosure of certain kinds of data. Verbal disclosure, making an official document available, and all other ways of disclosures are regulated. The Act also contains other prescriptions regarding official documents. Among other things it is explicitly stated that secret data which is kept within a public authority must not be disclosed to any other authority, or even to any other department within the public authority in question if the two departments are regarded as independent of each other. Although exemptions to this rule exist (Chapter 1 OSA).

As concerns records for automatic data processing a number of detailed rules are given. For instance there is a rule stating that any authority whose activities involve the use of automatic data processing shall organise such activities by taking into consideration the right-of-access to official documents prescribed by the FPA. The authority shall furthermore arrange data processing in such a way that it takes account the interest of private subjects to use a terminal or other technical aid within the authority for the purpose of gaining access to official documents.

Of relevance in this respect is also the fact that the Secrecy Act explicitly states that any authority shall make available to the public a description of registers that are kept, provide terminals for public use, or supply other forms of aids for private subjects who want to gain access to computer based registers.

4.3.3 Privacy

The suitability of including official material in public information systems cannot only be limited due to aspects of secrecy, it may also be questioned as a consequence of considerations concerning privacy. The protection of privacy, i.e. the right of the individual to enjoy a certain degree of integrity as a person is in most jurisdictions accepted as an important component of a law state, which must be given serious attention. Consequently, the issues related to privacy are in many countries dealt with in special legislation. Privacy issues are also acknowledged to be highly relevant in the handling of data in computer based media[43] and often indicate that documents concerning individual cases or ongoing disputes may have to be omitted from public information systems or, at least, transformed so that it no longer is possible to identify individuals before the material is made available.

Of relevance in this context is for instance *The Swedish Data Protection Act* (DPA)[44] which came into force as early as 1973. The DPA is based on the principle that anyone who is responsible for automatic processing of personal data shall have a licence issued by the *Data Inspection Board* (DIB) – a public authority established in 1973.

The basic provision of the DPA is that personal data files may only be created and maintained by persons who have registered with the DIB and received proof of registration (a licence) from the Board. In addition, the processing of certain kinds of sensitive data requires special permission (e.g. concerning a person's health, political opinion, etc.).

The DPA also provides a number of definitions, and mention can be made of the following terms: "personal data" which means any information relating to an individual; "personal data file" which means any file, list or other record undergoing automatic data processing that contains information relating to a data subject, "data subject" which means an individual who is the subject of data in a personal data file; and "file controller" which means any person for the purposes of whose activities a personal data file is kept, where the file is under his control. It should furthermore be observed that the DPA regulates only "automatic data processing". Noticeable is also that the DPA provides the basic regulation concerning illegal handling of computerised information, viz. so called *data intrusion*.

The Swedish DPA has for a long time been under debate. For a number of years it has also been generally accepted that the Act provides solutions that are to a large extent obsolete, despite numerous amendments and changes. For a long time, a number of upcoming difficulties have had to be

---

[43] *See, e.g.*, Directive 95/46/EC *supra* note 36.

[44] *Supra* note 40.

solved with specific ad hoc solutions of little or no consistency, decided and administrated by the DIB. In addition, a large number of court decisions, as well as administrative and Governmental decisions have affected the actual interpretation and application of the DPA.

This state of the matter is widely known and a recent example of this is provided by a problem inventory carried out by a special Project Group "Toppledarforum" comprising officials from the DIB, the Swedish Agency for Administrative Development, the National Tax Board, and several others. The Group came to the conclusion that "if measures [concerning updating of the current legislation] are not taken immediately, there is a great risk that regulations will become totally or partially obsolete – as is already the case with the Swedish Data [Protection] Act."[45] The Group proposed, among other things, "that the current Swedish Data Act [should] be replaced by all encompassing privacy legislation and that the necessity of special register legislation be re-examined".

As regards the time perspective, it was made clear that there was an urgent need to review the regulations concerning the exchange of classified information between authorities, revise the Data Protection Act and re-examine the processing of public administration matters using information technology. It was recommended that these issues should be given "top priority". Likewise, it was stressed that a holistic perspective should be applied.[46]

A similar conclusion was reached already in 1993, in a previous attempt to revise the Swedish Data Protection Act. It was then concluded that the DPA could be considered to be outdated, both from the technical and the substantial point of view.[47]

Thus, from the point of view of the legal information manager, the issues related to secrecy and privacy in many situations may lead up to the conclusion that certain material must be left out from public databases, or that such material in various ways must be edited. In such cases it may well be argued that the freedom of information principle better is ensured in

[45] Toppledarforum/Datainspektionen, *LEXIT – A pre-study*, 1995.

[46] *Id.* at 3-4, *and, passim.*

[47] SOU 1993:10, *En ny datalag*, at 13.

other ways, e.g. by means of making official records open on requests to the authorities, combined with administrative regulations in order to prevent unwanted effects and misuse of sensitive information. In most developed countries there also exist regulations suggesting that personal data should not be made public, except in certain well defined situations.

From the jurisprudential point of view the removal of personal data is not a serious limitation. That is to say that there are seldom reasons to include names or other forms of personal data in the material that is made official. From the practical point of view, however, the removing of personal data from the information presupposes editing, and it may also be a cumbersome and time consuming task. The important conclusion in this context is nevertheless that privacy aspects are natural starting points when materials to be excluded from public legal information systems are being identified and selected. And, from the point of view of the user, the fact that personal data has been removed from a public information system will seldom be looked upon as a limitation.

4.4 Proposed Legislation

4.4.1 A New Personal Data Protection Act

On April 2, 1997 a draft for an entirely new Swedish Personal Data Protection Act (SFS 1998:204) was presented.[48] The aim has been to produce a modern, technically independent legislation to protect personal integrity (privacy) in the processing of personal information. The Committee behind the proposal explicitly states that "we propose unambiguous provisions in the new Personal Data Protection Act which make clear that the Act should not be applied to an extent which would curtail rights protected by the Constitution", and among other things, mentions the right-of-access principle in this context. It is also made clear that the starting point for the Committee has been the fact that Sweden's viewpoints on the matter have been implemented in the 95/46/EC directive. A statement implicitly referring to the above mentioned Recital 72.

[48] SOU 1997:39, *Integritet, offentlighet, informationsteknik.*

The new Personal Data Protection Act is based on the regulation of the actual handling of data containing personal information, which is in line with the EC directive, and which is to some extent also similar to the general structure of the current DPA. As for the chosen model of legislation the Committee has, however, made it clear that the proposal should be considered as a non permanent solution and that in the long term, "a policy of constraint and legal steps against misuse would be preferable to the regulation of data handling of the kind which virtually anyone can engage in." Such an alternative model, it is argued, would instead allow more or less free handling of personal information, and would only seek to prevent the kind of personal information handling that could be seen as attempts to misuse such information.

It is furthermore stated that the new Personal Data Protection Act provides a framework stipulating guidelines for all processing of personal data, with the exception of purely private use of such data. As an example of the latter, the exchange of e-mail between private persons is mentioned.

It is also obvious that the general nature of the new legislation will make it necessary for the Government and the Swedish Data Inspection Board to issue more precise regulations within the new framework. Such an order is already established and the DIB can enact detailed administrative rules concerning subject matters within its authority.[49] From the proposed changes it also follows that the number of special register statutes presently in force (the Committee mentions some 35 examples of such statutes) will have to be reviewed in the near future.

As regards definitions, the new Act uses the expression "processing of personal data", which is said to comprise everything that can be done with such data, e.g. retrieval, collection, storage and dissemination. The Act is intended to cover all processing of personal data which is partly or wholly automatic. Manual processing of personal data on paper is only included if the data is to form a proper register.

The person responsible for the processing of personnel data (the controller) must ensure that the data is only collected for certain, expressly stated and justifiable purposes. The data may not be later on used for any

---

[49] These rules are published in *Datainspektionens författningssamling* (DIFS) – the official collection of regulations of the *Data Inspection Board.*

purpose incompatible with the purposes for which the data was originally collected. Superfluous data may not be processed, and the data which is processed must be accurate and relevant. Inaccurate, misleading or incomplete data must be corrected. The data may be stored only as long as it is necessary with respect to the purpose of the processing. Special rules are included for historical, statistical or scientific purposes.

Personal data may always be processed if the individuals in question (the data subjects) have given their consent. If such consent is lacking, the processing must comply with a number of explicitly mentioned purposes, such as:

- In connection with a contract.
- In order to fulfil a legal obligation.
- In order to protect vital interest of the data subjects.
- In order to carry out a task of public interest or in connection with the exercising of official authority.
- After a balance of interests where the interests of the data subject are weighed against the interests on the part of the controller.

Special restrictions apply with regard to the processing of so called sensitive data, i.e. data relating to a person's health or sex life, and data concerning race, ethnic origin, political opinions, religious or philosophical beliefs, or membership of a trade union. Sensitive data may be processed when the data subject has given his or her consent, or when he or she has manifestly made the data public, and in order to fulfil a number of other explicitly mentioned purposes.

The data subjects shall be informed about the processing of data relating to them although some exceptions exist in this regard (see below). As for the duties of the Data Inspection Board, the current obligation to issue licenses for the processing of personal data and similar activities shall be "kept to a minimum". Instead, the DIB should concentrate on supervision, information and advice. The DIB shall also issue instructions which clarify the provisions of the Act in various areas.

Penalties for violation of the new Act primarily comprise damages to abused data subjects. It is furthermore suggested that the rule concerning penalties for unauthorised use, etc. (previously section 21) should be incorporated into the penal code (Brottsbalken chapter 4, section 9c).

The new Personal Data Protection Act come into force on October 24, 1998, and apply in full to all processing commenced thereafter. For processing already underway when the Act comes into force, the former Data Protection Act shall apply until October 2001.

The proposal for a new Personal Data Protection Act also includes proposals for changes in the FPA, and minor terminological changes in other parts of the constitution.[50]

4.4.2 The Right-of-Access Principle

An explicit aim of the Committee working on the new Personal Data Protection Act has been not to alter the principle of the right-of-access. The Committee has thereby been working on the following premises

- Right-of-access shall be as broad as possible
- The rules must be clear and simple to apply

In order to accomplish this, the central concept of "public data", is proposed to replace the present "public document". It is thereby argued the term "public data" is technically neutral and that the Official Secrets Act is based already on it. A positive consequence of this is also that theoretical notions, such as potential documents, can be abandoned.

"Document" is nevertheless intended to remain as a concept defined as a "storing space" for data. A document has thus a defined content, viz. a content ascribed to it originally by the person who once wrote it. It is of no

[50] In *The Fundamental Law on Freedom of Expression* (In Swedish Yttrandefrihetsgrundlagen) *and*, in *The Instrument of Government* (In Swedish Regeringsformen).

consequence whether the document takes the form of a sheet of paper, or whether it exists in digital form.

Storage spaces which do not constitute documents are referred to as databases. What typifies a database is that individual elements of data can be arraigned in various ways and that they can be searched for. Registers are typical examples of databases. Manual databases and those maintained via digital technology have the same status.

It is proposed that the concept of storage should reassume its original meaning, but that it should also include electronic storage. The obligations of an authority to release public data should thus comprise the obligation to release it in the form in which it store it, either physically (on paper, CD-ROM, floppy- or hard disk) or logically (in an electronic file belonging to the authority).

In cases where the general public wants a certain type of information, authorities are currently assumed to have a certain obligation to make extra searches and compilations, over and above their normal course of work. Usually, anything that can be produced by "routine measures" is deemed to be a public document. This should apply also in the future, but it should be related to costs: an authority should have a duty to carry out any extra work which can be carried out without incurring significant costs. Since technology will provide even broader and cheaper opportunities for searching for and compiling of data, it is assumed that the future possibilities of the general public to gain insight into the activities of various authorities, and of sharing their knowledge, will increase.

Regarding the actual issue of disseminating public data to the general public, the proposal is said to promote the extension of the right-of-access principle. According to the proposal, the right-of-access should also include the right to obtain public data in electronic form. It is, however, admitted that such rights cannot be introduced immediately, and that the extension must be related to the technical capabilities of each particular authority.

The right to obtain data in electronic form will not include computer programs. The authorities will be obliged, however, to provide descriptions (system documentation) of how such programs work.

The proposals for the introduction of new concepts into the FPA, which is part of the Constitution, will require consequential changes also in the Official Secrets Act and the Archives Act.

4.5 Handling of Basic Data

The freedom of information principle is not the only issue to discuss when official legal information is analysed. It is also important to try to define the kind of information that should be provided by the state and, furthermore, analyse the ways in which the material ought to be managed and disseminated.

To start with, it is quite clear that the outcome of a discussion about these issues will always depend on the nature of the material in question. As concerns legislative material, for instance, it is obvious that the state must play a very active role in its dissemination. It is, however, also quite clear that as regards more peripheral data managed by public authorities, such as various kinds of background materials, as well as internal files, personal data, and so forth, their dissemination may raise well-motivated arguments concerning economic limitations, practical obstacles, privacy, etc. And, ultimately, when material of the latter kind is analysed, reflecting, e.g., basic personal data concerning employment, education, different forms of treatments, criminal records, etc., it sometimes becomes obvious that the data should not be made available without careful consideration and considerable restrictions.

Where to draw the line in this respect is, however, not easy to determine. In most cases opinions will very among various groups. From the point of view of the legal information manager or the law library it is, of course, interesting to get access to as much basic data as possible at a low cost, and it may thus be reasonable to argue that the state and the public authorities should play an active role in the dispersion of official data of various kinds. For various reasons other groups may, however, want to follow a more restricted policy. At the individual level the answers to these issues will vary a lot.

It is nevertheless noticeable that reasons for limiting access to the data may not originate from considerations concerning personal data only. Restrictions may also concern other forms of data generated by the public authorities, such as "materials relating to national security, external relations, the safety of the State and public security, matters sub judice, ...

commercial and industrial confidentiality, and in general any material required by law to be held in confidence".[51]

It is apparent that the various opinions concerning these matters sometimes clash. It is therefore relevant that various kinds of official legislative materials, as well as other kinds of public data, can be looked upon as potential income sources. Several arguments can therefore be raised, suggesting that the state should use this fact to make money by selling various kinds of public data. In practice it must therefor also be noticed that a discussion on the availability of public data is to some extent an issue of what is economically viable for the state to provide, and, conversely, a reflection of the fact that there exist data that are for some reason unsuitable for dissemination on a commercial basis.

The suggestion that the state should provide public data on a commercial basis is, however, by no means an uncontroversial standpoint. Noticeable is thus also that arguments concerning these matters may be reflections of political and ideological considerations. In this debate, various arguments have been raised. The EC synergy guidelines recommends, for instance, that the state should leave as much as possible to the market and commercial companies to handle it, by stating that "[t]he public sector should adopt policies and procedures which encourage investment by the private sector in the development of information services based on public data" and by suggesting that "when a public administration provides electronic information services directly, it should avoid any practice which leads to the distortion of competition." It is moreover recommended that "before establishing a new electronic service or continuing an existing one, public administrations should consider whether an existing private sector service can be used or adapted to meet their requirements".[52]

Closely related to the discussion of what kind of material the state should provide is the issue concerning the ways in which it should be distributed. When these aspects are investigated, it soon becomes quite obvious that all

---

[51] *EC Guidelines for improving the synergy between the public and private sectors in the information market*, 1989, at sec 1, which also makes clear that "[w]hen availability of data or information for use or exploitation is denied to the private sector, an explanation of the reason for non-availability should be given".

[52] *Id.* at sec 7, 8. *See*, for a collection of documents, including the above mentioned EC Guidelines, "http://www2.echo.lu/legal/en/access/access.html".

forms of public information cannot be left to be handled by the market. This is simply a reflection of the fact that commercial publishers must concentrate for natural reasons on information which is requested by larger groups and which can be sold at reasonable prices. Equally important is thereby the fact that there exist various forms of official information which is requested by users lacking financial resources, or which is requested only sporadically. In addition, the previously quoted arguments related to quality, authenticity, completeness, etc., may become relevant in this context. This in turn makes it clear that access to rarely requested information may have to be ensured by other means than pure commercial activities, and this again makes it natural to set the focus on the responsibility of the state.[53]

The issues that have been addressed in this context are, however, not always easy to manage. It must furthermore be observed that it is not sufficient to analyse the nature of a certain type of material in order to decide the extent to which the state should take an active part in the dissemination process. Also intended use and the types of requirements that have been articulated for a certain kind of material are often of relevance. To illustrate – it is obvious that freedom of information sometimes makes it clear that public data should be accessible without pay, e.g. when a state-run school wants to use a public legislative database for educational purposes.

From a somewhat different point of view it appears equally clear, however, that it is reasonable for the users to pay for the information, e.g. when the same public database is approached by a commercial publisher who wants to copy the database and use it on a continuos basis in order to refine, restructure and market it in his own name.[54] Another illustration of the latter is when large volumes of address information intended for so called direct marketing purposes are being requested.

---

[53] In this respect the EC Guidelines list as "reasons for which the public sector might develop and support electronic information services could include, amongst others, the following examples: i. where the service is deemed to be essential to the public interest, but the private sector is unwilling or unable to offer it on reasonable terms; ii. where it is an inseparable part of public sector tasks; iii. where a visibly neutral service, independent of the private information industry, is required". *Id.* at sec 8.

[54] "The public sector could, for example, develop databases and then consider offering them to the private sector, or could offer the distribution rights of public sector databases to the private sector. In order that the taxpayer may share in the rewards of success when databases which have reached commercial viability are transferred, a royalty payment in addition to the negotiated price may be considered appropriate." *Id.* at sec 9.

The discussion on availability, the responsibility for distribution, and the related price issues set the focus, in turn, on the issue of the extent to which the information should be refined and restructured, and whether or not the state has responsibility for such activities? In this respect it is quite obvious that commercial vendors have an interest in marketing and publishing official information in a refined form, and that from their point of view it is clear that the state should do as little as possible. The argument here is often that the state ought to provide various kinds of raw data as cheaply as possible. Many user groups, on the other hand, are likely to articulate well motivated requirements concerning various pedagogic structures, overviews, abstracts, translations, etc., which can be used as arguments in favour of an enhanced responsibility of the public sector in the distribution of digital material.

To some extent also the answers to these questions will be of a political nature since it is obvious that various conflicting interests are present, e.g. as to the type of requirements that the state should meet, and the extent to which the state should provide legal information free of charge.[55] In this respect, it is quite clear that the state cannot be expected to elaborate and restructure the material in a limitless way. Thus, also when these aspects are discussed it becomes rather obvious that there exists a borderline delimiting the undertakings by the state, and that the development of many kinds of customised solutions for different user groups must be left to the private sector.

Additionally, in the discussion concerning the handling of basic data, it is important to mention that the shift of media initiated by IT and telecommunications must eventually be reflected in the promulgation and publication of official legal material. As the development continues, it becomes increasingly obvious that the state cannot provide materials only in old-fashioned forms, and that the shift in media in other fields of society must also be reflected in the public sector. In this respect a variety of arguments, ranging from quality aspects, such as the speed of updating, and

---

[55] *See*, for various arguments, Seipel, Peter, *Rättsinformation som ansvar och kommers*, JT 1993-94 at 649-56, *and* Eilemar, Birgitta & Dereborg, Anders, *Regeringskansliets författningsdatabaser SFSR och SFST*, JT 1997-98 at 265-68.

potentialities concerning enhanced efficiency, to political arguments, and freedom of information, etc., reappear.[56]

To conclude, it is quite clear that many of the questions raised in this context still have to be answered. It is also noticeable that many of the issues are, doubtless, of such a kind that a continuos debate about various policies can be foreseen. If one tries to summarise this analysis, it is, nevertheless, possible to distinguish four rather distinct and interrelated issues, which should be able to function at least as points of departures for further discussions, viz. 1) what kind of information should be the responsibility of the state to provide, 2) how far should the public sector's responsibility stretch as regards refining and restructuring the material, 3) how and by whom should it be distributed, and 4) what kind of price policy should be followed?

4.6 Administrative Rules

From the point of view of the legal information manager one must also consider the fact that information processing within different types of organisations may have to be related to various kinds of administrative rules. In this respect the previously discussed principles of freedom of information, the rule of law, and other jurisprudential standards reappear, although often in a slightly more specific manner. In addition, various kinds of internal considerations, domain-dependent regulations, and similar matters may become relevant. In this respect also special kinds of considerations reflecting such things as corporate cultures, organisational standards, social environments, practical arrangements, etc., may have to be considered.

This normative framework will specify, however, not only the kind of material that a legal organisation may have to work with. It will also decide to some extent on the ways in which legal information can be utilised, managed, and generated within an organisation. To illustrate this it is enough to realise that the ways in which decisions are administrated within

---

[56] *See, e.g.*, Svensson, Britt-Marie & Wahlgren, Peter, *Regeringskansliets författningsdatabaser – en replik*, JT 1997-98 at 901-904.

various public organs and courts must be in line with the rules of formality of various kinds, as they are defined in procedural acts, administrative legislation,[57] and semi-authoritative rules, issued by, for example, court administration authorities, etc.[58]

To notice in a system development situation is thereby that rules of this nature will often be found in many different parts of a given rule system, and also that different rules may be of very different origin. Rules reflecting the practical aspects of the freedom of information principle may sometimes be found, for instance, in the administrative legislation, rules of relevance for the motivation of decisions made by courts or public authorities may have to be retrieved from certain procedural acts, restrictions concerning the possibilities of rationalisation and changing the nature of certain work tasks may be found in agreements between the employer and the union, and so forth. In this context mention can also be made of rules and guidelines issued by e.g. public administrative authorities, and branch associations, as well as various kinds of de facto standards for legal information management. To notice in this respect is furthermore that all these rules are likely to be quite detailed and specific.

Frequently it is also possible to detect authoritative rules which are tacit, i.e. rules that are embedded in the practical handling of various issues within a certain organisation. Rules of this kind may define, for instance, the type of decisions that a certain department of an organisation has to deal with, or describe the ways in which information and data should be retrieved, combined and disseminated within a certain organisation. This kind of rules may often be more or less unconsciously followed by those who are affected by them.

At a more special level administrative rules may thus also describe the type of data and files that the courts and public authorities are authorised to handle, etc.[59] Noticeable is thereby that authoritative rules of various kinds

---

[57] In the official report on a new Personal Data Act some 35 national, so called Register Acts are listed, SOU 1997:39 *supra* note 48 at 206-07.

[58] *See*, especially on rules and regulations of relevance for libraries, Roos, Carl Martin, *Biblioteksrätt*, 1995, and especially on methods and rules concerning investigations performed by practising lawyers, Heuman. Lars, *Advokatens rättsutredningar*, 1987.

[59] *See, e.g., Förvaltningslag* (1986:223), *and Förordning om registerföring vid allmänna domstolar* (1986:104).

can have far-reaching consequences on how legal information management can be organised within legal organisations. Examples can be provided by the rather detailed court rules concerning decision formulations stipulating, among other things, that certain forms and phrases should be used. In a similar way there may exist rules stipulating that regulative material issued by public authorities should be given a certain form and that it should be published in a certain publication series, and so forth.[60]

It is of relevance in this context also that libraries, publishers, as well as other organisations working with legal information must consider legislative rules concerning dissemination of information, licensing agreements, etc. Libraries, for instance, must adjust their activities not only to the administrative legislation, but they must also consider, e.g., regulations concerning the right to charge for their services, and, depending on their status, adapt to public service regulations, university rules, etc.

Publishers, in turn, must deliver the so called "duty copies" of all printed documents to a number of reference libraries.[61] Similar rules apply to publishers of other media in the sense that copies may have to be delivered to various kinds of archives.[62] Publishers of periodical materials must also adjust to constitutional rules concerning ownership, the responsible publisher, and so forth.[63]

It should also be remembered that there exists a large number of rules which make it necessary for organisations, public as well as private, to deliver information and data of various kinds to a large number of public authorities. These are responsibilities which, for natural reasons, affect the ways in which the internal management of information within the companies can be organised. Examples of rules of the latter kind can be found in tax legislation, copyright legislation, data protection laws, labour law, and in numerous regulations stipulating the duty of an organisation to deliver data for official census purposes.[64]

---

[60] In Sweden regulated by the *Författningssamlingsförordning* (1976:725).

[61] Roos, *supra* note 58 at 23-24. *See also*, SOU 1992:92, *Pliktleverans*.

[62] *See, e.g., Lag (1993:1392) om pliktexemplar av dokument, and, Förordning (1993:1439) om pliktexemplar av dokument.*

[63] In Sweden regulated by the *Freedom of the Press Act*, Chapter 5.

[64] In Sweden the great amount of data that private companies have to deliver for various reasons to

The complex nature of the legal domain makes it thus quite clear that all attempts to analyse information management of legal organisations at a general level must take a large number of administrative components into consideration. A legal information manager must also be prepared to accept that this may be a cumbersome and time-consuming task. This is simply due to the fact that the requirements will vary from organisation to organisation, depending on the domain in which the organisation operates and its various functions. In this respect, not only will the content of the information that should be considered as relevant differ, but the legal framework and the ways in which the material should best to be managed will also vary.

Sometimes it may also be necessary, or desirable, to try to reform the regulative framework in order to be able to implement IT-related tools in an efficient way. It should be therefore also kept in mind that the rule systems may be very complex. Consequently, from the point of view of the system developer, or the legal information manager considering the implementation of an administrative support system, it is always necessary to make a broad investigation concerning the kind of rules that may affect certain system implementations, and to realise that the inclusion of various kinds of operative, de facto, rules may be crucial for the success of a given legal information system development project.

4.7 Contracting Issues

In addition to various kinds of official and formal rules that may be of relevance in legal information management it is apparent that many professional activities concerning legal material normally include the handling of contracting issues which can be decided more or less freely between the negotiating parties.

The question about the kind of issues that have to be dealt with in this respect will vary, for natural reasons, depending on the type of product that

---

public authorities has spurred several organisations in the commercial sector to form a special organ, *Företagens uppgiftslämnardelegation* (FUD) for the surveillance and interpretation of rules affecting the information delivery of commercial companies to the public sector. These issues have recently also been addressed by a public investigation. *See*, SOU 1997:146, *Grunddata - i samhällets tjänst.*

is at hand, the intended use, etc. In this respect in principle all the components mentioned in chapter 3 may be of relevance, such as, e.g., licensing of information products, database subscriptions, pricing, liability, definitions of content, updating, etc. The multifaceted nature of the issues that may be of relevance also means that a more detailed analysis of contract clauses and various forms of agreements must be left out in this context.[65]

It should be noticed, however, that in practice it may be necessary to negotiate and reach agreements with several parties, such as customers, information providers, publishers, etc., and thus also that the issues relevant for discussion will vary according to the situation. From this it also follows that the types of questions that have to be dealt with may be of very different kinds, and, consequently, that legal information managers must be prepared to handle all aspects of information systems. It is also noticeable that the rules that have to be dealt with may sometimes be very detailed and, if the organisation is a library, for instance, various kinds of specialised rules about e.g. copying, lending policies, reading room access, special regulations concerning students, and so forth, may be of relevance.

In order to handle these situations it is normally very useful to develop checklists, like, for instance, the ones outlined in chapter 3. Likewise, it is in most cases very time saving to try to find negotiated standard agreements in which experiences and contract clauses have been aggregated and elaborated upon over time. From this it follows in turn that in many situations it may be a very good idea to investigate whether or not there exists a branch organisation whose services can be utilised.

4.8 Ethical Considerations

In this context it may finally be relevant to mention something about the ethics of legal information management. This is simply a reflection of the fact that all forms of information management – legal and non-legal – may raise questions about privacy and morals, and that these issues have often to

[65] A recent compilation of Swedish negotiated IT-contracts alone, encompasses some 100 pages. *See*, Wahlgren, Peter, *Materialsamling IT-rätt*, 1997 at 285-385.

be dealt with in a very careful manner, even if explicit legislative or administrative rules are lacking.

Also in the handling of ethical issues it is apparent that the questions will vary depending on the situation and the kind of information that is at hand. A legal information manager working in a law office, for example, has normally to deal with different kinds of issues than a law librarian, and the administrator of students' database accounts will have different types of priorities, as compared to the administrator of a decision support system intended for administrators of the social security legislation, and so forth.

A critical issue in many professional situations will nevertheless be privacy and the aspects related to privacy are likely to attract more and more attention and interest, and perhaps also become a matter of increasing controversy. An in-house network with communication servers, for instance, makes it easy for an employer to monitor the traffic on the net and thus also to keep track of the employees' search performances, their working hours, the use of different programs, etc. In a similar way, interests and performances of the customers, Internet browsers, participants in so called chat systems, and similar users, can be recorded.[66]

From the point of view of the law library it is thus also clear that privacy issues may become relevant when files and records concerning the users of a certain library are to be managed, and several arguments indicate that data of this kind should be dealt with in a careful manner. In this context, mention can also be made of various more or less informal rules concerning quite subtle aspects of legal information management, such as e.g. the handling of circulation lists and other forms of record keeping, concerning e.g. individual users' subscriptions, use of data-bases and journals, etc.

As concerns information management in the legal domain it must be admitted that many of the aspects that may be of relevance in this respect are still more or less tacit. A related example is nevertheless given by *The American Association of Law Libraries* (AALL) which refers to the statement of professional ethics promulgated by *The American Library Association.*[67] Standards which can, of course, also be transformed and

---

[66] *See* generally, Duke University, *Ethics and the Internet*, "http://www.duke.edu/~-wgrobin/ethics/surflaw.html", 1997.

[67] *See*, for information and further references to these organisations, AALL, *Online Information Service*, "http://www.aallnet.org/". *See, also,* especially on the American Library Association's

elaborated upon to be used for the handling of different undertakings in the field of legal information management in various IT based settings. In this context it is therefor motivated to quote them in full, and in accordance with these standards a librarian:

- "has a special responsibility to maintain the principles of the Library Bill of Rights[68]

- should learn and faithfully execute the policies of the institution of which one is a part and should endeavor to change those which conflict with the spirit of the Library Bill of Rights.

- must protect the essential confidential relationship which exists between a library user and the library.

- must avoid any possibility of personal financial gain at the expense of the employing institution.

- has an obligation to insure equality of opportunity and fair judgement of competence in actions dealing with staff appointments, retentions and promotions.

- has an obligation when making appraisal of the qualifications of any individual to report the facts clearly, accurately, and without prejudice, according to generally accepted guidelines concerning the disclosure of personal information."

In addition, the Association, in light of the special character and mission of its membership, espouses the principles that law librarians, while engaged in their professional work:

---

code of ethics, Lindsey, Jonathan & Prentice, Ann, E. *Professional Ethics and Libraries*, Onyx Press, Phoenix, 1985.

[68] *See*, on the principles of *The Library Bill of Rights*, AALL, *Handbook & Directory, The Library Bill of Rights*, "http://www.aallnet.org/handbook/policy_bill_of_rights.html", 1997 (footnote added).

- "have a duty neither to engage in the unauthorized practice of law nor to solicit an attorney-client relationship.
- have a duty to avoid any situations posing a possible undisclosed conflict of interest.
- have a special duty, given the nature of their patron base, to treat confidentially any private information obtained through contact with library patrons and not to divulge any confidential information to persons representing adverse interests.
- have a duty to exercise scrupulous care in avoiding any acts or even the appearance, of misappropriating the work product of library patrons or professional colleagues to their own credit or profit.
- have a duty actively to promote free and effective access to legal information.
- have a duty to society and the legal profession to work both individually and through their professional organizations toward improving the quality and minimizing the cost of the library component of the delivery of legal services."

5 Aspects Affecting Change

As mentioned in the introduction, legal information management cannot only be based on various aspects of legal work, technical matters, and analyses of the legal material. Nor is it sufficient to include a legal framework into the discussion. Also a number of other aspects must be taken into consideration, and in the following sections a number of such factors are discussed in some detail.

5.1 IT Maturity

As the first observation it can be remarked that the ways in which IT can be integrated into the legal profession will depend to a large extent on the IT maturity of the users, or the potential users. This is simply to say that an important premise for a successful system implementation relies on the condition that those who will be affected by the changes must be able and ready to understand and accept the new options.

For natural reasons difficulties which can be related to the issue of users' IT maturity will vary from one situation to another. A lack of understanding is probably not a huge problem when new types of IT solutions are introduces to a university library, for example, where each new generations of students tend to be more familiar with IT than the previous one, and where the number of staff usually is small, which makes it easy to keep the employees informed about the changes. On the other hand, problems may easily occur when systems are to be implemented into more traditionally organised legal organisations, e.g. courts and lawyers offices, where there may be less willingness to adjust to or accept the changes. This attitude which can be explained in some cases by the fact that many of the persons working in such spheres may have devoted a considerable portion of their professional carrier to acquire legal skills and reach the position of an independent decision maker. Likewise it is quite obvious that a large number of lawyers are more or less depending on their skill in retrieving legal information in an efficient manner. In such a context, the import of highly advanced IT devices, like all legal information management activities of a more radical kind, may even be interpreted as a threat or a challenge to the professional role of individual lawyers. Similar reactions may be revealed, of course, not only by legal decision makers but by any category of employees whose work situation becomes affected by new technology.

The fact that users of IT must be able to accept and understand the intended changes may appear as an obvious presupposition. It is nevertheless a factor that is easy to overlook and, doubtless, the inability to assess the importance of these aspects correctly have frequently produced negative effects, both in the sense that necessary and well motivated changes have failed, and that bad solutions have been implemented. The latter often due to the fact that the potential users or buyers of IT systems were unable to articulate their needs and, consequently, that the suggested solutions did not incorporate assumptions necessary for the legal domain.[1]

In this context it is also necessary to note that even if a lack of maturity in IT issues does not actually prevent system implementation, it is nevertheless an aspect which affects the ways in which reorganisation of the working methods will be apprehended. An all too critical or negative attitude among those who will be affected by the changes can easily make that well-motivated reorganisation of work will become less effective. Reflecting over these matters one may wonder whether the reason for the inefficacy of IT development within the legal domain so far has been due to the previously mentioned conservative attitude towards computers and IT,

---

[1] *See, e.g.*, concerning the support system MÅHS, developed for Swedish courts, Säfström, Charlotte, *MÅHS: Ilska på domstolarna mot nytt datasystem: – tidsödande och 70-talsmässigt*, 1996 at 28-29.

and the fact that the suggested solutions have not always been given a fair chance to show the advantages they may bring along.

It is however important to observe that a lack of maturity in IT issues must not only be perceived as an obstacle; it may also be seen as a component facilitating the introduction of new working tools. That is simply to say that such a state of the matter is often combined with an openness and an interest in methodological aspects and may therefore also facilitate the implementation of legal information technology – for most people it is desirable to be updated and to have access to the same facilities as others. Noticeable is also that the degree of readiness to accept IT-related changes may change in a surprisingly short time. The quickly growing use of CD-ROMs, on-line databases, and the Internet may serve as obvious illustrations of the above.

Looked upon from this point of view, it may even be concluded that a failure to react to more or less explicit signals coming from the employees concerning requests for updated information management may make that an organisation will find it difficult to maintain its working force, or even to recruit people. In other words it may be said that lawyers and other people working with legal material, like all other categories of professionals, will expect their work to be efficiently organised and that they normally also will be prepared to acquire skills enabling them to use modern IT tools.

The conclusion that can be drawn from all this is that development of IT and legal information management within an organisation must go hand in hand with the expectations of the users. In this context it must also be noticed that readiness to use IT and the accompanying expectations of changes belong to social phenomena. No organisation can function in a vacuum, and the ways in which the work is being organised elsewhere in the environment must also affect internal IT projects. When strategies for future legal information management projects are discussed, for instance, it is obvious that attitudes and expectations of clients, customers (e.g. library visitors) and co-operating organisations must be taken into consideration. An example of a supplementary, external factor that may boost the demand for changes within an organisation is thereby standardisation.[2]

---

[2] In Sweden, *Toppledarforum* – a working group for the co-ordination of IT activities in the government sector – has initiated a project with the objective of handling 95 per cent of official procurement activities through EDI (Electronic Data Interchange) by the year of 2000. This project presupposes, naturally, considerable standardisation of various components among the

As regards methods of gaining acceptance for legal information management activities several approaches can be adopted. Most important, however, is the awareness that readiness to use IT must be investigated at the earliest organisational stages of a project, and that, if found unsatisfactory, it must be remedied by supplying the subjects with information and education. It should also be noticed that IT readiness is a factor that to a large extent is possible to affect by means of adopting a plan or a strategy for the development of competence within the organisation in question. This means that preparations to meet the issuing changes must be looked upon as natural and essential ingredients of legal information management, not only when discussing the organisation of a project, but also at a more permanent basis.[3]

At the individual level, it is thereby obvious that changes in anybody's working situation will normally be looked upon as involving a measurement of difficulty. Learning new skills or adjusting one's working methods to new parameters, e.g. in the form of computer programs, new technology, or information products is not only time consuming – it may also be a stressful and annoying experience in which impediments and problems may easily multiply if the changes occur unexpectedly or at a bad time. In consequence, when a legal information management project is being planned, it is advisable to investigate the normal work load of the organisation, other ongoing activities, and whether any form of periodicity in the intensity of the work can be detected: all this in order to try to avoid bad timing for starting any projects involving changes.

In the early stages of system development projects it is therefore also highly advisable to present the new technique to the potential users in a realistic way. One strategy may be to discuss and make explicit the objectives of a given system development project to the intended users as early as possible. This should be done simply because educational activities,

---

suppliers, such as security, encoding, document formatting, etc. Similar initiatives have been launched in other countries. *See* "http://toppled.nutek.se/index.html". In this context it can also be noted that some "seventy-five percent of banks' requests for other banks' issuance, advice, confirmation and negotiation of credits are sent electronically", see, Katsh *supra* chapter 3 note 7 at 118, with further references.

[3] *See also*, for a discussion concerning a number of additional "critical success factors", Susskind *supra* chapter 1 note 13 at 223-61.

and information about the planned changes before and during the implementation of a system development project will always play a crucial role in the success of legal information management projects. It should also be noted in this respect that one must try to establish a certain degree of consensus, as regards the description of what is to be considered as relevant working methods and with regard to the ways in which problems typical of the domain in question ought to be addressed. It is also important that the objectives must be discussed in terms of functions, and not in purely technical jargon. In this way, many misunderstandings and unrealistic expectations may be avoided.[4]

An additional aspect related to gaining acceptance is that it should be possible to evaluate new solutions by testing and comparing their performance with the result of work achieved by using other kinds of methods (preferably traditional, pre IT-methods). Access to historical data and up to date documentation is therefore important in all system development projects. It should also be noted that this kind of information may have to be collected not only during the development phase of the project, but even before the practical work has actually begun.[5]

In order to establish the preconditions in this respect, a preliminary project investigation should consider and analyse a number of factors. What are, for example, the presuppositions concerning the organisational and administrative environment? How will the intended system be used? Will it be psychologically viable to integrate the new technique with the present form of the organisation, and, if not, will it be difficult to change the existing presuppositions?[6]

One way in which the aspect of maturity can be summarised is by recalling that the IT component cannot be looked upon as an isolated phenomenon. On the contrary, it should be underlined that it is IT, the legal material, and the persons involved in the use of the former that together

---

[4] Hamfelt, Andreas, Wahlgren, Peter, *Datorstödda beslut: Artificiell intelligens och juridik,* 1988 at 44 *and* Thompson, Donna M., Feinstein, Jerald L. *Cost Justifying Expert Systems*, 1990 at 114-15.

[5] *See*, especially as regards methods for the evaluation of library performances, Ekengren, Bo, Hammarlund, Nils, Janzon, Ona, Zetterberg, Marianne, Vessberg, Viveka, Hultberg, Alf, Törngren, Margareta, *RUT, Resultatmätning och utvärdering av mätmetoder*, 1993.

[6] Wahlgren, Peter *Beslutstöd för brottmål*, 1987 at 23-26 and 54-58.

make up the systems which are the focus of legal information management. This point of view again suggests that legal information management should be looked upon as a social activity.

5.2 *Aims*

In legal information management projects it is often quite clear that there exist conflicting interests, or – at least – that different objectives can be detected among the persons involved. For obvious reasons these difficulties in opinion often reflect different backgrounds of the individuals working on, or being affected by the project. Occasionally, the lack of a common background results in goal conflicts of an explicit nature. This is the case, for example, when the people involved in a system development project disagree about the purpose of the system or when the submitted methodological proposals are criticised. In other cases, the lack of a common background is of a less explicit nature, being reflected merely in misinterpretations of various contributions as well as mistakes occurring during system development.

For natural reasons it is not possible to make a complete inventory of how various motives may affect system development. Generally, it may be noticed, nevertheless, that lawyers as compared to technically-oriented personnel show different attitudes towards the question of what is to be considered as relevant objectives of undertakings related to legal information management. In this respect lawyers are more often inclined to perceive tangible systems intended to provide support for practical problems in day-to-day legal work as the main objects of concern. System developers with a technical background, on the other hand, often seem to consider the question of whether the addressed issue poses a practical problem to be comparatively less important. In their point of view a primary objective may be to tackle intricate computational difficulties, e.g. the possibilities to implement some exotic feature in a legal database. The differences in this respect become even more obvious if one investigates the ongoing research in the fields of computers and law, and AI and Law. For researchers with a technical background it may be more than sufficient to illustrate the advantages of their contributions by supplying a small-scale prototype, comprehensible only to those who master the programming language of the computer in use.[7]

The differences in opinions between technicians and lawyers concerning the objectives of legal IT development are not the only factors to be considered in legal information management projects. Conflicting perspectives on what is to be regarded as the main aim may also evolve within organisations, e.g. between various hierarchical levels of an authority. A lawyer working for a public authority may prefer, for example, a support system which will enable him to adjust his information retrieval process in an unrestricted way so that he can individualise his decisions in such a way that previously unidentified factors will be continuously reflected. The head of that very same institution may prefer solutions, on the other hand, that will limit the possibilities for the lawyer-employees to individualise the outcome of their decisions, e.g. in order to minimise the number of appealed cases and to achieve the highest possible efficiency within the organisation as a whole. In the long-time perspective the introduction of decision support systems (DDSs) in the field of law may also mean that an increasing number of tasks will be transferred from lawyers to paralegals or administrative staff[8] – a development which may easily be interpreted as less desirable from the point of view of the legal profession.[9]

Examples of various goal conflicts can also be perceived within various groups working on different tasks of the same organisational level. Some lawyers, handling, for example, administrative tasks may find that case management systems are their primary matters of interest. Others, active,

---

[7] The existence of various inclinations among the contributors has been commented on by Susskind who recognises two basic types of contributors: "pragmatists" and "purists". The main aim of the pragmatist is thought to be "to develop and implement working computer systems that can actually assist in solving legal problems", whereas the "major goals for the purist are to clarify the nature of legal reasoning, of human and artificial intelligence, and of computational models of law". Two types of purists – AI purists and jurisprudential purists – are identified. Although the author admits that many researchers combine both the pragmatic and the purist attitude, he claims nevertheless that the majority of the researchers in the field lean towards one side rather than the other. Susskind *supra* chapter 3 note 27 at 2-3.

[8] Such a development can already be seen, e.g. in the organisation of the Swedish legal domain, where a several kinds of cases which previously have been administrated by the courts now are handled by other kinds of authorities. *See, e.g.*, for a background, SOU 1991:191, *Domstolarna inför 2000-talet, Arbetsuppgifter och förfaranderegler.*

[9] *See, e.g.*, Wahlgren *supra* note 6 at 103-04. *Cf. also* Magnusson, Cecilia, *New Roles in the Shaping of the Law*, 1990 at 135-65,.

for example, in litigation, may arrive at the conclusion that efficient document retrieval, in combination with advanced word processing facilities, should be the major functions to be developed, and so forth.[10]

Different preferences appear also among technically oriented researchers. Some contributors would lay emphasis on advanced methods reflecting a high level of technical sophistication (e.g. "the surfing through the virtual legal landscape interface") and would devote less energy to document retrieval systems and word processing facilities, whereas others would, without hesitation, incorporate the functions originating from conventional computer technology into advanced AI-techniques. Another kind of differences in attitude exhibited by this group may be found when we look at the preferences shown in the selection of computer programming languages, the employment of data base systems, and similar matters.

In this context one must also recall that even various groups outside the organisation for which the development project is contemplated (e.g. customers, clients, business partners) may show inner conflicts of interests. Some people may react positively to the notion of IT based devices in the field of law. Others may be sceptical towards such solutions, and in some cases it may even be impossible to introduce computerised legal support systems for psychological or ethical reasons.

As a final comment on these aspects it may be argued that problems originating from differences in attitudes between lawyers and technicians, as well as between practically oriented and theoretically inclined contributors, must not be overestimated. At least this is a valid conclusion from the stand-point of a theoretically inclined observer. That is to say that although conflicting interests may create practical problems in actual system development projects, one must admit at the same time that the existence of various approaches can be often regarded as a positive factor for the notion of legal information management taken as a whole, in the sense that different contributions supplement each other. It is also clear that the apparent conflicts springing between different contributors can be often solved if practical concerns are viewed as short-time objectives and when theoretically defined goals are viewed as long-term objectives. Noticeable is

---

[10] *See, e.g.*, Wahlgren *supra* note 6 at 128-55.

also that in many projects several objectives may be approached simultaneously.

5.3 Economy

All changes concerning integration of IT and reorganisation of working methods cost money and resources, so that in order to find feasible solutions, considerable investments may be necessary. The economics of the project constitute therefore one of the basic factors that must be carefully considered in all legal information management activities. Economic resources do not only determine the ability to choose between large-scale projects and minor changes, but they also affect the possibilities of choice between standard IT components and customised solutions, as well as the ways in which systems can be developed. These aspects may likewise delimit the kinds of products and services that can be implemented and accessed.

Economic considerations must naturally include estimation of costs and possible savings related to the intended system development projects. It is, however, clear that depending on the nature of the domain and the task that has been undertaken, the parameters of costs and cost-cuts may appear in many different shapes. In the commercial sector, for instance, economic advantages may appear in the form of saved time, less constrained personnel resources, enhanced productivity, etc. Simultaneously, costs may originate from different sources, such as investments in software or hardware, licensing fees, IT system engineering, maintenance, etc.

It is also clear that the already existing physical environment, such as, for example, the already acquired computer system, may make the integration of the new technology with the old one be exceptionally costly, and cause that new generations of IT cannot be introduced without difficulties. It is also important to try to identify the more or less hidden costs related to the reorganisation of a working place. How can, for instance, the costs of educating of the personnel be estimated? What are the needs with regard to adjustments of the existing information systems, and reorganisation of the established working methods, etc? As a rule it must also be assumed that system development necessarily presupposes participation of in-house personnel and that IT implementation strategies will put a strain on the existing resources in many different ways.

Of relevance to system implementation are also the economic consequences connected with necessity of reforming the organisational structures, replacing people, and other similar aspects. Some organisational preconditions of this kind may be very expensive to change, which will seriously delimit the possibilities for legal information management. It should also be noted that in some cases it may be necessary to compare the prospective benefits following from the system development project with other kinds of options. For example, the operations of a commercial organisation (e.g. a law firm) may become constrained due to a demand of a fast return on the investments. Legal information management projects may therefore have to compete with other kinds of urgent and potentially profitable undertakings. Efficiency reasons may thus make not only that system development projects are initiated, but also that they are hampered.

Relevant to investigate are, of course, also the possibilities of redirection and reduction of costs. In certain kinds of organisations these possibilities may be considerable. This is for instance the case in commercial companies and law firms that can afford to let their customers and clients bear the costs, simply by adding the costs for information retrieval to the bill. In other types of organisations the possibilities of finding alternative means of financing may be more limited. The latter no doubt may be a quite common situation as regards law libraries.

Another complication that must be taken into consideration is that costs and benefits related to legal information management may assume indirect forms in the sense that certain benefits may only be described in terms of intangible, qualitative aspects. This is perhaps especially true in the legal sector, where it may be argued that a number of principles and procedures (e.g. the right of access principle, the aspect of "legal security" in the rule of law, the need to have access to various versions of the material, etc.) must be retained even after the introduction of new kinds of legal information management systems, and despite the fact that these principles and procedures may appear as economically inefficient from the point of view of the IT consultant.

Admittedly, it may be difficult to get the measure of the degree of influence improved working conditions have on the increased output of the employees, for example. Likewise it may be difficult to measure the economic value of the degree of satisfaction displayed by e.g. library visitors, customers, or clients. The adoption of the economic perspective in the legal sector may also contain an element of controversy. In other words, it may be argued that quality is the overall objective of the work and that the cost/benefit analyses must not be given too much influence.

From this does not follow, of course, that in the legal sector an improved response time of the legal information retrieval system, a higher percentage of found documents or cases and similar indications cannot be simultaneously a reflection of enhanced quality. On the other hand, pure economic gains, in the form of reduction in time spent on research, for example, may appear as unmotivated if arguments showing that quality aspects will be improved cannot be presented. Likewise it must be established that more efficient retrieval systems are not accompanied by negative side effects, e.g. problems related to information overload.

In addition, in the evaluation of cost and benefit aspects it must be remembered that it may be difficult for a single organisation to change some of the preconditions. This becomes obvious, for instance, when for reasons of competitiveness a certain technical standard cannot be adopted. For similar reasons, in some cases, it may be impossible to introduce some special kind of IT systems into an organisation, because co-operation with other organisations demands the use of computer standards of a different kind.

Economy is, naturally, also relevant with regard to more down-to-earth, single decisions, as for example, when a decision must be made whether or not to buy or subscribe to a certain IT service. In this respect there is little difference between the parameters that have to be taken into account in this case and when traditional investments in information are being considered, e.g. books and other forms of publications. In this context it should be pointed out, however, that trying to overlook the consequences of the choices may be even more important, due to the fact that investments in IT will affect the working methods and the efficiency of the organisation as a whole. In this respect the import of computers and telecommunication related products constitutes a fundamental difference when compared to investments in an environment previously not affected by IT.

5.4 *Pace of Change*

In addition to a survey of non legal factors it is important to devote some time to the development of the legal system as such. It seems especially interesting to investigate whether it is possible to detect any kind of regularities in the development of law and the legal system. The reason for this is simply that if such regularities do exist, there are good reasons for incorporating them into a theory of legal information management, and in the following sections some general observations on the development of legal systems are presented.

As a starting point it may be recalled the fact that in the legal domain the ability to cope with change is a constant challenge. The law must always be open to corrections and amendments, due to changing social conditions, changing presuppositions, and irregularities and errors discovered in the judicial process. In the foreseeable future it can be assumed that this dynamic aspect of law will become even more important. A factor to consider in any discussion about the future development of the legal system is therefore the accelerating pace of change that can be observed in many spheres of society.

The rapid pace of change in present-day society can be seen everywhere. It is reflected, for example, in the development of IT, the utilisation of elaborated communication facilities and the internationalisation of legal work. It is also apparent that the accelerating development of society, propelled by technical and scientific advancements continuously generates new products and new perspectives. Likewise, it is obvious that these subject matters generate new problems, and that the pressure on the legal domain to adjust to such changes increases. Illustrations of this may be found in almost any area.

The rapid pace of change is reflected not only in the higher frequency of emerging new issues in need of regulation. Also well-established branches of law are being affected by the development, and previous solutions must be transformed and adjusted in various ways. This is simply a consequence of the normative function of law – when presuppositions change, the accompanying rules must change also. The changes affecting the legal rule system may in turn be of different kinds – insignificant or minor, e.g.

inducing modification of existing concepts, or of a more extensive character, making it necessary to introduce entirely new systems of rules and novel concepts.

To try to predict in which areas the need for regulative efforts or "legal dogmatics" will increase due to a faster pace of development is not, however, a meaningful undertaking. In this respect the technical and scientific development is all too complex and unpredictable. Even though some of the subject matters which stand out today as major objects of concern will presumably attract a growing interest. Thus IT, gene technology, environmental issues and internationalisation may remain as topics of great interest also in the future. This may nevertheless change overnight and the development may take new routes. For example, an interdisciplinary effort to develop a combined field of communications theory, gene technology and holographic representation may give rise to entirely new legal issues. In the same way new presuppositions, as well as shift in interests, and changes in theoretical perspectives, etc., may also give rise to the emergence of new, functionally defined "interlegal" topics, of which IT-law is merely one recent example.

Following from the fact that it is more or less impossible to identify in advance the areas of substantive law that may be affected by the development, it may be concluded that other kinds of approaches should be preferable. One alternative strategy would then be to focus on the methodological aspects of the development. This simply because the rapid pace of change is probably also something that will be reflected in the ways in which legal work and jurisprudential research are being performed. Pace of change is therefor also something that is of relevance for legal information management.

5.4.1 Other Kinds of Rules?

At a general level it may also be assumed that a higher pace of change may be detected by looking at the ways in which the legal system is being developed. One obvious indication of this is that it becomes increasingly clear that traditional methods of legislation are insufficient. This is reflected, among other things, in the fact that many central complexes of legal problems remain unregulated, despite the fact that those who are in the highest degree concerned, continuously request legal initiatives. In other cases it becomes indisputable that solutions which the legal system can provide are more or less obsolete. It can be also noticed that the latter is most easily perceived in fields in which the development is rapid, and especially in the areas affected by IT.

Following this avenue of thought it becomes natural to wonder whether a higher pace of social development will not accentuate the need for more fundamental changes and continuous efforts aiming at more long-lasting solutions. This may appear as a paradox, but this need can be identified in more than one way.

Illustrations of the above are provided by regulation concerning protection of intellectual property (copyright based on the prohibition of reproduction at a time when the technical means for copying, transformation, and dissemination of information become available to everyone in practice); other examples are legislation on privacy (based on old assumptions concerning technical presuppositions and perhaps also on a misjudgement of threats and possibilities),[11] and regulation of international trade and exchange of information through telecommunications and the Internet (in reality non-existing when it comes to issues of identifying the appropriate point of jurisdiction, liability, etc.). In Sweden, this "quilty" approach is also reflected in many recent legislative proposals,[12] and further examples of potential difficulties can easily be found. What are, for instance, appropriate legal definitions of subject matters such as electronic agents, digital market places, and the so called web hotels?

Other types of problems may appear when established legal concepts encounter novel technique. How should such features as, for instance, marketing, contracting, and forms of payments be looked upon when transactions are based on electronic communication? To what extent is the meaning of these concepts affected? Additional complications may be related to the fact that many of the components that are emerging in the

---

[11] *See* Toppledarforum/Datainspektionen, *Lexit*, 1995 at 10, *and* SOU 1997:39, *Integritet, Offentlighet, Informationsteknik* at 3 and passim.

[12] *See, e.g.*, SOU 1992:110, *Information och den nya informationsteknologin: Straff och processrättsliga frågor*, *and* SOU 1996:40, *Elektronisk dokumenthantering*, in which piecemeal changes in about ten different laws are being suggested due to the advance of IT.

context of IT are very complex matters. An illustration of the latter can be provided, for instance, in the form of techniques that have been developed for the encryption of electronically transferred messages. This complexity entails, in turn, that it is not always clear which aspects should be regulated. Nor is it obvious what kinds of legal standards should be used.

All this point to the conclusion that it is desirable that the traditional legal "dogmatic" method, i.e. the systematic investigation of legislation, court practice, legislative preparatory works and legal doctrines, in many cases should be complemented and, furthermore, that the efforts of the lawyers should be concentrated to a higher degree on the elaboration of a legal system of a somewhat different kind. All this in order to minimise the risks of presenting less well-developed, short-sighted solutions, and in order to make the work more future oriented.

A more far sighted legal strategy presupposes, however, several things. It is not only obvious that a more intensive study and analysis of technical and scientific advancements is necessary in order to accomplish in depth understanding of the ongoing activities and emerging concepts. In some cases the discussion may have to be complemented, for instance, with thorough investigations concerning the ways in which different kinds of objectives, and conflicting interests should be prioritised and evaluated. All this in order to be able to develop useful and updated legal solutions and more adequate legal perspectives.

One may furthermore speculate on the question of whether a higher pace of technical development will accentuate the need for more fundamental jurisprudential analyses with more distinct, long-term objectives. That is simply to say that it appears natural to discuss whether or not the central tasks of the future jurisprudential undertakings (i.e. the part of the legal work which ideally is less bound to directives and short time objectives) will be to try to deepen the conceptual analyses of the law and of the activities that are to be regulated. In this respect it may even be relevant to draw a parallel to the development of the legal systems of the industrialised world during the last two centuries, reflected e.g. in the elaboration of more general rules and a less frequent use of casuistic legislation, which can be apparently related to a large extent to the technical and administrative development of our society.

It may be argued that a legal strategy which is based on domain specific competence to a higher extent should then be based on the ambition to try to develop a deeper and more thorough understanding of the subject matters that are to be regulated. Behind this lies the simple assumption that analyses which initially take various technical presuppositions into consideration will have considerably better possibilities to be successful, as compared with studies which, perhaps more or less unreflecting, start out from legal conceptualisations that may be quite obsolete.

From the general point of view, one additional assumption which is important to note in this context is that professional reorganisation presupposes systematic efforts and a high awareness of methodological aspects. One may therefore also speculate on whether or not evaluation of implemented legislative changes will be more frequently requested.

It can thus be assumed that a systematic accumulation of general knowledge about the effects of changes in legal systems, which is today a quite neglected issue, will facilitate the debate on what should be considered as good or bad solutions. Such efforts may, naturally, also contribute to a better awareness of measures and methods that can be employed in various undertakings. What does, for instance, a desirable regulation of the Internet look like from the social perspective, or what effect does in fact the existing legislation concerning data protection have on the distribution of personal data in that context?

Sometimes it is also necessary to be able to change the rules without unnecessary delay. This has, of course, always been the case but it may be assumed that demands concerning the ability to implement changes without delay will become more clear as the technical development continues. Meeting such demands is, however, not a simple task, since a number of qualitative aspects must be considered. Perhaps most important in this respect is that different attitudes towards legislative and analytic work should not result in vaguely formulated regulations based on vaguely described objectives. Likewise, it is obvious that a more IT-adjusted legal system cannot be based on concepts which are all too abstract.

One must also remember that demanding that the legal system should be able to react more promptly must not become an excuse for letting quantity come before quality. An unreflecting reaction on the part of the legal system could easily result in an increasing number of complicated and incomprehensible rules – a development which many would not welcome. The objective of a more elaborated jurisprudential perspective is first and foremost to provide presuppositions for more well-informed discussions and better founded suggestions for solutions. In many areas it may therefore be a better strategy to see similarities between different activities and different types of legal solutions and to try to develop a more uniform and systematic legal system. Such an undertaking may demand a growing amount of analytic effort as the material increases, but this approach may lead, on the other hand, to far more uniform and adequate solutions.

5.4.2 More Rules?

From a somewhat different point of view it may be argued that it is a mistake to try and anticipate such far-sighted solutions based on highly elaborate conceptual analyses. And even if such a methodology could be developed it may be argued that such an undertaking could only generate theories and solutions that would become all too abstract for those most highly affected. This is simply to say that discussions concerning the possibilities of adopting a more long term oriented legal strategy and developing the legal method in order to accomplish "better rules", may be seen as naive. Likewise it may be suggested that the arguments concerning a more elaborate legal perspective, as are outlined above, reflect an all too optimistic attitude towards the potentialities of jurisprudential work and the development of the law. It may thus also be suggested that another kind of development is more likely.

A different hypothesis would then be that the problems which the legal system faces are urgent, due to the fact that there are too few rules, or that rules are non-existent. In other words, it can be assumed that a radical change in the speed of rule production is the only realistic and feasible reaction that should be expected from the legal community when problems originating from the high pace of technical development are to be tackled.

A request for more rules may easily appear as controversial, however. Many people associate rules with bureaucracy and administrative work, so that suggesting that many of the answers to the problems encountered in the legal system would be solved in an increased production of rules is something that may provoke strong reactions.

On the other hand, there are various factors indicating that practical difficulties should be approached in the conventional manner and that, consequently, an intensified production of rules is the most logical development. It is, for instance, apparent that we all live in a thoroughly regulated society, and there is nothing in the development as such that would indicate that a society relying on digital information, IT, and telecommunications will be automatically able to cope with fewer rules, or with rules of a different kind. Naturally, it can also be argued that it is a good strategy to abstain from starting new methodological experiments in periods when problems are accentuated. On the contrary, in such situations it is often wise to carefully adjust to well known routines. Experiments with more theoretical, long-term oriented strategies of the kind outlined above, which may become, of course, more or less successful, may actually make that the situation will deteriorate.

From this does not follow that an attitude which accepts an intensive production of legal rules cannot be filled with risks. The result of this scenario may be the production of underdeveloped rule systems and rules of a fragmented kind. But again, such concrete solutions are perhaps to be preferred to a situation in which no legal solutions whatsoever are given. Likewise, concrete solutions may be better than regulations which are all too general or to difficult to grasp. To keep in mind is also that new issues which demand detailed and distinct legal answers emerge more or less continuously. To avoid to give explicit answers by means of referring to the fact that in-depth theoretical investigations have been initiated is obviously not the way in which a "law state" can excuse itself in the long run.

It must furthermore be underlined that the kind of development which accepts a drastic growth in the number of detailed legislative activities does not necessarily entail the fact that a more ambitious jurisprudential strategy has been abandoned. An intensive production of rules can also be combined with efforts to make the legal system more accessible and transparent, although the approach in the latter case may have to be of a different kind. In undertakings aiming to make the rule system more accessible it may also become important to investigate IT and its potentialities. The objective here will be of a different kind, however, since IT will be perceived in this case as something that can be utilised in order to identify, structure, and retrieve adequate information. Subject matters, such as legal information retrieval services, legal information management, and its potentialities will come into focus once more.

5.4.3 A Broader Approach?

To try to identify more or less well-defined legal strategies and foresee their possible influence on legal information management may reflect, perhaps, an all too theoretical attitude. In a balanced discussion about further development of the legal system the only realistic approach is maybe to try to combine the various perspectives outlined above. In practice this means that more elaborate and meticulous analyses are likely to be developed side by side with pragmatism in the form of traditional problem-solving mechanisms based on the application of detailed legal rules.

Looking closer at these subject matters, it may even be argued that a combination of the various perspectives is something that can be predicted for several reasons. For one thing, it is obvious that there exist different kinds of needs concerning legal activities. Law may be seen, for instance, as an instrument which fulfils primarily the function of setting guidelines for general conduct, i.e. providing a framework for activities so that all the parties involved are ensured a maximum security in the sense that it is possible to overlook the consequences of their actions. Alternatively, the task may be to provide solutions to problems or incidents that have already occurred. It is obvious that the legal considerations that come to the fore in such situations are of an entirely different kind. In the former case the objective may be described, in general terms, as long-term oriented solutions. In the latter case the existing rules must be considered, or, if explicit rules are lacking, the existing material in the form of court decisions, statements in the doctrine, etc., must be interpreted. It is also clear that in the majority of legal areas these various needs coexist.

From the theoretical point of view a combination of the different ways of viewing the various legal strategies may perhaps be also related to a process-like description of the legal system and the legal analysis. The development of the legal system may then be described as a process in which different ways of focusing succeed one another. Drawing a parallel to the notions developed within the general theory of sciences it may be speculated whether the legal system does not also go through phases of "normality" which are followed sometimes by more intensive periods in which the basic presuppositions, as well as the central concepts, are reformulated and recast in a rather drastic way.[13]

Such a way of looking at law involves the assumption of a certain amount of periodicity of development. In practice this means that periods of steady development in which detailed solutions are produced at a constant and slow pace, are followed by more intensive phases in which theoretical analyses, reconsideration's, and creative solutions, ultimately make it possible for a certain domain to achieve a certain level of stability.

The shift between these different phases may be caused by different occurrences. Periods of stability may be interrupted, for instance, as in the case of IT and telecommunications, when the development of things that are to be regulated accelerates. In a similar way, theoretical efforts and reconsideration may appear to be urgently needed, if the rule system has become incomprehensible or all too inconsistent.

[13] This may be compared with the terms of *normal science* and *paradigm shifts* which are used sometimes in the discipline of general theory of sciences. *See* Kuhn, Thomas, *The Structure of Scientific Revolutions*, 1970.

6 Conclusions

6.1 *Requirements of Legal Information*

The first objective of this investigation has been to identify various requirements that may be related to legal information, and in this way also enhance the understanding of such IT-related legal products and services that may be useful to develop. In this undertaking three levels of study have been addressed, at which different types of legal requirements can be found: the general, jurisprudential level where also the government's administration of public legal information is reflected; the level at which organisations working with legal information are placed; and, finally, the level at which an individual lawyer is situated.

The analysis of general requirements clearly shows that the so called *doctrine of legal source*s gives strong indications as to how legal information ought to be handled. Despite this, it is apparent that it is impossible to work out some universal code comprising an elaborate design strategy for legal IT-systems based on the existing descriptions of the content and hierarchical order of legal sources. In this respect the law is an all too complex phenomenon. It is also obvious that legal sources are ascribed various degrees of importance in different jurisdictions. An important drawback of a general design strategy based on an analysis of the doctrine of legal sources is furthermore the fact that conditions in different law areas vary, and that all development activities concerning legal IT systems must be adjusted to the domain in question.

The complications following from the domain dependent nature of legal information must not overshadow, however, the fact that the doctrine of legal sources actually provides a number of standards which have to be taken into consideration in all undertakings dealing with legal information systems. It must also be observed that the analysis of the doctrine of legal sources clearly indicates a number of quality aspects which reflect the requirements of society at an aggregate level. Important illustrations in this respect are the principles of freedom of information, standards concerning free exchange of information, the importance of promulgation, etc.

It is also noticeable that the doctrine of legal sources makes explicit a number of factors that can be utilised in order to delimit and select materials in the process of legal information management. Examples of such factors are descriptions of subject-matter relevance, formal and hierarchical relevance, obsolescence, and so forth.

The result of all this is that the doctrine of legal sources will provide in most cases the necessary starting point for an analysis of the relevant legal material in a given area of law. Likewise, there is little doubt that the doctrine of legal sources constitute the most reliable framework for legal information management.

The investigation of the organisational level makes it apparent, in turn, that in all realistic enterprises involving IT in the legal sector organisational requirements must influence the ways in which the legal material is selected. It is also obvious that organisational requirements may be of relevance for the ways in which the more subtle aspects of the material can be handled, relating, for example, to continuity, authenticity, and completeness.

The analysis further shows that requirements at the organisational level should determine the ways in which legal materials of various kinds should be combined and amended. It is likewise clear that the organisational framework will provide indications concerning the type of meta-information that must be included in a feasible legal information system. In this context it is also important to notice that different organisations within the same domain may exhibit quite different requirements due to the fact that their objectives differ. Worth mentioning is moreover the fact that the analysis of requirements at the organisational level makes it clear that various users within the same organisation may have different opinions about the ways in which the material ought to be best managed, and about prioritisation.

The fact that users' opinions vary is even more apparent when the requirements of individual lawyers are studied. At this level it may be even correct to say that at some point all lawyers will have their own opinion concerning the ways in which the legal material ought to be managed. This is not only a reflection of the fact that all individuals working with legal material will have different needs due to the fact that their working tasks differ, but also a consequence of the fact that various lawyers have different background knowledge and different opinions on law.

Another conclusion from the analysis of individual lawyers' requirements is that law should be perceived as a network of component structures appearing at different levels of abstraction. This is a consequence of the fact that users will require various legal components in different situations. For instance, in the initial phase of the analysis of a legal problem a lawyer will seek for a legal concept describing the problem at a general level. The objective will then be to be able to delimit the issue from the legal point of view. In order to obtain a more distinct picture of the situation in the following phase attention may have to be shifted towards legal rules and definitions of interrelated concepts (prerequisites). Thereafter, some methodological rule may have to be investigated, e.g. a rule concerning evidential value that may be ascribed to a certain fact which has been established. In the final stages of legal reasoning search activities may aim at explicit references (documents) of a formal nature, etc.

In this perspective, documents and text units, concepts, legal rules, and rule systems are only a few examples of the components of the complex network that constitute legal knowledge. Some levels of the network (e.g. document structures with explicit references between associated documents) are clearly visible, while others (e.g. rule-structures) can only be perceived after a thorough investigation of legal texts. It may be also noticed that some of the relevant component structures necessarily generate secondary structures. Document categorisation, for instance, implies supplementary structures, specifying authors, publication series, and so forth.

The general conclusion from the study of requirements of legal information is therefor not only that these requirements are domain dependent, but also that situations in which law is to be used, together with the identity of the users, must be accepted as the point of departure in the design of legal IT-systems.

6.2 Evaluation of Legal Information Systems

The second objective of this study has been to identify and analyse factors of relevance for the evaluation of legal information systems and legal IT products. The approach selected for this operation has been to develop a general model for evaluation. The starting point for this undertaking was the assumption that all legal information systems are to a large extent reflections of choices concerning i) information content, ii) methods and iii) organisational arrangements.

As regards the elaboration of the evaluation model documented in chapter 3 the above summary of the requirements of legal information (section 6.1) provides the basis for conclusions concerning information content standards.

The exploration of methods reveals, in turn, that demands concerning legal information systems vary to a considerable extent, depending on the user situation and the working tasks that are to be performed. An important observation is also that differences in expectations can be related to all aspects of technology, e.g. computers, communication facilities, software performance, etc. The analysis of methods furthermore indicate that IT maturity of the users (or the potential users) is an important aspect that must be included in any evaluation of system performance in this area.

A factor which complicate proper evaluation of methods is the rapid technical development. It is apparent that apart from more or less obvious conclusions concerning such things as access to high speed communication facilities, graphical interfaces, cut and paste standards, hypertext and clickable buttons, etc., it is useless to be more specific about technical standards. In this respect the pace of change is simply too fast and unpredictable.

In an investigation of methods one must also take into consideration the fact that at present several different technical standards may provide satisfactory solutions. It is, for instance, obvious that CD-ROM products and on-line databases can both provide feasible storing and retrieval tools for professional lawyers, which is even more apparent when different software products are investigated. In the process of evaluation, however, it is not possible to foresee which standards will survive, and which will be replaced by new techniques and new technical solutions.

When methodological aspects are scrutinised, it is nevertheless noticeable that a number of jurisprudential and practical presuppositions must be taken into consideration besides pure technical components. The complexity of legal information, for instance, may make it necessary to prioritise functions that may facilitate overviews. For similar reasons simplicity and focus on introduction facilities will always be crucial when a certain system is being evaluated. Likewise, for on-line applications 24-hour access, continuos assistance, e.g. in the form of a help desk, frequent updating of the content, print out facilities and similar aspects are likely to be requested by a large majority of professional users in this area. In this context it is furthermore realistic to suggest that due to the enormity of legal information priority should be given to solutions which make it possible to collect as much information as possible. These details, suggest in turn that it is realistic to predict further development of computer-based legal networks, and that communication facilities and interoperability of systems are important components of investigation when various legal information systems are compared.

In a survey of methods it is also relevant to remember that the analysis of legal requirements indicates that advanced legal information systems should be able to handle not only legal documents and legal texts, but also smaller components, such as legal rules, rule systems, and legal concepts of various kinds. This also indicates that it is possible to foresee that legal information applications will develop from pure IR-systems and simple administrative systems towards applications with much more integrated functions.

An additional factor to be considered is the fact that all lawyers will differ to some extent in their opinions about the law. This in turn makes it possible to predict that most users will be likely to appreciate customised systems rather than general-purpose systems, which is why in an evaluation of various suggested solutions priority should be given to applications that are open to such solutions.

The third aspect of legal information systems that have been included in the model of evaluation – the organisational component – sets the focus on several fundamental, but perhaps less frequently observed aspects that may be relevant to look into when a legal information system is to be investigated.

The factors that can be related to organisational components are numerous, but in the above analysis two aspects appear to be more important than others, viz. stability and competence. Stability is necessary since all professional use of a legal information system is likely to presuppose investments in terms of time, money, and education. From this it obviously also follows that it is desirable that the service is of a permanent character.

Stability of a certain organisation, e.g. a publisher or a database provider, is, nevertheless, difficult to measure and predict, especially in a long-term perspective, but it can be estimated to some extent by means of studying components such as the future plans, the size, and the economy of the organisation.

Competence, in turn, is a generic concept covering a number of aspects ranging from legal proficiency, technical competence, and combined skills concerning all aspects of legal information systems. Competence perceived in this form is not only of utmost importance when legal information systems are to be designed, but it is also a crucial element when a legal information system is to be integrated into the work process, and, of course, when a system is to be managed over a longer period of time.

From the fact that competence is such a broad concept it follows that it may sometimes be quite difficult and time-consuming to evaluate it. Various aspects are also of such a nature that their evaluation is only possible over a certain period of time. When this aspect is investigated, it may, nevertheless, be relevant to try to investigate components such as flexibility, service, etc.

Finally, the analysis of factors relevant to legal information systems shows that the investigation combining information content, technical aspects and organisational issues illustrates how a feasible model for the evaluation of legal information systems, IT products and services can be developed. It should also be noticed that the model of evaluation outlined here can be used not only when various legal information services are to be scrutinised and compared from the user's point of view, but that it can also be used by the legal information system designer, as well as the legal information manager.

The model of evaluation based on information content, methods and organisational aspects can thus be characterised as exhibiting an *overall structure* facilitating more systematic investigations. It is also noticeable that the model is *general* in the sense that it can be used for evaluation of legal information systems of various kinds, and that it reflects components that can be accepted by scholars of different traditions.

In addition, it may be suggested that the model is *transparent* in the sense that the components can be described in a non technical way, and that all legal and technical terms can be explained as they appear. It may furthermore be claimed that the model is *explicit* and *particular* by means of providing a basis for the elaboration of more or less step wise specifications. It is also apparent that the model is *flexible* since it can be modularised in such a way that one or more components can be changed, elaborated upon, omitted, etc. without disturbing the overall structure of the model.

In this context mention should also be made of the fact that the usefulness of the model is illustrated by an ongoing survey of legal IT-products on the Swedish market in which the model is a central component.[1]

6.3 Legal Issues

The third aim of this study has been to provide an overview of legal issues that may affect legal information management and effective utilisation of IT in legal work. In this respect the analysis reveals that legal rules that may be of relevance are of many different kinds and that the most frequently appearing issues are those that can be related to copyright, freedom of information, secrecy, privacy, administrative regulations, and contracting.

---

[1] *See supra* chapter 1 note 10.

A closer look at the investigation reveals that the legal system can sometimes facilitate legal information management, e.g. by means of securing access to official data, providing standard contracts, or procedures for copyright clearance, etc. On the other hand, it is equally clear that the legislative system may sometimes be regarded as a factor complicating the handling of legal information. This is, of course, a natural consequence of the fact that rules are often instruments that have been developed in order to balance different interests and that the reasons for various categories of legislation may sometimes be quite contradictory. The existence of conflicting interests becomes even more apparent when contracting issues are scrutinised. Thus, from the point of view of the legal information manager who is trying to collect as much information as possible, the intellectual property legislation, provisions concerning secrecy, privacy issues, etc., may be looked upon as annoying complications. At the same time these regulations are, of course, of vital importance for individuals that are producing and providing the material.

Another debatable aspect concerns the ways in which basic data of an official nature ought to be dealt with. The basis for the controversy is contained, among other things, in the principles of freedom of information and free exchange of information, as well as different opinions concerning the interpretation and extension of these principles. In connection with this there has been a continuos discussion as to the extent in which the public authorities should provide official information free of charge and whether it should be provided in electronic form. Likewise, there is an ongoing debate as to how far the responsibility of public authorities to edit information should go, e.g. in order to adjust the information better to the electronic media, or in order to satisfy the requirements of specific user groups.

Opinions differ greatly in this respect. The critical voices belong here to the companies trying to explore the market for electronic media in the legal domain by means of designing customised products, and by means of elaborating information packages for selected user groups based on official, unprocessed, basic data. What they mean is, of course, that the state should provide information in a "raw" form and that customisation should be left to the commercial companies to handle. At the same time large user groups, e.g. undergraduate schools, public libraries, etc., find it natural to argue that the state should take considerable responsibility in this respect. In order to balance these interests various countries have come up with different solutions, but in several cases the debate is still going on.

The type of legal problem that is the most difficult to solve depends, naturally, in each case, on what a given legal information manager or a certain library is trying to accomplish. Is it simply a question of giving the public access to information on a lending basis? Or is it a more ambitious project involving e.g. the design and creation of intricate databases, pedagogic interfaces, and dissemination of educational materials? In the latter cases administration of intellectual property aspects may grow drastically. Not only may the procurement of information, (from many different contributors perhaps), give rise to comprehensive licensing issues and cumbersome negotiations. It is also clear that the products that are being produced will have to be protected in various ways.

Trying to predict which legal issues will be the most crucial in the future is, however, unrealistic. In this respect the development of IT and the future roles of legal information managers and law libraries are too difficult to foresee. On the other hand it is realistic to expect a continued discussion on the extent to which it will be possible to seek protection for various new kinds of information structures, lists of links, meta indexes, etc. Likewise, new forms of library activities, such as, e.g., the lending of computer programs to university students or the compilation of own databases will raise new issues that must be dealt with. The development and utilisation of IT also make it possible to foresee that these issues will become even more central in the future.

The intricate nature of the legal system and the rapid change of IT and accompanying legal issues thus lead to the conclusion that non-experts with a responsibility for IT development projects must be prepared to seek assistance and advice, e.g. from lawyers specialising in IT-law, library associations, reproduction rights organisations, etc. It may furthermore be concluded that all legal information managers and law libraries with the ambition of participating in the future development in a creative manner should seek to develop, or get access to IT-copyright expertise.

6.4 Aspects Affecting Change

The fourth objective of this study was to provide a discussion of "external" (i.e. not necessarily law-domain dependent) aspects that may affect the future development of the legal work process in an environment increasingly affected by IT. In this undertaking various aspects such as IT maturity, aims, economy, and pace of change have been addressed, and in the following sections the conclusions from this analysis are discussed in some detail.

6.4.1 IT Maturity

As concerns the important aspect of IT maturity it is quite obvious that all law librarians or legal information managers must follow the technical development very closely. There is simply no other way in which to survive in the rapidly changing legal domain. It must be noticed, however, that IT maturity is quite a complex component, which is why it is necessary to continuously watch over a number of features. It is not only that the legal information manager must be proficient in technical matters, but also that the readiness of end users, as well as potential users, must be taken into consideration. No IT projects or administrative changes can be completed without acceptance of the users.

From this in turn follows that distribution of information concerning the technique and its potentialities, as well as education of the users, must be considered as important undertakings for anyone trying to introduce IT, or any other new forms of legal information management, into an organisation. As a consequence, legal information managers must not only be able to keep up with IT development, but they must also be able to disseminate their knowledge further in their organisations.

To be able to motivate others and to successfully introduce changes may be, however, difficult. In this context it should be recalled that conservative attitudes towards IT and methodological changes are not unusual within the legal domain. In some cases the new technology may even be looked upon as a threat, which indicates in turn that psychology and tactics may be important aspects. To observe in this respect is thereby the fact that an all too enthusiastic approach may create difficulties in some cases, and also that demands in this area may change more or less overnight due to the fact that IT maturity is something that changes very fast.

The way in which the aspects of IT maturity ought to be handled in practice must be furthermore related in each case to the kind of organisation in question. In a small, in-house library, serving e.g. a law firm, the legal information manager may have to be very active in order to explain and promote various changes related to technical proposals. This would simply be a reflection of the fact that in many cases it is natural to assume that the person responsible for the law library should be the firm's leading authority on these matters. From this it naturally also follows that the legal information manager in a small organisation may be less restricted with regard to the selection of technical solutions for implementation, in the sense that the proposed changes may be accepted in a more or less uncritical way.

In a law library serving, for example, a university or a large company, on the other hand, the situation may be entirely different. Here, it may be necessary to adjust to and stay in line not only with the development of the legal education taking place, but also with standardisation and IT strategies decided upon elsewhere. It may be difficult in such cases to influence the aspects of IT maturity so that the primary objective of the legal information manager may be instead to adjust the services to that which is expected from the users and other co-operating parties. This is, of course, not to say that the development in larger organisations cannot be influenced, but only to point out that it may be sometimes necessary to adjust one's efforts to other ongoing activities concerning similar matters, and that methodological aspects of information retrieval, selection of legal sources, and evaluation of legal IT may also constitute primary concerns of the users of a law library.

Another presupposition therefore suggests that representatives of the law library must be highly communicative and that they must be prepared to co-operate smoothly and without unnecessary friction with various user groups and their representatives concerning technical and methodological matters. This is without doubt also something that will become increasingly important as IT maturity becomes more wide-spread in society.

The need to be able to communicate and explain any proposed changes presupposes, in turn, access to the channels of communication. This is a precondition which might pose only minor problems in a small organisation, but which can constitute a considerable problem in a large organisation.

In this respect the legal information manager may have to consider various strategies. It is obvious, for instance, that existing facilities, e.g. e-mail, internal newsletters, and the like, should be used as much as possible in order to make announcements and to disseminate information. Complementary activities may include arrangements of demonstrations, internal courses and undertakings in order to provide individual training for users. In addition, authoring of articles, participation in management groups, arrangements of departmental meetings, on-line training sessions, offering of legal research seminars, co-operation with other administrative departments, and even organisation of social gatherings, may belong to feasible means in which information can be disseminated.

An important and related task is to provide background information for various groups within the organisation, not only by means of providing traditional information services, but also in order to illustrate the advantages and potentialities of new forms of services as such. In this respect it is recommended that the legal information manager should monitor various media for client related articles, keep track of ongoing activities outside the organisation, conduct user surveys, etc.

6.4.2 Aims

Anyone working with legal information management must acknowledge the fact that the aims of an organisation, as well as the objectives of individuals, may pose problems for suggested system implementations as well as for other kinds of changes. This is simply to say that the relevant aims may change and that different objectives may sometimes clash.

In order to handle this state of the matter a variety of strategies must be adopted. Perhaps most important for the legal information manager is to try to participate in the dialogue or the debate within the organisation in order to understand the various implicit and explicit objectives.

It may also be relevant in this respect to motivate, establish, and develop the perspective of legal information management in order to facilitate for the members of an organisation the articulation of their needs in relevant (IT related) terms.

This would mean in practice that a legal information manager should try to initiate meetings with other managers and that ultimately, he or she should strive to become a part of the management team in order to understand and be able to raise questions concerning the direction and focus of the activities. For the same reason considerable efforts should be made in order to try to pinpoint the objectives of the individual lawyers, e.g. by means of finding forms for continuos discussions. This may be accomplished by means of demonstrating interest in individual attorneys' work, and trying to offer adequate support to end users, whether in litigation, client advice, or business development.

Better understanding of matters such as mentioned above will furthermore make it possible to function as an interpreter or intermediary between various groups within an organisation, e.g. between technicians, administrators, and lawyers, or between law teachers and students. This is a role which presupposes, among other things, the ability to explain various technical matters pedagogical. If successfully carried through, however, such undertakings may facilitate not only legal information management activities, but they may also be profitable for the development of an organisation as such.

6.4.3 Economy

Important to observe is furthermore that although some undertakings concerning legal information management can be initiated without major investments, it must be remembered that any serious legal information management project will depend on the fact that economic resources are available. Noticeable in this respect is thereby that legal information managers are rarely in the position of being able to make decisions regarding their own budget. Proposals for the introduction of new technologies may meet with various degrees of enthusiasm, which makes it therefore necessary to be able to properly motivate any proposed changes. It becomes obvious here again that an essential part of a long-term strategy of legal information management must be to show that investments in IT and information management can be profitable as compared to other potential activities of a given organisation active in the legal domain.

A natural strategy for legal information management is therefore to continuously collect data, which can facilitate evaluation of changes in terms of effectiveness and economy. Relevant facts may include, e.g., money spent on law report subscriptions, average time spent on inter-library loans, numbers of requests for various types of information, etc., which may be later compared with the performance and costs of new information systems and consequences of other types of changes. It should also be noted here that collection of data of this kind can be initiated, disregarding whether any actual changes are being scheduled for the near future.

In this respect it may be furthermore suggested that legal information managers should be active in planning activities, such as setting individual and departmental goals concerning efficiency and performance in economic terms, preparing detailed budgets, controlling the budgets, and revising and modifying the objectives. It can also be pointed out that it may be valuable to record library time spent on client research and other activities, to control library accounts, and check the usage of library collections and resources. In connection with the above it may be necessary to identify less efficient on-line searchers, to control increasing on-line costs, and to keep statistics of various kinds which can make it possible to follow up and measure the performance of the library and of various IT related services over time.[2]

It should be observed in this context that it at present there can be detected tendencies to reduce the library budget within organisations. Likewise, experiments with outsourcing have been reported, in which services that are normally related to libraries are bought from external

---

[2] Fact and categories of relevance in this respect are quite well documented and described, *See, e.g.*, AALL, (ed.) *Making Information Work: A Tool Kit*, AALL, Chicago, 1996, SUB, *Mått och Mätningar: Biblioteksservice vid universitets- högskole- och forskningsbibliotek*, Stockholm, 1994 (Stockholms universitetsbibliotek rapport, SUB 25/1994), *and* Ekengren, Hammarlund, Janzon, Zetterberg, Vessberg, Hultberg, Törngren, *supra* chapter 5 note 5.

organisations. This strategy leads to a dismissal of law librarians from their work. A recent and much debated example of such tactics is the firing of the library staff at Baker & McKenzie's Chicago office[3]– an example of a tendency which has lead to the creation of a "Task Force" by the American Association of Law Libraries (AALL), relating to the "Value of Law Librarians in the Information Age".

As a result of this, the AALL has put together a "tool kit" in which, among other things, a number of "key points" concerning the reasons why law librarians are needed have been elaborated in economic terms and other aspects related to efficiency. In summary, it is thereby suggested that librarians should underline the facts that they are able to guarantee the following:[4]

- "saving money for their firm and its clients by quick and efficient research, usually at a lower billing rate than attorneys,

- negotiating with publishers about the most favourable prices or contracts,

- selecting the most efficient way in which to use the firm's electronic databases, and training attorneys to use them profitably,

- being responsible for keeping up with the on-going information change, using the appropriate protocols, and practising the most efficient research methods for efficient identification of information,

- providing professional information management to ensure that the firm continues to receive the highest return on its investment in information resources – an aspect which is especially important in times when research funds are limited and information sources are more or less unlimited,

---

[3] See e.g. Gill, Donns, *Challenges Face Law Librarians, as Research Goes Electronic* and *Shelving the Library Staff at Baker & McKenzie,* Chicago Lawyer, July 1995.

[4] AALL, *supra* note 2.

• overseeing the organisation's information needs, and making sure that the most cost-effective research materials and on-line data bases are secured and used to support the firm's work,

• conducting reference interviews in order to help attorneys identify information that would best satisfy their needs, then using or guiding lawyers towards the most cost effective resources for locating that information,

• collecting information for the expansion of new businesses, and providing non-legal research directly to clients for a fee,

• co-operating with their colleagues at other firms in the borrowing and sharing of resources through inter-library loans, thus expanding the available information and making it accessible to their firms without increasing the costs."

It should be noticed, however, that economic aspects may make legal information management difficult for several reasons. The fact that important objectives of active legal information management include rationalisation and enhanced effectiveness may also cause problems. In this respect problems may actually emerge alongside the appearance of IT maturity of the employees at a law firm. This is simply due to the fact that the proficiency of the individual end users increases, their need for assistance from legal information managers may decrease. In this respect it is obvious that the development of IT and activities connected with legal information management may become a threat to the persons involved in the development of such activities. Or, to put it differently, the ultimate result of the introduction of thinking in terms of effective legal management and advanced IT tools in relation to individual end users, may well be that librarians and legal information managers may become superfluous, or at least not so frequently sought after.

If one analyses this aspect somewhat more deeply, and accepts the fact that the development of IT entails the fact that many of the functions previously thought of as being the responsibility of the library can be overtaken by individuals, it becomes clear that the only way a legal information manager can motivate his or her existence in the long run, is to be well ahead of all the others within the organisation, that can benefit from the knowledge and the activities that he or she may initiate.

6.4.4 Pace of Change

Conclusions of relevance for legal information management can also be drawn from the above outlined discussion with regard to the rapid development of legal systems and the growing pace of change that may be observed in many social aspects.

The most striking thing is that changes in the legal system must be looked upon as natural and continuously occurring events. It is likewise clear that these changes may be of many different kinds. As concerns the traditional perspective of the law library one must be aware that established ways of systematising the legal material may have to be altered in a very short time. Obvious is also that methodological considerations may have to be revised more or less continuously.

At a somewhat deeper level this means that anyone working with legal information must be prepared to accept the fact that well established presuppositions may change very quickly. Sometimes new developments may make it necessary to define new legal areas and find new perspectives in order to study the emerging subject matters. A clear illustration of this is found in the attempts to implement various kinds of EU directives, and in the integration of international and national legislation. At a more specific level it can be observed, for example, that legal aspects of gene technology appear presently to form a separate field of interest.

To be able to cope with more or less constant change, from the point of view of the legal information manager it is, of course, highly relevant to try to understand the ways in which the legal system may be reorganised and restructured, and predict when shifts of various kinds are likely to occur. For natural reasons this is extremely difficult but at least it must be assumed that it is possible to achieve greater readiness for changes, as well as a higher ability to adjust to changing presuppositions.

The way in which to enhance one's ability to foresee changes is to try to have good knowledge of the general development of society in order to predict the emerging areas where legal conflicts may become frequent. A further consequence of this is that the objective should not only be to collect material that may come in handy, but to concentrate on collecting the means and services that may assist one in the retrieval of legal materials of various kinds. In other words, the overall strategy should be to focus on general methodology.

Another conclusion is that the ability to handle and effectively reflect changes in the development of the law presupposes in many cases an in depth knowledge of the law and the legal methods. Contemplating further over these issues and the constant growth of the material, it may thus be predicted that legal information management will emerge, in many situations, as a crucial component of legal work. It may even be argued that effective legal information management presupposes legal education – or vice versa – that legal education must be based, to a large extent, on skill in legal information management, as well as that rapid changes, due to the import of IT, make it necessary to look upon these issues from an entirely new perspective.

From the point of view of the law library, it may thus be suggested that, among other things, the traditional collection of substantive legal material may have to be substituted by a more reactive activity in that the legal information manager may have to concentrate on responding to user requests to a larger degree than before.

Likewise, it appears obvious that the law library may have to be looked upon as a place where knowledge of methodological matters is collected, made refined and available. It can no longer be looked upon only as a place for storing legal information of a static nature.

6.5 Outlook for the Future

6.5.1 Digitalisation and Law Libraries

If one analyses the phenomenon of digitalisation a bit more carefully it becomes quite obvious that changes which may be brought about by this development have only just started. Fundamental changes in information management can already be noticed in many areas making that law is not an isolated domain in this respect, even though the pace of change has obviously been more moderate here than in other areas. It is also clear that the development of IT and telecommunications, as well as the utilisation of specially designed systems for legal work will have secondary effects. As the products become more sophisticated, and the tools become integrated into the legal education, it is beyond doubt that future generations of lawyers will have a completely different view of law, legal information retrieval and the related issues. Of great importance in this respect is, of course, also the fact that the methods used for structuring and management of legal knowledge will change.

In this situation completely new demands will appear, concerning, among other things, the ability to handle methods for identification, collection and presentation of various kinds of components of legal knowledge. From the point of view of law libraries this obviously entails that the prevailing methods of text and document management must be complemented by methods for the management of more elaborate structures of different kinds. Such development will result, in turn, in radical changes in work processes and the organisation of legal work.

As concerns the concept of law libraries and issues of their definition, it may be concluded that, although the traditional meaning of the word "library" remains uncontested, an open-minded attitude towards this concept is preferable. This point of view becomes especially relevant when we think about the changes brought about by the IT development – changes indicating that the traditional perspective must be complemented with a new outlook, and that a shift from passive storing to active structuring and management of the material must be accepted. And, as mentioned before, this also means in practice that law libraries must concentrate on accumulating knowledge about legal methods, and they must also be prepared to develop skills in handling such methods.

It may furthermore be concluded that law libraries will meet competition of a new kind. It is therefore of relevance to discuss the extent to which it is possible and desirable to modify the services traditionally provided by law libraries. For example, what are the demands concerning the adjustment of library activities towards more active management of legal knowledge, aiming to accomplish products and services of a more elaborate kind? At another, more detailed level it is the question of the kind of functions that one should realistically concentrate on. Other questions come to mind too. For example, what kind of legal obstacles exist to a more active organisation of legal knowledge within the framework of law libraries? To what extent is it necessary to adjust one's work to the emerging international standards, and what are the requirements concerning education and technical resources?

It is important to notice, however, that changes that may be brought about by technical development will not replace or alter all the previous functions of the law library. For the foreseeable future digitalisation and other changes related to legal information discussed in this study will complement the law library and add new components to it. This is simply to say that organisational issues concerning the distribution of material, accommodation for visitors and students, loan policy, inter library co-operation, acquisition policy and practice, publishing, binding, shelf arrangements, cataloguing, circulation of material, etc., will be important tasks also in the future, and that in most cases the established functions will have to be administrated simultaneously with the integration of the new techniques. It should also be noticed that during different stages of their carriers lawyers will request different types of services, both traditional as well as IT related, depending on their working tasks and their economic resources.

When it comes to dissemination of knowledge it may be desirable to develop efficient and secure channels for internal information exchange, as well as initiate various activities in order to advertise and actively distribute legal information. From this it also follows that it may be necessary to highlight certain fragments of information and that a conscious and perhaps also customised indexing may be important in order to make it possible for the users to retrieve and utilise information in an efficient manner. In this respect the library staff must strive to stay ahead of the users as regards the surveillance of law publications, identification of new services and other activities that may affect the ways in which information is accessed and interpreted. It is also obvious, of course, that effective collection of legal information presupposes being able to compare various information services, and a skill in negotiations with information producers and publishers about acquisition, subscriptions, database licensing, etc.

In this respect, digitalisation implies many new potentialities, of which only a few can be foreseen. What is easy to understand, however, is that knowledge concerning these potentialities must increase and that accumulation of knowledge and experience from information search, as well as of other aspects of legal methodology will become an important task. Likewise, it is rather clear that it will become necessary to expand educational activities in order to improve the competence of the library staff, which will without doubt apply to all types of law libraries.

Finally, it can be concluded that library organisation is quite a complex matter. It is therefore obvious that law libraries would benefit from co-operation and from utilisation or formation of institutions that could bring various kinds of know-how together such as, for example, competence centres and law library associations. The importance of such organisations can be expected only to increase in the future,[5] and they are, of course, vital when contracting issues, such as, for example, the national library licenses or policies for lending services, etc. are to be handled.

6.5.2 Legal Information Management

Another predictable consequence of the digitalisation is the emergence of new professions in the legal sector, such as legal information managers and consultants for the design, analysis, and publishing of electronic materials.

[5] Specialised law library organisations are rather recent occurrences, although *The American Association of Law Libraries* was founded in 1906. In Europe *The British and Irish Association of Law Libraries* was established in 1959, and *The International Association of Law Libraries* in 1969. Wiegand *supra* chapter 2 note 1, and Wedgeworth *supra* chapter 2 note 2.

The concept of legal information management, as it is developed in this study, is characterised by an active attitude towards legal information. Thus, legal information management presupposes controlling a set of methods of various kinds, stretching from the handling of well established types of legal information, e.g. legal documents, law journals, and traditional publications, to proficiency in IT-related products and services. Legal information management is therefore by necessity a very dynamic activity and presupposes an open attitude towards more or less constant changes. In addition, it should be underlined that legal information management is a social activity in the sense that, if it is to be meaningful it must be conducted in close co-operation with the producers, administrators, and end users of legal information.

In a somewhat broader perspective it may be argued that the emerging concept of legal information management is a necessary reaction to the challenges facing the legal domain, and illustrated by, among other things, a dramatic increase in the production of legal information, the internationalisation of law, and new emerging forms of IT related products and telecommunication services. In this context it is also noticeable that the increasing pace of development in all these aspects makes a more active attitude crucial, and that the importance of the issues referred to in this study can be expected to grow with time.

The fact that legal information management stands out as a necessary component of the future development of the legal domain makes it possible, in turn, to predict that it will eventually be perceived as a separate profession – probably through a natural extension and transformation of law librarianship as it is seen today. Early examples of the broadening of the scope of librarianship are presently reflected in initiatives aiming at the interconnection of law library resources with the presentation of new, library-related services on the Internet.[6]

Tentatively, the objectives of legal information management can be said to be twofold. Perhaps the most obvious fact is that the legal domain and legal work are driven, to a large extent, by the desire to utilise existing technical means and other methodological potentialities as efficiently and as

---

[6] *See, e.g.,* the projects mentioned in chapter 3, note 45, *supra.*

early as possible. From this point of view it appears that the elaboration of the concept of legal information management is a natural consequence of economic and practical considerations, and, in consequence, that enhanced efficiency is a clear objective.

The second objective of legal information management is of a jurisprudential qualitative nature. That is to say that as the development continues, it becomes more and more apparent that it is important for the legal domain to acquire knowledge about a number of things. It is, for instance, indisputable that it is necessary to try to better understand how IT and digitalisation should be utilised in order to serve the legal community in the best possible way. It is also clear that there exists a number of fundamental jurisprudential principles that must be vindicated and nourished also in a digital environment. And, as has been argued throughout this study, this means that one must learn more about the actual needs of the users of legal information –in order to be able to develop the right kind of services and products.

In practice this means that one of the objectives of the legal information manager is to participate in the development of legal information services, and, in the long-term perspective, that it is advisable to try to elaborate standards and quality aspects related to IT and law. Likewise, it appears indisputable that many aspects of legal information management must become an integral part of legal education, by showing law students how to understand and use various IT related services. From the jurisprudential point of view this also entails that legal information management must be looked upon as an important aspect of the legal method.

The "external" aspects treated in this study show furthermore that the role of the legal information manager is becoming extremely difficult and challenging, since the number, complexity, and diversity of the subject matters to be handled are rather high. Many topics also demonstrate an extremely fast pace of development. Another consequence of all this is that successful performance presupposes not only that legal information managers must be very active in order to improve their competence and professional roles, but also that the management must be prepared to accept fundamental changes in the traditional role of the librarian.

6.6 Future Work

In this book some approaches that may be utilised in order to evaluate legal IT-systems are described. The focus is set on system components (content, methods and organisation), user requirements, and various external factors. The objective has been to provide the means for the critical and consistent scrutiny of the products and services that are being developed.

As for the future, it is, however, important to take into consideration the fact that the rapid development of IT and telecommunications, as well as the increasing internationalisation of law, makes it necessary to revise and adjust many of the more detailed aspects of the employed method. Likewise, it may be concluded that this must be done in a more or less continuous manner. Additional factors to be considered in this respect is the growing competition and increased commercialisation of the legal information market.

Another conclusion from the above is, of course, that enhanced and up-to-date knowledge of IT-components and various types of user requirements will doubtlessly be important when various products and services are to be evaluated also in the future.

In the long-term perspective, however, it may be argued that one should be even more ambitious, trying to utilise the results of the analyses and evaluations in a broader sense. Most important in this respect appears to be that it is desirable that the analyses include *development methods* for legal IT-systems, as well as *long term effect.*

The need to include development methods in the discussion is motivated by the obvious fact that there exists a close relationship between the characteristics of legal IT-systems and the various strategies and methods that are employed in order to design and develop them. This is simply a way of saying that it should be important to scrutinise, among other things, the ways in which preliminary studies are completed, organisational analyses carried out, legal information is being selected, adjusted and transformed, implementation strategies and educational activities are performed, as well as a number of other aspects.

In a similar way the necessity to aggregate and systematise the knowledge about effects of legal information systems follows from the fact that it is important to understand the ways in which various legal IT-systems affect the legal community. In many situations it is quite apparent that legal IT-systems are likely to have a considerable impact on the way legal work is carried out. Likewise, the ways in which the systems are designed and utilised may affect the substantial aspects of law, and for obvious reasons it is also interesting to try to manage these consequences. In this wider perspective the nature of investigations that have to be completed differs depending on the situation. When a legal IT-system is implemented in a teaching organisation, for instance, it is natural to investigate whether the system has had a positive effect on the actual learning, how the course administration and the teachers' resources have been affected, and so forth. Likewise, it is relevant to scrutinise the economic consequences, the emerging legal problems, the effect of IT investments on the future plans and flexibility of the organisations, etc.

Another reason why the study of effects appears to be a crucial issue is the obvious fact that in some situations it may be necessary to regulate the consequences of legal IT-systems in order to vindicate various kinds of legal quality aspects. The relationship between the proposed future study objects may thus be reflected as in figure 6.1.

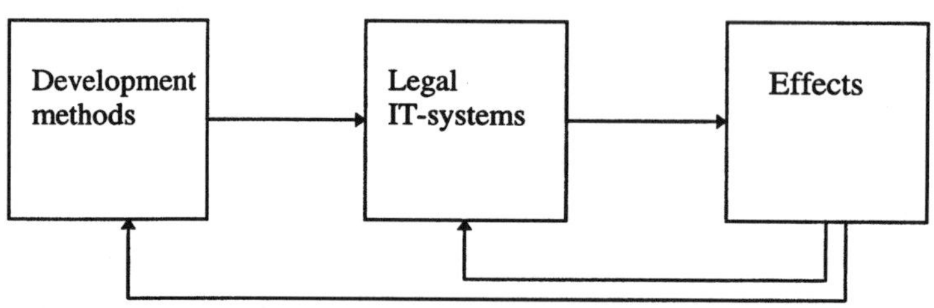

Figure 6.1: An evaluation of IT-systems with any practical ambitions should include not only system components of a tangible nature but also system development methods and effects.

It may finally be argued that an approach of the kind outlined here should eventually lead to the formation of standards, not only for legal IT-systems as such, but also for development methods. Likewise, it can be suggested that the effects of legal IT systems should be observed and regulated (figure 6.2).

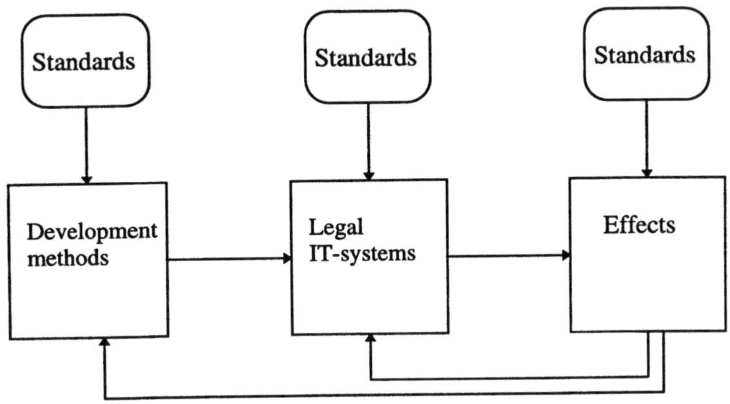

Figure 6.2: Components and objects of interest in the future study of law libraries and legal information management.

Literature References

AALL, *Handbook & Directory, The Library Bill of Rights,* "http://www.aallnet.org/handbook/policy_bill_of_rights.html", 1997.

Agreement on Trade-Related Aspects of Intellectual Property Rights (TRIPS) "http://www.wto.org/wto/intellec/1-ipcon.htm".

Alchourrón, Carlos E. & Bulygin, Eugenio, *Normative Systems*, Springer-Verlag, Wien, 1971 (Library of Exact Philosophy 5).

Arbetsgruppen för datoriserad rättsinformation, *Sammanträdesprotokoll May 10, 1989,* photocopy (Ju-dep RIA91A Unr:1 m bilaga).

Arbetsgruppen för ett nytt Rättsdatasystem, *Gruppens överväganden i den första etappen av arbetet*, photocopy, February 24, 1997.

Arbetsgruppen för ett nytt Rättsdatasystem, *Kravbeskrivning för ett moderniserat Rättsdatasystem*, photocopy, July 3, 1997.

Baur, Jürgen, *Legal Decision Support Systems – Implemented Systems,* In Skantze, Pernilla (ed.) Essays in Legal Information Management, The Swedish Law and Informatics Research Institute, Stockholm, 1996 (IRI-report 1996:2) 33-54.

Bechthold, Stefan *The Link Controversy Page* "http://www.jura.uni-tuebingen.de/~s-bes1/lcp.html", December 1997.

Bergström, Ann Marie, *IT-stöd blev åklagarnöd*, Jusektidningen nr 4, 1997, 4.

Berne Convention for the Protection of Literary and Artistic Works Paris Act of July 24, 1971, as amended on September 28, 1979, "http://www.wipo.int/-eng/iplex/index.htm".

Bernitz, Ulf, Heuman, Lars, Leijonhufvud, Madeleine, Seipel, Peter, Warnling-Nerep, Wiweka, Victorin, Anders & Vogel, Hans-Heinrich, *Finna rätt: Juristens källmaterial och arbetsmetoder*, Juristförlaget, Stockholm, 4 ed., 1996.

Bertnes, Pål, A. & Kongshavn, Halvor, *Praktisk rettskildelære: Juridisk kildesøking i Norge, øvrige nordiske land og EF*, Det juridiske biblioteksfond/Ad Notam Gyldendal AS, Oslo, 1992.

Bing, Jon, *Legal Decisions and Computerized Systems*, In Seipel, Peter (ed.) From Data Protection to Knowledge Mashines: The Study of Law and Informatics, Kluwer Law and Taxation Publishers, Deventer, 1990 (Computer Law Series 5) 223-50.

Bing, Jon, *Handbook of Legal Information Retrieval*, North Holland Publishing Co., Amsterdam, 1984.

Bing, Jon & Harvold, Tryggve, *Legal Decisions and Information Systems*, Universitetsforlaget, Oslo, 1977 (Publications of the Norwegian Research Center for Computers and Law no 5).

Blume, Peter, *Fra tale till data: Studier i det juridiske informationssystem*, Akademisk forlag, København, 1989.

Blumer, Thomas, J., Bolis, Monica & Hyde, Janice, I., *International Access to Legislative Information: Vol. II, Collection, Storage, Retrieval and Delivery of Public Information*, UNIFO Publishers Inc., Sarasota, Florida, 1994.

Blunt, Adrian, *Law Librarianship*, K.G. Saur Clive Bingley, New York, ..., 1980 (Outlines of Modern Librarianship).

Borgström, Håkan, *Nitlotter för miljarder*, Ny Teknik 21/97, 21-23.

Brownlie, Ian, *Principles of Public International Law*, Clarendon Press, London, 4 ed., 1990.

Brümmer, Anna & Åstrand, Lotta, *Biblioteken på Internet: en undersökning av elektroniska biblioteks hemsidors form, innehåll, struktur och användarstöd*, "http://www.ub.lu.se/UB2proj/LIS_collection /AnnaLotta/toc.html".

Business and Government Information Center, University of Nevada, Reno, *Website Evaluation Criteria*, "http://gordo.library.unr.edu/ ~bgic/fed/criteria.Html".

Business Software Alliance, *Press Release*, Washington/Stockholm, photocopy, May 7, 1997.

Chiang, Win-Shin, S. & Price, Kathleen, *International Access to Legislative Information: A Preliminary Investigation*, UNIFO Publishers Inc., Sarasota, Florida, 1992.

Clinch, Peter, *Using a Law Library: A Student's Guide to Legal Research Skills*, Blackstone, London, 1992.

Cohen, Morris, L. & Olson, Kent, C., *Legal Research in a Nutshell*, West Publishing Company, St Paul, Minn., 5 ed., 1992.

Council of Europe, *The Selection, processing, presentation and archiving of court decisions in legal information retrieval systems*, Council of Europe Publishing, Strasbourg, 1996, Recommendation No. R (95) 1 and explanatory memorandum.
Cwiklo, William E. (ed.) *Computers in Litigation Support*, Pertocelli Books Inc., New York, 1979.

De juridiska fakulteternas europautredning, *Europagemenskap och rättsvetenskap*, Iustus förlag, Uppsala, 1992.

Delegationen för översättning av EG:s regelverk, *Anvisningar för översättningsarbetet*, photocopy, n.p., 1995.

Denning, Peter J. & Metcalfe, Robert M. (eds.) *Beyond Calculation: The Next Fifty Years of Computation*, Springer-Verlag, New York, 1997.

Dertouzos, Michael L., *What Will be: How The New World of Information Will Change Our Lives*, HarperEdge/Harper Collins Publishers, New York, 1997.

Dickinson, Gail K., *Selection and Evaluation of Electronic Resources*, Libraries Unlimited, Inc. Englewood, Co., 1994.

Diesen, Christian & Wahlgren, Peter, *Multimedia som juridiskt läromedel*, photocopy, Stockholm university, 1996.

Dir. 1995:91, *Regeringens direktiv till Datalagskommittén*, Stockholm, 1995.

Ds 1996:71, *Rättsligt skydd för databaser*, Stockholm, 1996.

Duke University, *Ethics and the Internet*, "http://www.duke.edu/~wgrobin/ethics/surflaw.html", November 1997.

Dworkin, Ronald, *Taking Rights Seriously*, Harvard University Press, Cambridge, Massachusetts, 1977.

EC, *Council Directive 91/250/EEC of 14 May 1991 on the Legal Protection of Computer Programs*, Official Journal of the European Communities no. L 122 , 17/05/91 p. 42 (Article 8 was repealed by Directive 93/98), (also available at "http://www2.echo.lu/legal/en/ipr/ipr.html").

EC, *Council Directive 92/100/EEC of 19 November 1992 on the Rental Right and Lending Right and on Certain Rights Related to Copyright in the Field of Intellectual Property*, Official Journal of the European Communities no. L 346,

27/11/92 p. 61 (Articles 11 & 12 were repealed by Directive 93/98), (also available at "http://www2.echo.lu/legal/en/ipr/ipr.html").

EC, *Council Directive 93/83/EEC of 27 September 1993 on the Coordination of Certain Rules Concerning Copyright Applicable to Satellite Broadcasting and Cable Retransmission,* Official Journal of the European Communities no. L 248, 06/10/93 p. 15 (also available at "http://www2.echo.lu/legal/en/ipr/ipr.html").

EC, *Council Directive 93/98/EEC of 29 October 1993 harmonizing the term of protection of copyright and certain related rights,* Official Journal of the European Communities no. L 290 , 24/11/93 p. 9 (also available at "http://www2.echo.lu/legal/en/ipr/ipr.html").

EC, *Council Directive 95/46/EC on the Protection of Individuals with Regard to the Processing of Personal Data and the Free Movement of such Data,* Official Journal of the European Communities of 23 November 1995 No L. 281 p. 31 (also available at "http://www2.echo.lu/legal/en/dataprot/directiv/directiv.html").

EC, *Directive 96/9/EC of the European Parliament and of the Council on the Protection of Databases,* Official Journal of the European Communities of 27/3/96 no L 77 p. 20 (also available at "http://www2.echo.lu/legal/en/ipr/ipr.html").

EC *Guidelines for improving the synergy between the public and private sectors in the information market, 1989,* (available at "http://www2.echo.lu/legal/en/access/access.html").

Eckhoff, Torstein, *Rettskildelære,* Johan Grundt Tanum Forlag, Oslo, 1971.

Eckhoff, Torstein & Sundby, Nils Kristian. *Rettssystemer: Systemteoretisk innføring i rettsfilosofien.* Tanum-Norli, Oslo, 1976.

Eek, Hilding, *Folkrätten,* Norstedts förlag, Stockholm, 4 ed., 1987 (Bring, Ove, Hjerner, Lars (eds), Institutet för rättsvetenskaplig forskning LI).

Ekengren, Bo, Hammarlund, Nils, Janzon, Ona, Zetterberg, Marianne, Vessberg, Viveka, Hultberg, Alf & Törngren, Margareta, *RUT, Resultatmätning och utvärdering av mätmetoder: A test and evaluation of the American handbook "Measuring Academic Library Performance – A Practical Approach",* Stockholm, 1993 (BIBSAM-rapport nr 6).

ELVIL, *Proposal for The European Legislative Virtual Library, ELVIL,* photocopy, Stockholm University, 1996.

Freivalds, Laila, *Inledningsanförande,* In Wahlgren, Peter (ed.) Det goda kunskapssamhället: Ett perspektiv på rättsinformatiken, The Swedish Law and Informatics Research Institute, Stockholm, 1988 (IRI-report 1988:5) 7-20.

Frändberg, Åke, *Till frågan om de juridiska begreppens systematik: En studie i juridisk begreppsbildning*, Tidsskrift for rettsvitenskap, 1985, 79-116.

Gates, Bill, *The Road Ahead*, Viking, London, 1995.

Gentzschein, Anna, *Internet Links: Legal Implications*, The Swedish Law and Informatics Research Institute, Stockholm University, 1997.

Gentzschein, Anna, *Rättsbankens litteraturdatabaser*, JT 1997-98, 587-96.

Gunnarsson, Britt-Louise, *Lagtexters begriplighet: En språkfunktionell studie av medbestämmandelagen*, Liber Förlag, Lund, 1982.

Göranson, Ulf, *Juristen i biblioteket*, In Jareborg, Nils (ed.) Rättsvetenskapliga studier tillägnade Carl Hemström, Iustus förlag, Uppsala, 1996, (De Lege: Juridiska fakulteten i Uppsala, Årsbok årgång 6, 1996) 83-91.

Hafner, Carole D, *An Information Retrieval System Based on a Computer Model of Legal Knowledge*, photocopy, University of Michigan, 1978.

Hagerlid, Jan, *Studenternas bibliotek: En analys av högskolebibliotekens utveckling*, BIBSAM, Kungliga bibliotekets sekretariat för nationell planering och samordning, 1996 (Slutrapport).

Hamfelt, Andreas & Wahlgren, Peter, *Datorstödda beslut: Artificiell intelligens och juridik*, The Swedish Law and Informatics Research Institute, Stockholm, 1988 (IRI-rapport 1988:4).

Hart, H. L. A., *The Concept of Law*, Oxford University Press, Oxford, 1961 (Clarendon Law Series).

Head, John W. & MacCabe, Gerard B. (eds.) *Insiders Guide to Library Automation: Essays of Practical Experience*, Greenwood Press, Westport, Connecticut, 1993 (New directions in information management no. 30).

Hearst, Marti A., *Interfaces for Searching the Web*, Scientific American, March 1997, 60-64.

Herlitz, Nils, *Om lagstiftning*, Norstedts, Stockholm, 1930.

Heuman, Lars, *Advokatens rättsutredningar: Metod och ansvar*, Juristförlaget, Stockholm, 1987.

Hodd, Rebecca A. & Karp, Rashelle S., *Library Automation Technology*, In Head, John W & McCabe, Gerard B. (eds.) Insider's Guide to Library Automation: Essays of Practical Experience, Greenwood Press, Westport, Connecticut, 1993 (New directions in information management no. 30) 317-44.

Holborn, Guy, *Butterworths Legal Research Guide*, Butterworths, London,..., 1993.

IMPRIMATUR *Intellectual Multimedia Property Rights Model And Terminology for Universal Reference*, Project 20676 European Commission DGIII, "http://www.imprimatur.alcs.co.uk/", 1997.

International Convention for the Protection of Performers, Producers of Phonograms and Broadcasting Organisations, Done at Rome on October 26, 1961 "http://www.wipo.int/eng/iplex/wo_rom0_.htm".

International Review of Law, Computers and Technology, Carfax Publishing Co, Oxfordshire, 1996 - (bi-annual), (Previously the International yearbook of Law, Computers and Technology).

IT Kommissionen, *Official Letter to The Government*, photocopy, The Ministry of Communication, Stockholm, October 8, 1996.

Janlert, Lars-Erik, *Hemma i cyberspace*, Scandinavian University Press, n.p., 1995 (Forskningens frontlinjer).

Jareborg, Nils, *Värderingar*, Norstedts förlag, Stockholm, 1975.

Jensen, Eva, *Myndigheternas databaser: ensamrätt och tillgänglighet*, Norstedts juridik, Stockholm, 1997.

Katsh, M. Ethan, *Law in a Digital World*, Oxford University Press, New York, ..., 1995.

Konkurrensverket, *Beslut 1995-06-26: Wolters Kluwer Sverige ABs förvärv av samtliga aktier i Juristförlaget JF AB*, photocopy.

Kracht, D., de Vey Mestdagh, C.N.J. & Svensson, J.S. (eds.) *Legal Knowledge Based Systems: An Overview of Criteria for Validation and Practical Use*, Koninklijke Vermande BV, Lelystad, 1990.

Kuhn, Thomas, *The Structure of Scientific Revolutions*, The University of Chicago Press, Chicago, 2 ed., 1970.

Lindberg, Agne & Westman, Daniel, *Praktisk IT-rätt*, Norstedts juridik, Stockholm, 1997.

Lindahl, Lars. *Definitioner, begreppsanalys och mellanbegrepp i juridiken*. In Rationalitet och emperi i rättsvetenskapen. Stockholms universitet, Stockholm, 1985 37-49 (Juridiska fakulteten i Stockholm, skriftserien nr. 6).

Lindsey, Jonathan & Prentice, Ann, E. *Professional Ethics and Libraries*, Onyx Press, Phoenix, 1985.

Lundberg, Johan, *Internet, domännamn och svensk rätt: Särskilt om så kallade domänstölder*, Iustus förlag, Uppsala, 1997.

Lunneborg, Rolf, *Fogdarnas nya system fick dumpas*, Svenska dagbladet, April 23, 1997.

Lynch, Clifford, *Searching the Internet*, Scientific American, March 1997, 44-48.

MacEllven, Douglass, T., *Legal Research Handbook*, Butterworths, Toronto, ..., 2 ed., 1986.

Magnell, Viktor, *Rättskällebegreppet: I sökandet efter en modell att analysera olika rättssystems rättskälleläror*, Stiftelsen skrifter utgivna vid juridiska fakulteten vid Stockholms universitet, Stockholm, 1994 (Skriftserien nr 44).

Magnusson, Cecilia, *New Roles in the Shaping of the Law*, In Seipel, Peter (ed.) From Data Protection to Knowledge Machines: The Study of Law and Informatics, Kluwer Law and Taxation Publishers, Deventer, 1990 (Computer/Law Series 5) 135-65.

Magnusson Sjöberg, Cecilia, *Rättsautomation: Särskilt om statsförvaltningens datorisering*, Norstedts juridik, Stockholm, 1992.

Magnusson Sjöberg, Cecilia, *Corpus Legis – A Legal Document Management Project*, In Brinnen, Martin (ed.) Telekommunikation, Norstedts, Stockholm, 1996 (Nordic Yearbook of Law and Informatics) 161-77.

Modéer, Kjell Å., *Historiska rättskällor: En introduktion i rättshistoria*, Nerenius & Santérus förlag, Stockholm, 1993.

Moen,William E. & McClure, Charles R. *Government Information Locator Service (GILS): An Evaluation of the Federal Government's Implementation of the Government Information Locator Service (GILS): Final Report*, General Services Administration, Office of Information Technology Integration, Washington, DC, June 30, 1997, "http://www.access.gpo.gov/su_docs/gils/gils-eval/html/toc.html".

Moys, Elisabeth M., *Manual of Law Librarianship: The Use and Organization of Legal Literature*, Gower Publishing Company Limited, Aldershot, 2 ed., 1987.

Moys, Elisabeth M., *Moys Classification and Thesaurus for Legal Materials*, Bowker Saur, London, 3 ed., 1992.

Mueller, Heinz Peter & Kehoe, Patric E. (eds.) *Law Librarianship: A Handbook, vol. 1-2*, Fred B Rothman & Co., Littleton, 1983 (AALL Publication series no 9).

Negroponte, Nicholas, *Being Digital: The Road Map for Survival on the Information Superhighway*, Hodder & Stoughton, London, 1995.

Network Computer™ *Pressrelease May 20, 1996*, "http://www.nc.ihost.com/".

Nilsson, Åsa, *Vingklippt MÅHS gäckar domstolar*, Computer Sweden nr 2 1997.

Nordisk Årsbok i rättsinformatik, Norstedts, Stockholm, 1984 - forthcoming (Nordic Yearbook of Law and Informatics).

Olsson, Anders R., *IT och det fria ordet – myten om storebror*, Bokförlaget juridik och samhälle, n.p. 1996.

Oudet, Bruno, *Multilingualism on the Internet*, Scientific American, March 1997, 67-68.

Paliwala Abdul, Cartwright, Andrew & Terrett, Andrew, *User Needs in Electronic Law Reporting: A Research Study of The Law Reports*, 1997 JILT (2) "http://elj.warwick.ac.uk/jilt/leginfo/97_ 2pal/".

Palm, Johan & Wahlgren, Peter, *Utvärdering av juridiska databaser och IT-produkter: Rättsbankens rättsfallsdatabaser AD01 och HD01*, JT 1994-95, 1098-1104.

Palm, Johan & Wahlgren, Peter, *Lexis-Nexis*, JT 1995-96, 200-06.

Paris Convention for the Protection of Industrial Property of March 20, 1883, "http://www.wipo.int/eng/iplex/wo_par0_.htm".

Peczenik, Aleksander, *Rättsnormer*, Norstedts förlag, Stockholm, 1987.

Pehrson, Lars, *EG-samarbetet och den svenska rättskälleläran*, JT 1991-92, 626-37.

Poler, Ellen, *Frames and License Agreements*, "http://www.collegehill.com/ilp-news/poler1.html", October 1997.

Resnick, Paul, *Filtering Information on the Internet*, Scientific American, March 1997, 54-56.

Roos, Carl Martin, *Biblioteksrätt*, Nerenius & Santérus Förlag AB, Stockholm, 1994.

Rosén, Jan, *Swedish Software Law: As Related Primarily to EC Directives*, Juristförlaget/Stiftelsen Skrifter utgivna av Juridiska fakulteten vid Stockholms universitet, Stockholm, 1995 (Skriftserien nr 46).

Rosenoer, Jonathan, *CyberLaw: The Law of the Internet*, Springer-Verlag, New York, ..., 1997.

Ross, Alf, *Directives and Norms*, Routledge & Keagan, Paul, London, 1968.

Saxby, Stephen John, *Public Policy and Legal Regulation of the Information Market in the Digital Network Environment*, Norwegian Research Center for Computers and Law/Tano, Oslo, 1996 (COMPLEX 2/96).

Seipel, Peter, *Law Libraries and Information Technology*, JT 1993-94, 312-29.

Seipel, Peter, *Rättsinformation som ansvar och kommers*, JT 1993-94 at 649-56.

Seipel, Peter, *Informationssökning och rättsutbildning*, In Koivumaa, Ari (ed.) Rättslig informationssökning i databaser: Juristens nya verktyg, Norstedts juridik, Stockholm, 1994 (NÅR 1994) 31-50.

Seipel, Peter, *En strategi för datarätten: IT:s juridik*, The Swedish Law and Informatics Research Institute, Stockholm, 1995 (IRI-PM 1995:13).

Seipel, Peter, *Juridik och IT: Introduktion till rättsinformatiken*, Norstedts juridik, Stockholm, 6 ed., 1997.

Shabtai, Rosenne, *The World Court: What It Is and How It Works*, Martinus Nijhoff Publishers, Dortrecht, ..., 5 ed., 1995.

Skantze, Pernilla, *CELEX*, JT 1995-96, 517-24.

Skantze, Pernilla (ed.) *Essays in Legal Information Management*, The Swedish Law and Informatics Research Institute, Stockholm, 1996 (IRI-report 1996:2).

Skantze, Pernilla & Westman, Daniel, *Infolex*, JT 1995-96, 1193-1200.

Skantze, Pernilla & Westman, Daniel, *CD-Lag X*, JT 1996-97, 821-27.

Smith, J.C., *Review of Wahlgren, Peter, Automation of Legal Reasoning*, JT 1993-94, 247-56.

SOU 1973:23, *Bättre överblick över lagar och andra bestämmelser: Betänkande avgivet av utredningen om författningspublicering m. m.*, Stockholm, 1973.

SOU 1991:72, *En kreativ studiemiljö: Högskolebiblioteken som pedagogisk resurs: Förslag till synpunkter från högskoleutredningens arbetsgrupp för högskolans biblioteksfunktioner*, Stockholm, 1991.

SOU 1991:106, *Domstolarna inför 2000-talet: Arbetsuppgifter och förfaranderegler, Del A, Betänkande av Domstolsutrendingen*, Stockholm, 1991.

SOU 1992:110, *Information och den nya informationsteknologin: Straff och processrättsliga frågor: Betänkande av Datastraffrättsutredningen*, Stockholm, 1992.

SOU 1992:92, *Pliktleverans: Slutbetänkande av Pliktleveransutredningen*, Stockholm, 1992.

SOU 1993:10, *En ny datalag: Slutbetänkande av Datalagsutredningen*, Stockholm, 1993.

SOU 1996:40, *Elektronisk dokumenthantering: Betänkande av IT-utredningen*, Stockholm, 1996.

SOU 1997:39, *Integritet, Offentlighet, Informationsteknik: Betänkande av datalagskommittén*, Stockholm, 1997.

SOU 1997:146, *Grunddata - i samhällets tjänst: Betänkande av Grunddatabasutredningen*. Stockholm, 1997.

Standardiseringskommissionen i Sverige (ed.) *Informationsteknik – ordlista: Dataordboken*, SIS, Stockholm, 1989 (Svensk standard SS01 601).

Stefik, Mark, *Trusted Systems*, Scientific American, March 1997, 68-71.

Strömberg, Tore, *Rättsordningens byggstenar: Om normtyperna i lag och sedvanerätt*, Studentlitteratur, Lund, 1988.

Strömholm, Stig, *Rätt, rättskällor och rättstillämpning: En lärobok i allmän rättslära*, Norstedts juridik, Stockholm, 5 ed., 1996 (Institutet för rättsvetenskaplig forskning CIX).

Sundby, Nils Kristian, *Om normer*, Universitetsforlaget, Oslo, 1974 (Næss, A. (ed.) Filosofiske problemer XLIII, Scandinavian Studies in Philosophy).

Sundström, Margaretha, *Fogden överger problembarn*, Dagens IT, 1997, nr 8, 4.

Susskind, Richard, *The Future of Law: Facing the Challenges of Information Technology*, Clarendon Press, Oxford, 1996.

Susskind, Richard, *Expert Systems in Law: A Jurisprudential Inquiry*, Clarendon Press, Oxford, 1987.

Svensk juristtidning, AB P A Norstedts & Söner, Stockholm, 1976, 1977.

Svensson, Britt-Marie, *Rättsbankens författningsdatabaser SFST och SFSR*, JT 1996-97, 1044-49.

Svensson, Britt-Marie & Wahlgren, Peter, *Regeringskansliets författningsdatabaser – en replik*, JT 1997-98, 901-904.

Säfström, Charlotte, *MÅHS: Ilska på domstolarna mot nytt datasystem: – tidsödande och 70-talsmässigt*, Jusektidningen nr 4, 1996, 28-29.

Tekniska litteratursällskapet, *Bibliotek i Sverige*, TLS, Stockholm, 3 ed., 1997 (TLS Handbok 24).

The American Association of Law Libraries, *Handbook & Directory, The Library Bill of Rights*, "http://www.aallnet.org/handbook/policy_bill_of_rights.html", 1997.

The American Association of Law Libraries, *Online Information Service*, "http://www.aallnet.org/", 1997.

The Swedish Law and Informatics Research Institute, *Studiematerial i rättsteknik*, Stockholm, 1996.

Thomas, Philip A., *How to use a Law Library: Introduction to Research Skills*, Sweet & Maxwell, London, 1996.

Thompson, Donna M. & Feinstein, Jerald L., *Cost Justifying Expert Systems,* In De Salvo, Daniel A. & Liebowitz, Jay, (eds.) Managing Artificial Intelligence and Expert Systems, Yourdon Press, Englewood Cliffs, 1990 (Yourdon Press Computing Series) 93-121.

Toppledarforum/Datainspektionen, *Lexit – A pre-study,* Stockholm, 1995.

Tysver, Daniel, A., *Ticketmaster v. Microsoft Dispute* April 1997, "http://www.bitlaw.com/hot/ticketmaster.html".

Wahlgren, Peter, *ADB, telekommunikationer och juridiskt arbete*, The Swedish Law and Informatics Research Institute, Stockholm, 1983 (IRI-report 1983:3, also published as Teldok information nr 3).

Wahlgren, Peter, *Rättsdata: En användarundersökning,* The Swedish Law and Informatics Research Institute, Stockholm, 1983 (IRI report 1983:6).

Wahlgren, Peter, *Beslutstöd för brottmål: En förstudie om kunskapsbaserad systemutveckling*, The Swedish Law and Informatics Research Institute, Stockholm, 1987 (IRI report 1987:5 and DV-rapport 1987:9).

Wahlgren, Peter (ed.) *Det goda kunskapssamhället: Ett perspektiv på rättsinformatiken*, The Swedish Law and Informatics Research Institute, Stockholm, 1988 (IRI report 1988:5).

Wahlgren, Peter, *Automation of Legal Reasoning: A Study on Artificial Intelligence and Law*, Kluwer Law and Taxation Publishers, Deventer, Boston,..., 1992 (Computer Law Series 11).

Wahlgren, Peter, *Evaluation of Computerised Legal Networks.*, University of Strathclyde, Glasgow, 1995. (Paper presented at Electronic Communications, 10th BILETA Conference).

Wahlgren, Peter, *Notisum – Rättsnätet via Internet*, JT 1997-98, 254-62.

Wahlgren, Peter (ed.) *Materialsamling IT-rätt*, The Swedish Law and Informatics Research Institute/Jure, Stockholm, 1997.

Wahlgren, Peter, *Sveriges rikes lag: Lagbokskommentaren*, JT 1997-98, 875-82.

Wedgeworth, Robert (ed.) *World Encyclopedia of Libraries and Information Services*, American Library Association, Chicago, 3 ed., 1993.

Westman, Daniel & Wahlgren, Peter, *Sveriges rikes lag CD-ROM: C-LAG X*, JT 1995-96, 206-13.

Wiegand, Wayne A. & Davies, Donald G. Jr. (eds.) *Encyclopedia of Library History*, Garland Publishing Inc., New York, 1994.

Wikander, Cecilia, *RIXLEX – riksdagens databaser*, JT 1995-96, 902-08.

Vogel, Hans-Heinrich, *Juridiska översättningar*, Juristförlaget i Lund, Lund, 1988, (Skrifter utgivna av juridiska föreningen i Lund nr 100. Acta Societatis Juridicae Lundensis).

Woodcock, Erik, *Pacta*, JT 1996-97, 194-204.

Wren, Christopher, G., *The Legal Research Manual: A Game Plan for Legal Research and Analysis*, A-R Editions Inc., Madison, Wisconsin, 2 ed., 1986.

Youngs, Raymond, *Sourcebook on German Law*, Cavendish Publishing Limited, London, 1994.

Österman, Roger, *Akelius skatt*, JT 1996-97, 514-19.

Internet References

As available January 1998

American Association of Law Libraries (AALL)
http://www.aallnet.org

AustLII Australasian Legal Information Institue: A joint facility of the Faculties of Law at the University of Technology, Sydney and the University of New South Wales
http://bar.austlii.edu.au

Awapatent: Frågor om IT-Juridik? (Online Q&A about Law)
http://www.awapatent.se/dnet.html

Blue ribbon Campaign for online freedom of speech, press and association
http://www.eff.org/blueribbon.html

Business and Government Information Center, University of Nevada, Reno, Libraries (Website Evaluation Criteria)
http://gordo.library.unr.edu/~bgic/fed/criteria.html

Catalaw (Metaindex Law)
http://www.catalaw.com

CCTA: Governmental Information Service: Organisational Index, etc.
http://www.open.gov.uk/

Center for Democracy and Technology
http://www.cdt.org

Chicago-Kent College of Law
http://www.kentlaw.edu/

Duke University Law School
http://www.law.duke.edu/

ECSC - EC - EAEC – Common Command Language
http://www2.echo.lu/echo/ccl/en/ccl.html

ELVIL, European Legislative Virtual Library
http://www.sub.su.se/sam/elvil.htm

Ethics and the Internet (Duke University)
http://www.duke.edu/~wgrobin/ethics/surflaw.html

Europa, The European Union's Server: Information
http://europa.eu.int/geninfo/info-en.htm

European Commission DG XIII/E-4 Telematics for Libraries
http://www2.echo.lu/libraries/en/libraries.html (a project list is avaialable at http://www2.echo.lu/libraries/en/projects.html)

European Commission, Legal Advisory Board: Intellectual Property
http://www2.echo.lu/legal/en/ipr/ipr.html

European Union Website "Europa"
http://europa.eu.int

Georgetown University Law Center
http://141.161.67.230/topics/news.html

Government Information Locator Service (GILS)
http://www.access.gpo.gov/su_docs/gils/gils.html

Högskolan i Jönköping, Biblioteket, länksamling juridik
http://www.hj.se/hs/bibl/juridik.html

IMPRIMATUR project
http://www.imprimatur.alcs.co.uk/

Information Market Europe: An interactive service of DGXIII of the European Commission
http://www2.echo.lu

Infotorg: Rättsbanken: Swedish Legislation via Sema Group Info Data AB
http://www.infotorg.sema.se/

Internet Legal Resource Guide
http://www.ilrg.com/

IT kommissionen
http://www.itkommissionen.se

Juridiskt forum: Swedish legislation via Juridisk Informationsteknologi AB
http://www.jit.se/aspscripts/default.asp
Law Book Network: Buy and sell law books on the World Wide Web
http://lawbook.com/

Law Library of Congress
http://lcweb2.loc.gov/glin/lawhome.html

Law Library of Congress: Global Legal Information Network (GLIN)
http://lcweb2.loc.gov/glin

LawRunner: A Legal Research Tool for the WWW
http://www.lawrunner.com/

Legal Dot Net
http://www.legal.net

Legal Information Institute, Cornell Law School
http://www.law.cornell.edu/

Lexis-Nexis Communication Center
http://www.lexis-nexis.com/lncc/

LIBRIS - bibliotekens litteraturdatabas
http://www.libris.kb.se

Network Computer Inc.
http://www.nc.com/nc.html#what

Rättsnätet: Swedish Legislation via Notisum AB
http://www.notisum.se/

Sveriges Riksdag: (The Swedish Parliament)
http://www.riksdagen.se

The 4Internet Network
http://www.4Internet.com./

The Journal of Information, Law and Technology (JILT)
http://elj.warwick.ac.uk/jilt/

The Link Controversy Page
http://www.jura.uni-tuebingen.de/~s-bes1/lcp.html

The Rixlex Database - Swedish Legislation via the Swedish Parliament
http://rixlex.riksdagen.se (English version
http://www.riksdagen.se/rixlex/index_en.htm)

The SGML/XML Web Page by Cover, Robin
http://www.sil.org/SGML/sgml.html#toc-general

The United States Sentencing Commission
http://www.ussc.gov/

The World Wide Web Virtual Library: LAW
http://www.law.indiana.edu/law/v-lib/lawindex.html

Toppledarforum
http://toppled.nutek.se/index.html

UC Berkley Library Web: Government & Social Science Information
http://www.lib.berkeley.edu/GSSI/eu.html#documents

United States Information Agency
http://www.usia.gov/

World Intellectual Property Organisation
http://www.wipo.int/eng/index.htm

World Trade Organization
http://www.wto.org/

Yahoo: Top:Government:Law:Legal Research:Libraries
http://www.yahoo.com/Government/Law/Legal_Research/Libraries/

INDEX

A

B

D

E

I

J

P

Q

R

S

T

U